DATE DUE			
Apr30 '82			

PROFILES FROM THE NEW YORKER

with a preface by CLIFTON FADIMAN

"[These profiles] have pertinence and value for what they show of contemporary history. There is an impish mastery of unuttered revealment about these things, indeed, which gives them a fresh interest in repeated reading." *The New York Times*

PUBLISHED BY ALFRED A. KNOPF

Take Them Up Tenderly

Margaret Case Harriman

Take Them Up Tenderly

A COLLECTION OF PROFILES

NEW YORK: ALFRED · A · KNOPF

1944

THIS BOOK HAS BEEN PRODUCED
IN FULL COMPLIANCE
WITH ALL GOVERNMENT REGULATIONS
FOR THE CONSERVATION OF PAPER, METAL,
AND OTHER ESSENTIAL MATERIALS

Manufactured in the United States of America.

Published simultaneously in Canada by The Ryerson Press

First and Second Printings before Publication
Third Printing, October 1944

TO MY FATHER, FRANK CASE

Take them up tenderly,
Sift them with care,
Slice them so slenderly—
Got to be fair!

—Variation on an old theme by Thomas Hood, to be inscribed on a Profile-writer's tomb

Contents

Foreword
PAGE xi

1. *Mr. Miller and Mr. Hyde:* GILBERT MILLER
PAGE 3

2. *The Old Max:* MAX GORDON
PAGE 31

3. *The Candor Kid:* CLARE BOOTHE
PAGE 44

4. *Hi-Yo, Platinum!* MOSS HART
PAGE 79

5. *Miss Lily of New Orleans:* LILLIAN HELLMAN
PAGE 94

6. *Veni, Vidi, Vicky:* HELEN HAYES
PAGE 110

7. *The Wise Lived Yesterday:* COLE PORTER
PAGE 135

8. *Big-Time Urchin:* LARRY ADLER
PAGE 150

9. *Words and Music:* RODGERS AND HART
PAGE 166

10. *The Squarest Little Shooter on Vesey Street:* OSCAR HAMMERSTEIN II
PAGE 186

11. *The Boys:* JOHN-FREDERICS
PAGE 203

12. *Hollywood Agent:* LELAND HAYWARD
PAGE 213

13. *Miss Fixit:* FANNY HOLTZMANN
PAGE 224

14. *Sweetheart:* MARY PICKFORD
PAGE 243

15. *Dance Team:* THE DE MARCOS
PAGE 252

Except "The Squarest Little Shooter on Vesey Street," the original versions of the Profiles in this book originally appeared in the New Yorker.

❁ *Foreword* ❁

A GOOD DEAL has been said and written about Profile-writers ever since Harold Ross, that lovable old volcano, first gave the name "Profiles" to the biographical sketches he publishes in the *New Yorker*. Writers of Profiles, it is generally agreed, are a writing race apart. They are not fan-magazine authors, they have not reached the full dignity of biographers, and they are definitely not interviewers. If you think Profile-writers are interviewers, just call a Profile-writer an interviewer once and then dodge the bared fangs and the unsheathed claws.

An interviewer writes what he is permitted to write by the person he interviews, and hedges himself in safely by an array of authorized quotes. Male interviewers are generally attractive and bored and wear their hats on the backs of their heads like Joel McCrea in the movies. Female interviewers are more eager, with buck teeth, ruffles around the neck, large notebooks, and flat-heeled shoes. Profile-writers, on the other hand, look like almost anybody. That bruised appearance they sometimes have, which is often mistaken for skepticism, is actually the result of continually bumping up against one astonishing fact after another, which gives a permanent downward curve to a Profile-writer's face and makes him look, a good deal of the time, like a man who has taken too many rides on a scenic railway.

Profile-writers interview their subjects too, long and thoroughly. They also interview a number of (a) people who have long known and loved the subject, and (b) people who have long known and hated the subject. From this contradictory material the Profile-writer then sets down what seems to him a reasonable notion of what the guy or the dame is really like. Very few people agree with him. If a Profile is admiring —as many are, notwithstanding a superstition that they are all assassinations—readers complain that it is not admiring *enough.* If it suggests that the subject does not belong wholly among the seraphim, the writer is assailed by letters, telegrams, and phone calls from readers demanding to know why the Profile did not clearly place its subject once and for all among the devils in hell—the only fitting location, in their opinion. "You were too kind!" this bloodthirsty crew will wail; or, "Why didn't you see *me* before you wrote the piece? *I* could have told you what that so-and-so you were writing about did to my poor old mother!"

Once, after a few of these double-talking barrages, I wrote on the back of a laundry list a small parody that still expresses the impersonal view I try to take of the whole thing. It went;

There's so much good in the worst of us,
And so much bad in the best of us,
It turns out that a lot of us
Can make a pretty good living writing about the rest of us.

Profile subjects complain very little, considering the thoroughness of our reports about them. One time a lady in the cosmetic business withdrew her advertising from the *New Yorker* because, in a Profile about her, I quoted Consumer's Research as having pointed out that a bottle of her skin tonic, which sold at retail for eighty-five cents, cost her three cents to manufacture. "It costs me *twelve* cents a bottle to make that lotion!" the beautician stormed over the phone to a *New Yorker* editor. After a while she put her advertising back in the magazine. A sadder memory for me is the time I got sixty-one editorial queries on a twelve-page Profile. To explain the stigma this carried I shall have to describe briefly the *New Yorker's* system of editing Profiles.

The first version of a Profile comes back to its author with numbers pencilled in the margins corresponding to the numbers of notes and queries from editors, which are typed on separate pages and attached to the manuscript. A good Profile-writer is likely to get from ten to fifteen editors' queries on a piece, not counting checkers' queries, which come later and amount to several million. An average Profile-writer gets from twenty to thirty editors' queries. Practically perfect writers like Wolcott Gibbs and St. Clair McKelway seldom get more

FRAGMENT OF EDITORS' NOTES ON A PROFILE

(Author's cries are in handwriting)

to" etc.? Wording here, and
sense to me. Naq, uaq, uaq.

new. A friend of mine took
ive years ago in Lowell, Mass. ← Where the Nasals speak only to the Lowells?
ll
n't say nuffin
s on Lowelling alo-ong....
Just these two? And how → Just two and a werewolf.

tually knows his women
of the girls by name
, calls 'em all Charlie.

is almost a New Yorker
d. Thurber broods.
reet. But does Mr. G.
Lincoln brooded before
coined word.
ean nothing to me.

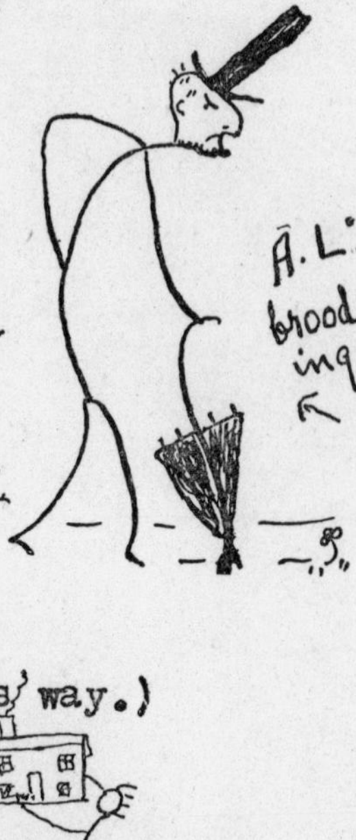

rther on, the house
rectly instead of this way.)
Sussex brought in
directly →

Father.

25. What does she mean, "put a stop
the sentence doesn't quite make

26. Courses in enunciation are not
an enunciation course twenty-f
because she was nasal.

Oh, nasal Lowell, nasal Lowe
She don't do nuffin, she d
She just keeps Lowelling, kee

27. How many servants in the house?
big is the house actually?

SO-O big.

28. One wants to know how much he a
employees... Does he know many
when he meets them outside? Nop

Mr. brooding

29. I'm getting petty now, but this
word which doesn't apply to Mr.
People brood up and down 52nd S
brood? I doubt it. Think A.
New Yorker

30. Just as a male reader scanties
For Your Information: Scanties.

31. This isn't clear to me. (And,
in Sussex should be brought in
House

32. What became of his mother?

She afterward became his

than five or six. Friends, my twelve-page Profile came back with six pages of editors' queries—sixty-one queries in all, meaning that the editors had found it obscure or intolerable about every forty-nine words. This was before the checkers had even had wind of it. In my black disgrace, I sat down with the manuscript and the editors' notes one bleak night and stonily answered all the queries just the way I felt like answering them. For anyone who may be interested in a glimpse of souls in turmoil (the writer's and the editors'), I have appended to this foreword a page from these famous queries along with my wounded replies. The Profile, whose subject wild horses will not tear from me, never appeared in print.

Neither does it appear in this book, for obvious reasons. I have also omitted the cosmetic lady and a number of other Profiles which have been published, because I wanted the book to be entirely about theater people. Theater people are the most entertaining to write about, and they are the *nicest* people to write about. They are full of charm and full of humor about themselves, and they have a disarming way of accepting a necessary spray of stinkweed as though it were a nosegay. I am convinced that this is not due only to love of publicity. I think it's just that theater people are wonderful people. Even the stinkweeds.

While I was rewriting the pieces collected here, and bringing them up to date, I kept remembering one question *New Yorker* readers invariably ask when they meet a Profile-writer face to face. Generally they ask it just after the last installment of a two-part or three-part Profile has appeared. The writer, who has sweated for some months to produce a fair, diverting, and accurate picture of, let's say, Helen Hayes, meets up with a reader who has just finished reading the final installment of Miss Hayes's Profile.

"Tell me," this reader inquires earnestly, "what is she *really* like?"

This book is an attempt to give a straight question the straight answer it deserves.

MARGARET CASE HARRIMAN

[illegible]

While I [illegible] the pieces collected here and keeping them up to date I kept remembering [illegible] [illegible] readers [illegible] [illegible] [illegible] to [illegible] [illegible] installment of a two-part or three-part [illegible] the writer who [illegible] for some [illegible] [illegible] and accurate [illegible] of [illegible] [illegible] up [illegible] [illegible] [illegible]

"Tell me," [illegible] "what is it really like?"

This book is an attempt to give a straight answer [illegible] straight [illegible] it deserves.

[illegible]

Take Them Up Tenderly

❁ 1 ❁

Mr. Miller and Mr. Hyde:

GILBERT MILLER

GILBERT MILLER, the theatrical producer, is a man whom people love to explain. When Miller's friends run out of listeners, they can be happy just explaining him to one another in earnest little chats like one that took place on a certain evening between a fashionable young woman and a successful playwright in the lobby of the Henry Miller Theatre after the first act of *Harriet,* a Gilbert Miller production.

"Gilbert sometimes seems abrupt and even rude, but I feel that it's simply because he's terribly *shy,*" said the lady, uttering this familiar defense of bad manners in the illustrious as earnestly as though she had invented it.

"He has none of the defenses of artificiality," the playwright said. "He is Nature's child, fundamentally kind, generous, intensely loyal to his friends, inevitably misunderstood."

"Yes, isn't he!" the lady agreed enthusiastically. "I think of Gilbert as terribly naïve in a sort of *Irish* way—you know, *fey.* And, of course a complete artist in the theater, don't you think?"

"Absolutely," said the playwright. "His taste is exquisite and his attention to detail is staggering—"

"And he is definitely not a snob, as some people accuse him of being," the lady interrupted. "He loathes the social game, and I always feel he would be much happier staying home and playing his Viennese records. He's a *simple* person, really, just a simple, sensitive, charming person."

"Oh, come," said the playwright, seeming to tire of a dialogue over which he had only partial control, "Gilbert's a son of a bitch, and we both know it."

The interesting thing about this conversation, to other students of Miller, is that all of it is true. He is a variable man, and his transitions from one mood to another are so swift and often so apparently causeless that, as one lacerated pal put it, "You can't depend on his friendship, but you can't depend on his enmity either." A Hollywood acquaintance, watching Miller in action, expressed an opinion that mystified several people for a while. "That Miller, he's a regelar Freddie March," he said, leaving his interpreter to explain that Miller's behavior suggested Fredric March's in the title roles of the picture *Dr. Jekyll and Mr. Hyde.* The comparison is irresistible to anyone who knows Miller. Normally (or as Dr. Jekyll), he is jovial, entertaining, chatty, and unruffled by any cracks about himself that he may hear popping around him. When Arthur Richman, who wrote *The Awful Truth,* one of Miller's successful productions, remarked to a friend, "You have to know Gilbert to dislike him," Miller heard about it and called up Richman to compliment him on a good line, laughing good-naturedly. His laugh is rich and throaty, a plump man's laugh, and his voice is high—two characteristics that contrast strangely with the swarthiness of his appearance and the glitter of his small, exceptionally bright eyes. He looks a little like one of the larger and later Roman emperors, and he moves purposefully but with a disillusioned air, like an overburdened sheep dog.

When he is overtaken by his personal Mr. Hyde, his wrath descends impartially upon the great and upon the humble who cannot answer back. In 1927, Miller brought Leslie Howard from England to play opposite Jeanne Eagels in *Her Cardboard Lover.* After the opening night at the Empire Theatre Howard was the town's pet, and John Donnelly, house manager of the Empire, hung a portrait of him in the theater lobby. A picture in the Empire lobby, along with those of Sarah Bernhardt, Maude Adams, John Drew, and other great players who have acted there in the fifty years since the theater was built, means almost as much to a young actor as a niche in Westminster Abbey might mean to a Bloomsbury scribbler. Donnelly's tribute to Howard was justified, but Miller, coming into the theater later that day, saw the picture and was annoyed because he hadn't been consulted about it. With a bull-like lunge, he climbed onto a cushioned seat under Howard's portrait, tore the picture from the wall, and threw it to the floor, smashing the glass and the frame. "Who did this?" he yelled, scrambling down from the seat. Donnelly, attracted by the noise, admitted that he had hung the picture. What Miller said to him is obscured by time and by the fact that people who have witnessed Miller's rages wince, close their eyes, and shake their heads when they are asked to repeat his actual words. Such words, they think, are better forgotten. When the storm was over, the Howard picture was repaired and rehung, with Miller's approval and even, as he was then able to point out, at his suggestion.

A refinement of the Miller temper came to light one Christmas not long ago when he was angry with a member of his office staff about something or other and gave him the task of counting out gifts of money for the office personnel and sealing each amount into an envelope bearing the recipient's name. The employee sorted and enclosed money for the whole office force before he discovered that there was no Christmas present for him at all. Miller's methods of getting rid of erring employees range from sudden dismissal to a kind of patient campaign warranted to make the hireling sick of his job. It was probably such tactics of Miller's that led Robert E. Sherwood, the playwright, who is a gentle and slow-speaking man, to make a famous remark one time when he was faced by the distasteful chore of firing the director of one of his own plays. "I haven't the temperament or the experience to handle a situation like this," Sherwood told the director forlornly, "and when it arises I do not ask what would Jesus do, or what would Abe Lincoln do, but I ask what would Gilbert Miller do—and then I cannot do it."

Miller's two most intimate friends are E. Ray Goetz, the retired producer, and Alexander Ince, the Hungarian publisher, for whom Miller backed the late *Stage* magazine. Both men deny that their chum's unpredictable temper is the reason he is not universally adored. Goetz says it is because Miller has a preoccupied air that makes people think he isn't listening when they try to talk to him. "Don't fool yourself," Goetz adds. "He can quote every word two years later." Ince, a slight, lively man, is more eloquent. "People in the theater are full of emotions they got to use," he says, "and they can't love anybody they can't feel sorry for once in a while. Take Charlie Dillingham. He was constantly broke, so everybody loved Charlie Dillingham. Take Max Gordon. He went broke, got sick, and was quivering in a hospital for months, so everybody loves Max Gordon. Al Woods—one million people will tell you about the time they dashed into Al's hotel room just in time to grab him as he was throwing himself out of the window. So everybody loves Al Woods. But Gilbert Miller? Listen. When Gilbert lost his money in the stock market in 1929 and 1930, he had four hits running in New York—*Journey's End, Berkeley Square, Dishonored Lady,* and *Candlelight*—and six shows doing from fair to terrific in London. When he had one of his worst years in the theater, in 1933, he made a fortune in foreign exchange, selling the dollar short all over Europe. Also, he was born to an advantageous position in the theater as the son of a famous actor, and he is married to Kitty Bache, the daughter of the late Jules Bache, the financier. Can anybody feel sorry for such a man? No. Therefore"—Ince smiles and spreads his hands—"very few people love Gilbert Miller."

The society of Europeans, relaxed and worldly, soothes and becomes Miller, who knows Europe better than he knows Shubert Alley. His familiarity with the French, German, Hungarian, and Viennese theater and his gift for languages distinguish him from theatrical producers like Al Woods, for instance, who is said to have moved fretfully from the Crillon to Claridge's, the first time he visited Paris, because he couldn't pronounce "Crillon." Miller speaks French, German, Italian, and Spanish well, and can get along in Hungarian. A great raconteur in congenial company, he likes to tell stories involving the use of two or three languages, and this has always made a hit with the cosmopolitan people he came to know in his travels before the war. When one of his preoccupied moments overtakes him, he can also interrupt, outshout, or brush off the same people in any one of five languages, and there are some admirers who find his ruthlessness refreshing. "You see,"

Miss Margaret Case of *Vogue* recently explained to an acquaintance who had received the full Miller treatment and was vibrating under it, "Gilbert is not quite a *civilized* person." Miss Case's tone was fond and implied that "civilized" was, in her opinion, just another word for "hackneyed."

Some of the friends who like to interpret Miller have reasoned it out that his unhackneyed behavior is a luxury he allows himself as a solace for a lonely and neglected childhood, but people who grew up with him say that he was never any more frustrated than any other celebrity's child. Miller's own account of his early days is voluble but hampered by his conversational style, which is lively but cluttered. Ask him where he was born, and you are likely to get three unrelated anecdotes, two in French and the other about Charles Dillingham's reply to the difficult actress who complained to him that she was playing to an empty theater. "Dillingham asked her why she didn't call up her first husband and get him to paper the house," Miller chuckles. "Her first husband was a paperhanger, you know, and she was trying to forget it."

For the record, Miller was born in New York sixty years ago this July, the second son of Henry Miller, the actor-manager, and the former Bijou Heron, who had been an actress until she married Miller and retired from the stage. Gilbert had an older brother, Henry, junior, who was called Jack and who died years ago at the age of twenty-eight, and a younger sister, Agnes. Agnes married Tim McCoy, the movie cowboy hero, who later became a lieutenant colonel in the Army, and had two sons by him, D'Arcy and Gerald McCoy. When the McCoy marriage ended in divorce some years ago and Agnes remarried, Gilbert Miller persuaded her to let him send Gerald to Yale and to change his name legally to Miller. Gerald Miller is now in the Army and his brother, D'Arcy McCoy, is serving in a Canadian tank corps. Agnes Miller's second marriage was also unsuccessful, and, resuming her maiden name, she joined the WAC last year and became an officer candidate at the First WAC Training Center in Des Moines. The maternal grandmother of Gilbert, Agnes, and Jack Miller was Matilda Heron, one of the first actresses to play Camille in

America, and the first translator of *La Dame aux Camélias* into English. Miss Heron's version, in which she coolly changed the name of Dumas's heroine from Marguerite Gautier to Camille, has become the standard English translation, and Gilbert Miller still enjoys meeting baffled Frenchmen who ask him what this Camille is doing in the place of Dumas's Marguerite. "My grandmother fixed that," he tells them.

Henry Miller was not wholeheartedly a family man and he seems to have regarded his children, especially Gilbert, with a quizzical detachment that occasionally flowered into insult. Once, when the elder Miller was starring in *Cyrano de Bergerac,* an admirer called on him in his dressing room at the theater and noticed a wig block, the featureless dummy actors keep their wigs on when they are not in use. "What's that?" the visitor asked. "It's a bust of Gilbert," Miller replied at once. Bee Drew Devereaux, who is John Drew's daughter, and was a childhood friend of Gilbert, insists that Henry Miller was sacrificing truth for the sake of a laugh, for Gilbert, she says, was a handsome boy, closely resembling her cousin, John Barrymore. Miller admits his former beauty and calmly accepts the start of surprise with which strangers receive news of it. "Would you believe it?" he says amiably. The Henry Millers and the John Drews were friends, and Mrs. Miller and her three children spent several summers in the 1890's at Mrs. Raynor's boarding house in Westhampton, where the Drews also boarded with their daughter and their nephews and niece, Lionel, John, and Ethel Barrymore. Mrs. Miller and Mrs. Drew were Auntie Bijou and Aunt Dodo to all the children, but for Mr. Drew, who was always known as Uncle Jack to his family and close friends, Gilbert invented a special nickname; he called him Uncle Turveydrop, after the Dickens character who was "a model of deportment." Lionel Barrymore, who, it was generally conceded among the Westhampton group, would never amount to much, was known as Sloppy Joe. The Drews and the Barrymores called Gilbert Gillypod, and Ethel Barrymore, who has since starred in Gilbert Miller productions of *The Constant Wife* and other plays, could always brighten the darkest moment of a rehearsal by calling Miller Gillypod again. At the sound of that name, spoken in Miss Barrymore's thrilling voice, he would relax into a sigh and a reminiscent beam. Miller's chief recollection of Jack Barrymore during the Westhampton days is that he and Jack built a boat in which they sailed away forever, across Moriches Bay, leaving a note that said, "Pursuit is useless. Do not attempt it." They didn't come home until suppertime, as Miller recalls it.

When Gilbert was twelve his mother took him to Europe, where he spent the next seven years going to Catholic schools in Germany, France, and Spain. In Dresden he made himself unpopular with his teachers by rolling derisively in a classroom aisle, one time, when a German pupil rose and delivered in a Teutonic roar a poem beginning, "*Muttersprache wunderbar, ach! Wie klingt es schön und klar.*" This guttural shout, describing the beauty of the mother tongue and how softly it falls on the ear, was too much for Miller. He still speaks German the way Beethoven might put a nickel in a juke box, tentatively and full of hate. He was happier at a French school in Passy, where a sympathetic *frère* announced, on Gilbert's arrival, that he was putting him at table in the refectory with "seven other little Americans" to ward off homesickness. Gilbert rapidly learned French and Spanish, both with a strong Argentine accent, from the seven other little Americans, all of whom turned out to be from Buenos Aires. He lost the accent later and his French is now Parisian. The Henry Millers separated while Gilbert was abroad, and when he returned to America, at the age of nineteen, he went to live in a bachelor flat on Murray Hill. He carried a cane, was addicted to overcoats with fur collars, and had such a natty, international air that his father took to referring to him as Count the House.

To the impartial biographer, Gilbert Miller's career, from the time he was nineteen until his thirty-second year, resembles the progress of a man walking under water. In 1904, he joined the Marines and served two years in Haiti. Back in civilian life in New York, he worked in a bank for a while and then underwent a brief spell of acting. His Continental aura had impressed Amelia Bingham, a popular actress of that day who was planning to produce and star in a play with a French name, *Olympe,* and Gilbert found himself playing a footman in the show. Later, in stock companies, road companies, and a production called *Julie Bon-Bon,* he quickly became known as one of the worst actors anybody connected with these enterprises had ever seen, and his performances were not improved by the occasional appearance of his father, who would turn up in a front row and just sit staring at him. "Your carriage has improved, and so has your diction," he told Gilbert after beholding him as the juvenile lead in *Zira,* a romantic comedy. "You have gained poise. There are unquestionably many parts you can play. What I have just witnessed is not one of them." When Gilbert was twenty-three, Henry Miller removed him from the stage, as a gardener might pick a bug off a rose, and put him to work as company manager of the Henry Miller outfit. Nine years later, in 1916, Gilbert made his first independent attempt to better his condition when his father, in collaboration with Al Woods, arranged for a London production, with an English cast, of *Daddy Long-Legs,* the sentimental comedy which the elder Miller and Ruth Chatterton had played in New York and on tour. Choosing a weekend when his father happened to be out of town, Gilbert went to Al Woods and got him to agree to send him to England as company manager for the show. When Miller *père* returned to town and heard about it, he rang up Woods violently. "Don't *do* this horrible thing!" he shouted. "Don't you know my son will ruin the whole production? Stop everything until I get there—I'm coming right down to your office in a taxi." In spite of the scenes that followed, Woods stood by his agreement with Gilbert, and soon the young company manager gratefully sailed for England.

He regards this assignment as the beginning of his career as a producer, but circumstances and the passing of time have slightly obscured his gratitude to Woods. In 1929, in New York, Gilbert Miller produced *Candlelight,* a play to which Woods owned the moving-picture rights. Soon afterwards Woods sold the picture rights to Metro-Goldwyn-Mayer for $20,000, agreeing to pay his partner half. Woods had by that time fallen upon a run of hard luck, and his long-simmering debtors attached the Hollywood money before he could pay Miller his share. Woods now admits his fault in not paying up promptly and agrees that Miller had a just complaint, but it was Gilbert's method of complaining, he says, that broke his heart. Miller sued him. Woods went into bankruptcy, and some theater people, including Woods, believe that he might have avoided financial ruin if Miller's lawsuit had not given him the final shove.

The London job with *Daddy Long-Legs* is a milestone to Miller chiefly because it brought about his first business contact with Charles Frohman, Inc. Frohman was an old friend and associate of Henry Miller, and Gilbert had once had a rocking horse named Charlie Frohman, after the producer, but the relationship never got out of the nursery until *Daddy Long-Legs* proved to be such a hit at the Duke of York's in London that Gilbert extended his lease on the theater, which was owned by the Frohman company. After the death of Charles Frohman on the *Lusitania,* in 1915, control of the company had passed to Alf Hayman, its cigar-chewing, tough-talking general manager, to whom Henry Miller once frostily referred to as "the imitation rough diamond." Shortly before his own death, six years later, Hayman sold the company to Adolph Zukor and Jesse Lasky of Famous Players-Lasky, a corporation which had absorbed Paramount, at that time a film-distribution and sales company. The Paramount-Famous Players-Lasky combination became Paramount Pictures in 1935. In 1920, Zukor and Lasky, travelling abroad, looked up Gilbert Miller, the lessee of one of the London theaters they had acquired along with Charles Frohman, Inc. Miller had by then managed for his father the English productions of such plays as *Nothing But the Truth, Monsieur Beaucaire,* and *Too Many Cooks,* and he had developed business and social relations with Englishmen important in the theater, including Charles Hawtrey, Charles B. Cochran, and Henry Ainley. He had also served in the war, in Paris, as a first lieutenant in the Intelligence Division of the American Army. In 1921 he returned to the United States as general manager of Charles Frohman, Inc., a position he occupied until 1932, at a salary of $1,000 a week plus fifty per cent of the Frohman profits. His contract allowed him to spend six months of each year in Europe, and he celebrated its signing by leaving almost immediately for Budapest, where he bought Ferenc Molnar's play *The Swan,* which Victor Jacobi, the Hungarian composer, had told him about in New York.

The Hollywood bosses objected to paying good money for *The Swan* until Zukor said, in one of those canny, elliptical statements peculiar to Hollywood, "Give Miller his head, and if he's wrong maybe we're paying him too much money anyway." Miller's production of *The Swan,* with Eva Le Gallienne, Basil Rathbone, and Philip Merivale, ran seven months in New York, and it was followed by other equally successful Hungarian, Viennese, and French adaptations, which included *The Grand Duchess and the Waiter, The Play's the Thing, The Captive, The Late Christopher Bean,* and *Her Cardboard Lover.* Miller did well, too, with English plays—*The Constant Wife, Our Betters, Journey's End, Berkeley Square,* and, more recently *Oscar Wilde* and *Victoria Regina.* Since 1921—eleven years with the Frohman company and twelve as an independent producer—Miller has presented over ninety plays in New York, of which only about twenty were written by Americans. He commissioned young American playwrights, notably Philip Barry, Sidney Howard, and Robert E. Sherwood, to adapt several of his early imported Continental successes, but he was cool toward their efforts to write original plays. A number of people who know the theater believe that it was partly Miller's discouraging attitude that inspired some of these writers and their colleagues to form the Playwrights Company, their own highly successful producing organization.

The formation of the Playwrights company in 1938 almost exactly coincided, in fact, with a battle between Miller and the Dramatists' Guild which had been simmering for a couple of years. In 1936 Miller had refused to sign the Guild's basic agreement, which stipulated, among various things, that producers deal with British and other foreign playwrights according to the same (Guild) rules that protect American authors. This clause was designed to safeguard British playwrights, who sometimes dreamily sold their works to American managers for less money than native boys and girls demanded. Miller and the Guild officers bickered along for two years, and during this time Miller arranged for the New York production of two British plays, one by Frederick Lonsdale, the other by J. B. Priestley. Neither Lonsdale nor Priestley found fault with his contract, but the Guild objected and its president, Robert E. Sherwood, brought matters to a head in an interview published in the *Times* and in other New York papers in September, 1938. Sherwood declared that Miller should have pointed out to the British playwrights that the contracts had been drawn up according to his own rules rather than the Guild's, and added that he, and possibly quite a number of fellow playwrights, would just as soon have no further dealings with such a producer. After a few more parleys, Miller signed the basic agreement that month. The two plays which had hastened the crisis turned out to be scarcely worth it all. *Once is Enough*, by Lonsdale, ran for three months, and the Priestley drama, *I Have Been Here Before*, lasted two weeks.

The war has closed most European dramatic sources, and their loss is a blow to Miller, who has always been better at putting on plays he has seen acted on some other stage than at putting on those he is obliged to read from scripts. He is a great reproducer, but theater people say that as a director he finds it almost impossible to visualize a play he has never seen. As he likes to direct, this has led to embarrassments. *Harriet*, which he directed during its early weeks of rehearsal, was the first play in a long time he had to put on cold, with no performances in London, Budapest, or Vienna to remember. Three weeks before the play opened in New York last year, Helen Hayes, who played Harriet, was seen to sit down tensely in a corner of the rehearsal stage and fold her lips. This amounts to antics for Miss Hayes, who is revered by everybody in the theater as one of its gentlest and most tactful actresses. Presently she pounded the arm of her chair with her fist and said, "It's no use, Gilbert, we've got to get a *director!*" She is said to be the only player living who can make Gilbert Miller meek, and next day Miller called in Elia Kazan, the young Group Theatre director who, the same season, successfully staged *The Skin of Our Teeth*. Kazan gathered the cast around him and started over from the beginning. Miss Hayes and Miller are good friends and share many pleasing memories of the four-year run (in New York and on tour) of *Victoria Regina*. Once, when a party was given at the Waldorf-Astoria to celebrate some anniversary of *Victoria*, Miss Hayes left at about two in the morning and charged Miller to see that her husband, Charles MacArthur, got home all right. By five o'clock, when MacArthur was ready to go home, it seemed wise to convoy him there, and Miller nobly drove him all the way to the Hayes-MacArthur residence in Nyack, returning to fall groggily into his own bed in New York. Almost at once the telephone woke him, and Miss Hayes demanded to know where Charlie was. Miller said he had driven him home to Nyack. "To Nyack!" Miss Hayes wailed. "Good heavens, Gilbert, I *told* you we were staying at the Waldorf-Astoria!"

Miller has been married three times. His first wife was Jessie Glendinning, a young actress in his father's company. By that marriage, which ended in divorce, he has a daughter, Dorothy, and a grandson who live in Toronto. Miller's second wife, from whom he was also divorced, was Margaret Allen, whom he met during his first trip to England. In 1927, Kathryn Bache married him in spite of the worried protests of her father, who warned her, among other things, that the theatrical business was a flimsy and undependable source of income. Miller cozily remembers that after the stock market crash, two years later, his father-in-law said to him, apropos of some investments Miller had made through the Bache brokerage office, "*You* don't have to worry—you've got a good business!" Until Mr. Bache's death this year he and the Millers were an amiable trio, and they all lived together in Bache's house on Fifth Avenue, of which the Millers occupied the two top floors. The house also contained Bache's art collection, which he had presented to the State of New York with the understanding that the house was to become a museum after his death. This gesture was not without its practical side, since it enabled Bache to live in the house on museum terms, or tax-free. On certain days specified by the

Bache office in Wall Street, the public was admitted to the first three floors to view the collection, and some thirty or forty students, painters, and possibly a few housewives curious to see the inside of a Fifth Avenue mansion would wander through the rooms in the wake of a guide or a teacher from an art school. Sometimes sensitive newcomers were brought to a sudden, astonished halt in a small study on the second floor, where they were faced by two life-sized, tinted, terra-cotta heads of Bache and Mrs. Miller, standing importantly between a Frans Hals portrait and a Rembrandt Christ.

The Millers now have a dwelling on Park Avenue, and except for their recent period of mourning, live a full life socially, entertaining, dining out, and going to the theater, where Miller, for whom all theater seats are too small, is often possessed by a creeping form of his Hyde alter ego and is saved from an outburst only by his talent for going to sleep quickly and sleeping throughout a performance. One night the Millers went to see *The Skin of Our Teeth,* which Gilbert, who had turned it down when Thorton Wilder offered it to him, so volubly disliked that Mrs. Miller wanted to leave after the first act. Her husband said no, their seats were in the first row and they would be missed, and he couldn't risk offending his old friends Tallulah Bankhead and Fredric March. As the curtain rose again he dozed off, unaware that the play was proceeding toward the scene in which Miss Bankhead lures Mr. March off the stage into the orchestra pit, which happened to be directly at Miller's feet. He woke up with a start, under the impression that the actors had suddenly chosen to continue the play sitting on his knees, and found March and Miss Bankhead icily regarding him from about a yard away. The Millers left quietly at the next intermission.

Generally Mrs. Miller is philosophical about her husband's drowsiness in the presence of entertainment. One evening, a guest in the Miller apartment pointed to the host, who was sleeping quietly beside a blaring radio. "Gilbert has perfected the knack of sleeping through dramas," his wife explained. "Now he's practicing to be able to sleep through musical comedies too."

Although Gilbert Miller is physically built along lethargic lines, his wildly fluctuating moods change as swiftly as the reflections of a man passing a series of Coney Island mirrors. Within the space of a half hour, Miller can be cushiony and smiling, blackbrowed and stubborn, and contorted into fury. Sometimes he manages to combine all three aspects in a single antic. Frederick McKay, a friend and associate, once happened to be in Miller's office in Rockefeller Center when a secretary brought in the wrong papers, or made some such mistake. Miller raged at her so mercilessly that McKay, embarrassed, turned to leave. Miller grabbed his wrist. "Don't go," he commanded, and at that moment the telephone rang. Still holding McKay's wrist and hastily telling the secretary to wait where she was, Miller picked up the receiver and carried on a cooing and sociable conversation with the Palm Beach acquaintance who had rung him up. Then he replaced the receiver and, without loosening his grip on McKay, resumed his tirade against the secretary where it had been interrupted.

Middle age, occasional ill-health, and seventeen years of quiet matrimony have mellowed his temper, so that now he almost visibly counts ten before he yells, but his awareness of this improvement sometimes irritates him to a frazzle. "Goddamit, I can't even get *mad* any more!" he shouted at his wife one day not long ago when things were annoying him. He has always had a disarming way of admitting that his disposition is far from angelic. Several years ago he asked a friend in Washington to sound out one Frank P. Morse, a Washington broker whom both men knew, as to whether Morse would like to come to New York to be Miller's general manager. The friend reported that Morse had declined, saying frankly that Gilbert's fits of temper were more than he would care to stand. "But doesn't he realize," Miller gravely inquired, "that I would be away in Europe six months of every year?"

Miller's lightning changes of character remind some people of Dr. Jekyll and Mr. Hyde, but European pals who have seen him glow with pleasure and burn with rage think of him indulgently as being more like the kind of waltzing mouse that circulates dreamily for a while and then suddenly, in another mood, dashes itself to pieces. Toward Europeans, whom he loves, Miller comes nearest to being consistently gentle. In 1938, when the news got around that Hitler intended to occupy Austria, Miller heard the tidings in Vienna. For all anyone knew then, the Germans planned to march on into Hungary as well, and Miller worriedly sent word to his friend and Hungarian representative, Alexander Ince, who was in Budapest, saying that Hitler was coming to Vienna and that Ince had better join Miller there immediately and fly to Paris. Ince wired back, "Sorry I cannot join you in Vienna. Wally Beery is coming to Budapest." This lightheartedness was typical of the times and of the world that Miller, as a producer active and well known on both sides of the Atlantic, had come to inhabit and enjoy. In 1938, his production of *Victoria Regina* was in its third season in New York, with Helen Hayes, and its tenth month in London, with Pamela Stanley. His newer play, *Oscar Wilde*, was a success on Broadway and he had two companies of *Tovarich* touring American cities. He was also planning a London production of that box-office boon, *The Women*, through an arrangement with Max Gordon, who had presented it in New York. "I don't produce plays in England, and Gilbert had the high hat on there" is the way Gordon, a picturesque talker, explains the deal. Miller's high hat had gleamed in most of the European capitals by 1938. *The Women* would be his seventy-third London production, and his success, in London and in New York, with English adaptations of plays by Middle-European playwrights such as Molnar, Lajos Biro, and Melchior Lengyel had made him equally prominent in Vienna, Budapest, and Prague. He had been having a fine time in Vienna until the Führer flounced in, and the rumble of war was less strong in his ears than the strains of the *Wienerwalzer*, which he likes to hum along with an orchestra, swaying his big body and keeping time with a plump hand. He left Vienna reluctantly, flying to Paris in one of his own planes. He generally travelled in a Stinson, sometimes flying it himself, occasionally taking along Frank Steinman, his pilot. Miller was a great one at trading in old planes for new, and at one time he owned five. Most of them were upholstered in red leather and had windows you could turn up and down, like the windows in a limousine.

The war burst upon Miller and his wife the following year in a way that was almost personally insulting, though accidental. Flying from Zurich to Paris, with Miller piloting, they were fired on by French antiaircraft guns as they crossed the French frontier. Mrs. Miller describes the incident coolly today, apparently unaware that the implied picture of the Millers' prewar social schedule is more staggering to the average listener than the fracas at the frontier. "We had flown from London to Geneva to see the Goya collection that had been evacuated from Spain," she relates. "Then we went on to Lausanne for dinner and ran into Grace Moore, and she gave us two tickets she couldn't use for the Toscanini concert in Lucerne the next night, so we flew to Lucerne in the morning. Somebody in Lucerne told us about a wonderful fair they were having in Zurich, so next day we went to the fair." She pauses reflectively here and murmurs, "It was really too beguiling." Then she continues, "That night we were dining at the British Embassy when a naval attaché, Captain Holland, told us we'd better get out of Zurich because the war situation looked bad, so we took off in the morning for Elsie Mendl's at Versailles. Of course we knew there was a rule that private planes mustn't fly over the militarized zone at the frontier, and we made the detour, according to Gilbert's map. But they had changed the detour in case of war, and it seems we were flying right smack across the military zone. A lot of guns roared at us and bullets began whizzing past the plane. Luckily we weren't hit, but I was never so glad to get anywhere in my life as I was when we arrived at Elsie's and found them all sitting around having champagne, and everything back to normal."

Miller learned to fly at the age of fifty, and says that he was inspired by the example of Leland Hayward, the Hollywood agent and amateur pilot, a younger and more erratic man. "If that nut could fly a plane, I figured I could too," is the way Miller puts it. The two men have a common commercial interest in aviation. Hayward is chairman of the board of Southwest Airways, which operates, for the United States and British governments, four training fields near Phoenix, Arizona, and Miller is a large stockholder in the company. Flying instructors say that Miller is a good pilot, but some erstwhile passengers feel that he has a tendency to dream at the controls, and at least one claims to have seen him set the instruments and relax cozily, at six thousand feet, to read the manuscript of a new play. One time, flying alone through fog from London to visit Lord Brownlow, a friend who lived in the country, he got lost when his map blew out of a window and, coming down to ask directions, he landed in a hedge surrounding a cottage. The lady of the house came out and regarded him coldly, her hands on her hips. "Why don't you look where you're going?" she demanded. Miller arrived at Brownlow's six hours late, in such a temper that he made another bad landing, this time on his host's private field. According to E. Ray Goetz, who was present, the plane bounced in the air three times while Brownlow and Goetz looked on in horror, expecting it to turn over and burst into flames. It came to rest at last, upright, and Miller piled out, cursing, and strode savagely toward his host. "What's the idea of letting your field get in that condition?" he roared.

Miller has a curious indifference to maps, and once, undertaking to fly a friend from Paris to Nuremberg to lunch at a restaurant he had heard about, came down by mistake in Düsseldorf, a couple of hundred miles away, thinking it was Nuremberg. It was lunchtime, so they lunched cheerfully in Düsseldorf. Miller has turned over to the American and British governments the planes he owned at the outbreak of the war. A man who felt relieved by this news was a Hungarian friend whom Miller had taken for a flight over Manhattan some years ago, swooping around thrillingly to point out all the sights. When they came down, Miller, eager to keep his guest amused, suggested, "What do you say we go and have a Turkish bath?" The Hungarian wiped his brow. "No thanks, I've had mine," he said.

Miller's name first appeared on theater programs as a producer in 1927, when he had been general manager of Charles Frohman, Inc., for six years and had been producing plays under the Frohman name for that length of time. The Frohman company was owned by Adolph Zukor and Jesse Lasky, who also controlled Famous Players-Lasky and Paramount, and the idea was to have Miller put on in New York plays that Hollywood could then turn into pictures. Hollywood people like the prestige of a Broadway run as a prelude to a movie *première*, and they are not unhappy if the play, as well as the picture, makes money. When Miller's cosmopolitan tastes led him to produce plays that were such unlikely material for closely censored Hollywood as *Casanova, The Swan, Grounds for Divorce,* and *Easy Virtue,* Zukor began to worry a little, but the plays were financially successful and he could scarcely complain. When, however, Miller followed these productions with *The Captive,* a play about Lesbians, Zukor jumped up and down.

The Captive played eighteen weeks to packed houses, while Zukor visibly aged. Finally, the New York Police Department, prodded by anti-vice societies and newspaper editorials, raided the show one night and hauled Helen Menken, its star, and the rest of the cast off to night court. James F. Reilly, who was then Miller's general manager, had the presence of mind to tell the box-office man not to deposit the evening's take, and stuffed the cash, which amounted to some $2,400, into his pockets. Then he telephoned Miller at home to break the news that Lieutenant James C. Coy had a warrant for Miller's arrest. The boss was giving a dinner party in the bachelor flat on Park Avenue where he lived at that time. He excused himself to his guests and took a taxi to the police station, arriving importantly in white tie and tails. After Miller had made a strong speech protesting the arrest, Reilly turned up with the box-office money and bailed everybody out, including Miller. *The Captive* was withdrawn and Miller was required by the district attorney to sign an affidavit that he would never again produce the play in New York State. The police took the scenery to a public dump on Long Island and burned it.

The somewhat unexpected result of *The Captive* debacle was that the words "Gilbert Miller Presents" appeared forthwith on the programs of two other Frohman shows then running in New York, *The Play's the Thing* and *The Constant*

Wife. Miller now says that he just went ahead and had the programs printed that way. "Zukor was in Hollywood; he couldn't say anything. And I am a great believer in the *fait accompli*," he adds. Presumably he wouldn't have cared if Zukor *had* objected, for his spirits were high and untrammelled that season. It was in the same year, 1927, that he married Kathryn Bache, and he was feeling as fine, free, and independent as any bridegroom, and more so than some.

Miller stayed on as general manager of Charles Frohman, Inc., for the next five years, and produced many successful plays for the company. In 1932, four years before Charles Frohman, Inc., was dissolved, he resigned and put on his first independent production, *The Late Christopher Bean*. Since then he has produced such memorable plays in New York and in London as *The Petrified Forest*, *Reunion in Vienna*, *Payment Deferred*, *Men in White*, and *Harriet*. His American stars have included Helen Hayes, Katharine Cornell, Ina Claire, Alfred Lunt and Lynn Fontanne, Ethel Barrymore, Ruth Gordon, Jeanne Eagels, and Eva Le Gallienne. Among the English actors he has introduced to America are the late Leslie Howard, Basil Rathbone, Sir Cedric Hardwicke, and Charles Laughton. Theatergoers think of "a Gilbert Miller opening" as reverently as they mention "a Helen Hayes opening" or "a Katharine Cornell opening," and until the war put a stop to dressing up, most first-nighters would as soon have gone to a Miller opening naked as without their white ties and chinchilla wraps.

Opening nights and even tryouts are sacred to Miller, too, and he once, in England, gave his old friend Frederick McKay the full Jekyll-and-Hyde, or waltzing-mouse, treatment because McKay had booked passage for America on a ship whose sailing time prevented him from going with Miller to Bournemouth for the out-of-town opening of *Tovarich*. It happened that Miller, in an earlier, expansive mood, had sent McKay to his London tailor with instructions to order a fine suit of dress clothes as a present from his pal. McKay had done so, and had also ordered two or three business suits, to be charged to his own account. In the stormy scene over the *Tovarich* mixup, Miller reminded McKay of his gift of the dress suit and accused him of foul ingratitude. McKay, escaping, called up the tailor and told him to put the dress suit on his own bill, as well as the other clothes. After McKay had sailed for America as scheduled, Miller, suspecting some such gesture, telephoned the tailor and ordered him to charge all of McKay's suits to *him.* McKay beat him to the payment, and Miller, arriving in the United States some time later, made one of his abrupt and awkward attempts to square things. His olive branch was an invitation to dinner at the Bache house, after which he took McKay to his own room and offered him all the clothes Miller himself had grown too fat to wear.

This was quite a gesture, since Miller generally hangs on to the clothes he has outgrown, never knowing when a spasm of dieting may lose him ten pounds and enable him to fit himself joyfully once more into the waiting garments. His English valet, who was with him twelve years, now has a war job in England, and Miller is attended by a morose Irishman. Burgess Meredith tells a story of happier days, when he and Miller once crossed on the same boat to Europe. There was a trapshooting tournament on deck one morning, and the assembled contestants gaped when Miller arrived wearing a hunting jacket and followed by his English valet, carrying a gun case. When Miller's turn came, he selected a gun and frowningly took aim. "One moment, sir!" cried the valet, bringing a little box out of his pocket. Miller laid down his gun, opened the box, took out two cotton ear plugs, and gravely placed them in his ears. Then he handed the box back, raised his gun again, waited for the bird, aimed, and fired. "The only proper ending to that story would be to have him miss," Meredith says, "but it wouldn't be true. He's a hell of a shot. As I remember it, he won the tournament."

Tales of American grandeur in Europe between the two wars sound thin these days, but Miller and his wife developed a refinement of *luxe* that is still interesting for its simplicity. Other people travelled with forty trunks and a staff of servants; the Millers travelled empty-handed because they had five establishments running at once—a house in Mayfair and one in Sussex, a flat in Paris, a villa in Biarritz and another at Le Touquet—and each one was partly staffed and fully equipped with clothes and toilet articles. The Millers never had to carry so much as a toothbrush when they went from one of their homes to another. Miller's contribution to Drungewick Manor, the place in Sussex, was a landing field, which is now plowed up and turned into a vegetable farm. He still owns Drungewick and the house in London, which is currently occupied by the Norwegian Military Command, a branch of the Norwegian Government in Exile. It's hard to tell, of course, who now owns the places in France.

When *Victoria Regina* opened in London, Princess Beatrice, a daughter of Queen Victoria, received the Millers in her box and graciously pointed out two errors in the play. John Brown would have worn green, not black, at Balmoral, she said, and the Queen would have addressed him as "my good Brown," not "my dear Brown." Miller corrected the mistakes, and frivolous friends who heard about the incident addressed Mrs. Miller for some time afterward as "my good Kitty." The late Duke of Kent and his duchess, who were the gayest members of the British Royal Family, used to drop in on the Millers so often that Kitty Miller was soon qualified to join in the current hostesses' whisper, which went, "They're charming, but *what* party-crashers!" The Millers knew the Duke when he was just Prince George, and one story other expatriates of the period never tired of telling involves the following dialogue between Miller and an American friend he encountered:

Miller: You know what the Prince calls Kitty?

Friend (*interested*): No! What does he call her?

Miller: Kitty!

Miller defends himself against accusations of snobbishness in much the same way that a pretty girl modestly disclaims her looks, and he denies now that this conversation ever took place. He adds crisply that what the Prince actually called Kitty was Flash.

As a clubman, Miller is not a conspicuous success. He belongs to the Buck's Club in London and to The Players in New York, and he was once proposed by Leonard Thomas for membership in the Racquet and Tennis. So far, however, the

Racquet Club has limited its theatrical members to two, Lieutenant Commander Robert Montgomery and Fred Astaire. Members of actors' clubs are cool to Miller, partly because actors like to tell stories and he is a poor listener. At The Players, one time, an acquaintance started to tell him an anecdote involving several people and prefaced it not only by mentioning their names but also by giving a short description of each. "Yes, yes, I know them all—get on with it," Miller interrupted curtly, and killed the story on the spot. A more urbane man might have stifled his boredom and waited politely for the point, but Miller has no more social armor than an angry baby. At a party in Hollywood not long ago, Louis B. Mayer, who is accustomed to reverent handling, crossed a patio to speak to Miller. Miller feels slightly hostile toward Mayer, who, he says, has always been a great one to borrow English actors imported by Miller and never return them. As Mayer approached with outstretched hand, Miller looked at him and said, "What? You here begging again?" Later, Mayer's daughter, Irene Selznick, reproached Miller. "You mustn't speak that way to a man of my father's age," she protested. "Look," Miller said, "I'll be fifty-nine next July. Your father says he's fifty-two. If he wants to be fifty-two, he's just a kid to me." Miller's hapless impulses have occasionally lost him a valuable actor. Several years ago Herbert Marshall came to New York from Hollywood to go into a Miller production. He stalked back to Hollywood at once when Miller greeted him with a long, abusive, and ribald tirade against the one movie actress Marshall happened to prefer to any other. The two men are on fairly good terms now, however. Nearly everybody finally forgives Miller, sometimes for business reasons, often because he can be so charming that they forget their wounds.

Miller likes to think of himself as a raconteur, gourmet, and boon companion, and some people who know him well agree that those words describe him, though one intimate, pondering the term "gourmet," finally said, "Well, he's a terrible eater all right, if that's what you mean." Miller once opened a restaurant of his own in Paris, in partnership with Walter Wanger, a gourmet from Hollywood. It was called Les Frolics, and the two owners closed it up after they arrived one evening and found the two best tables occupied by a maharaja and his suite. "Why do you suppose we opened a restaurant except to get the best tables?" Miller demanded of his headwaiter as he firmly paid him off.

Miller has made as much as $700,000 in one of his good theatrical seasons, and has lost almost that amount in one or two of his bad ones. He holds ninety-nine-year leases on two London theaters, the Lyric and the St. James, and in the first two years of war, when English people stayed home nights, he lost $200,000 on those two theaters alone. Now that the British are going to the theater again, he has begun to recover his losses. He also operates the Henry Miller Theatre in New York, which his father built with the financial backing of Klaw & Erlanger and of Mrs. Elizabeth Milbank Anderson, Jeremiah Milbank's daughter, who owned the lot on West Forty-third Street where the theater now stands. After Henry Miller's death in 1926, Gilbert bought out the Klaw & Erlanger interest and was sole lessee of the theater until its lease expired. He now manages it through an agreement with the Milbank Memorial Fund, paying its executors twenty-five per cent of the gross take of each play he produces there. The Henry Miller has housed many of Gilbert's successes, but it has also been the scene of such successive and instantaneous Miller flops as *Delicate Story*, which ran three weeks, *Heart of a City* (three weeks) and *Flare Path* (ten days). *Delicate Story*, a Molnar trifle in six scenes, was described on the program as having been "translated and staged by Gilbert Miller," and its dialogue unfortunately included, in scene 5, the line "Are you trying to use the world tragedy to excuse your filthy behavior?" On opening night this was enough to send Richard Watts, the *Herald Tribune* critic, quietly up the aisle and out, and witnesses declare that Miller, who saw him leaving, pounded after him, hoarsely muttering, "I didn't write that line, I never *heard* it before!"

It sometimes seems that people begrudge Miller even his most heartfelt utterances. After the successful opening of *Harriet* at the Henry Miller last season, Miller gratefully went backstage to see Helen Hayes and said, among other tributes, "*Dear Brutus* was your youth, Helen, *Coquette* was your adolescence, and *Harriet* is your maturity." Miss Hayes's husband, Major Charles MacArthur, who was also present, shook his head. "You've got it wrong, Gilbert," he murmured. "*Dear Brutus* was Helen's youth, *Coquette* was her adolescence, and *Harriet* is *your* maturity."

Most theatrical producers like to gamble for relaxation as well as for a living, and Miller's outside speculations have included horse racing and foreign exchange. He and Frank Curzon, a London theatrical manager, were joint owners of Primrose House, a racing stable at Newmarket, England. Call Boy, Golden Boy, and Scofflaw were all Primrose House horses, and Miller still regrets that he sold his interest to Curzon in 1926, just a year before Call Boy won the Derby. As a businessman active in England and America, he has long been obliged to deal in two kinds of currency, and he began to study exchange seriously some years ago when he noticed that fluctuations in value were occasionally hurting his profits. In 1934, when President Roosevelt announced the devaluation of the dollar, Miller had already sold the dollar short in England, a piece of foresight which made him a tidy sum. Six months later the United States Treasury's decision to buy up silver found Miller loaded with silver he had bought on margin through his London broker and was now able to sell at a profit. One December evening in 1935, he was dining in a Baltimore restaurant before the tryout of a new play. His companions were Ray Goetz and George Marshall, the Washington laundry man who also owns a football team. The talk turned to fairly deep things, and Miller said, "The trouble with you two boys is you live too dangerously. Ray, here, retires at the height of his career just because he thinks he has enough money to live on, and you, George, put your money in a ball team. I call that dangerous living." The headwaiter interrupted Miller to tell him that his hotel had transferred a telephone call for him to the restaurant, and to usher him to a booth. It was a transatlantic call, relayed from New York, and Miller's London broker was on the wire. The United States Government had stopped pegging the price of silver, he informed his client, the silver market had collapsed, Miller's losses were amounting to $25,000 a day, and the London firm regretted that it could no longer cover him. Miller hung up, called his New York broker at his home, and arranged to sell enough stocks, bonds, and so on to meet the catastrophe. He says now that it took about everything he had, including some of his wife's jewels, and that he came out of the telephone booth broke. "Well, boys," he said to Goetz and Marshall, "we might as well go on over and see the show."

The play that tried out in Baltimore that night was *Victoria Regina,* and it ran four years in New York and on tour and made $2,671,778 gross. About half of Miller's share went to the government in taxes, and it was soon after the play's phenomenal success that he formed Heron Productions, Inc., as a means of simplifying his bookkeeping. Helen Hayes and Charles MacArthur are said to own thirty-five per cent of *Harriet,* but neither owned any of *Victoria,* and Miss Hayes worked throughout the run of the play on a straight salary of $1,500 a week, plus ten per cent of the weekly gross. All of this brought her an average of $2,400 a week in New York and $3,200 weekly on tour. There is a story, possibly apocryphal, that Miller, one Christmas, tried to make her a present of ten per cent of *Victoria,* and that she declined it sweetly with a note saying, "No thank you, Gilbert, I have the same troubles you have."

Miller's love of the theater is genuine, and the theater's rewards, though erratic, have been enough to enable him to answer Hollywood offers with the single, stunning, and implausible statement that riches do not tempt him. His apparent indifference to selling plays to the movies also acts on film producers like catnip on a cat. In 1936, as he was about to sail for Europe after the New York opening of *Tovarich,* Metro-Goldwyn-Mayer telephoned him from Hollywood and offered $80,000 for the picture rights to the play. Miller refused the offer and sailed. In Brighton, about a week water, another call from Metro offered more money, and a few days afterward Metro phoned him in Karlsbad and raised the bid again. By the time Miller arrived in Prague other picture companies had started bidding by transatlantic telephone and he finally sold the play to Warner Brothers for $100,000, a fairly big price in those days. "Never go to Hollywood to sell a picture," he was heard to muse after that. "Go to Vienna and make 'em call you up from Hollywood."

Miller wears a telephone as constantly as any movie producer, and his wife sometimes frets when this habit makes them late for engagements, but her fretting is indulgent. Her husband has an eye for a production at home as well as on a stage, and his efforts can be winning. During the first winter they spent together in London, when they were living in a hotel and the foggy weather began to depress Mrs. Miller, he would bustle around every morning, fixing up the living room to cheer her, before he let her maid wake her up. When she joined him there for breakfast she would find the curtains drawn against the fog, a fire dancing on the hearth, dozens of red roses in vases everywhere, and a portable phonograph playing a Viennese waltz. Remembering that, she lets him telephone as much as he wants to, although she flinches slightly from his choice of a cozy telephone nook; he makes most of his calls on an extension in the lavatory adjoining his private office.

The Millers spend most of their time in New York, taking their vacations on a farm they own in Sandy Hook, Connecticut. Their present dwellings are simpler than the Bache mansion, which was baronial, with a vast entrance hall and yawning black fireplaces big enough to stand a horse in, and used to frighten some of the Millers' Middle-European guests. "There are oubliettes in this house," Ludwig Bemelmans declared one night at a party there, glancing nervously over his shoulder. "I am talking to Goetz one minute ago, a picture turns on the wall, and he is gone." Ince, Molnar, and many of Miller's other Continental friends have come to live in New York since the war. Molnar was temporarily annoyed with Miller last winter for turning down his latest play, *The King's Mate*. "Oscar Serlin produced it and lost fifty thousand dollars," Miller remarks when the subject comes up. Nobody has ever successfully mistaken Miller's love of Viennese waltzes, red roses, and red-coated Hungarian gypsy musicians for the kind of sentimentality that might seduce him into putting on a friend's play if he thought he was going to lose money on it. He can be as ruthless in five foreign languages as he can be in his native tongue, and as unpredictable. One time, during a rehearsal of a play adapted from the French, he turned from arguing in French with a Parisian actor and absent-mindedly shouted an order, also in French, to Peter Mason, a timid Negro who worked for him as porter, errand boy, and harassed handyman. Without stopping to ask questions, Peter streaked up the aisle and out of the theater, returning soon with a handful of pencils, a package of cigarettes, a quart of ice cream, and a newspaper. Miller took the newspaper and waved aside the other offerings. "I didn't know what the boss was sayin'," Peter explained to an interested onlooker, "but when he yells like that he mostly wants one of them four things."

Miller knows that his manner confuses people and he thinks it is because he often doesn't know whom he is talking to, having a poor memory for names. He cites as an instance a tangle he once got into when he engaged an actor for a New York play by cable from London. His New York office signed the actor he had named in the cable, and Miller, arriving home, discovered that he had remembered the name of the wrong actor. He had to pay the wrong actor a weekly salary for the run of the play besides paying the right actor, when he finally recollected who he was. Theater people don't care much for eccentricities that include forgetting their names, and there are one or two who would just as soon forget Gilbert Miller's if it were economically advisable.

Old friends from Europe understand Miller better. "He is a refugee, like the rest of us," one of them said thoughtfully not long ago, watching Miller beat time to a czardas orchestra playing a waltz from *Der Rosenkavalier*. Europe being what it is, his foreign cronies often snatch him out of his memories with a demand for quick action, and they usually get it. Shortly before his death last winter, Dr. Rudolf Kommer telephoned him and asked his aid in smuggling a young German anti-Nazi out of the Reich. Miller will almost tenderly help people out of trouble, but he likes to have an eagle-eyed control over what they do afterward. The young man having arrived safely in America, Miller spoke crisply to Kommer. "Tell your friend," he said, "that New York is overrun with refugees asking for jobs. Tell him to get out of New York. Farmers need workers. Tell this boy to get *out* of New York." Next day, the young German called on Miller at his office to thank him for his help. "Doctor Kommer has given me your message," he added, "and I have obeyed. Tomorrow, Herr Miller, I leave for Hollywood."

2

The Old Max:

MAX GORDON

THEATRICAL PRODUCERS, as portrayed in the movies by actors like Adolphe Menjou, are generally either frantic fellows rushing around to avert last-minute disasters and living largely on aspirin and bicarbonate of soda or suave, world-weary celebrities who seldom appear in anything but white tie and tails. Max Gordon, the producer of such hits as *Roberta, Design for Living, The Women, My Sister Eileen, The Doughgirls, and Over Twenty-One,* resembles neither of these types. He is a sturdy, compact-looking man in his fifties with a leisurely and friendly air that prompts people who know him to refer to him comfortably at times as "the old Max." He wears eyeglasses and grayish or brownish clothes that are all so much alike that a friend once complained that he always seemed to be wearing the same suit. "It *is* the same suit," Gordon told him rather indignantly. He is pleased by his reputation as the most unaffected man in show business and is likely to emphasize his own artlessness to a fancy degree. His private office, one of two shabby rooms above the Lyceum Theatre, contains a desk he bought when he started in the theatrical business thirty years ago, a few chairs upholstered in threadbare plush, and a cuspidor. This apartment is even less pretentious than another office he had a few years ago whose walls, covered with photographs of stage celebrities, were panelled in imitation pine. Gordon always asked newcomers what they thought of that office, and once when a caller hesitantly replied, "Well, the pine panelling is very elegant," the old Max rapped his knuckles against it and smiled proudly. "It's phony," he announced.

Visitors to the office generally find Gordon sitting in a sunny window with his feet propped against the desk, reading *Variety* or *Racing Form* or doing nothing in particular beyond gazing at his hands with the idle air of a man about to file his nails. To anyone who expresses astonishment at this aimlessness in so prominent a man, Gordon enjoys explaining a favorite theory of his: that the men who accomplish the most are those who seem least busy. "President Roosevelt, Bernard Baruch, men like that," he expounds, "you walk into their offices—I've been there—and their desks are absolutely clean, not a paper on 'em." Here he waves a hand toward his own desk, which is remarkably cluttered. He disposes easily of that *non sequitur,* however. "There is positively nothing of importance there," he says.

In spite of his simplicity, Gordon has been described affectionately by people who know him well as an intellectual snob. He has a passion for anyone whom he suspects of being an authority on something or other, and he will bombard such a personage on sight with questions so direct and all-encompassing as to produce a certain bewilderment in his victim. Not long ago, at a cocktail party given by Arthur Schwartz, the composer, his host pointed out Arthur Garfield Hays, the attorney and liberal, standing at the other end of the room chatting with a group of people. "I want to talk to that fella," Gordon said, and waving aside Schwartz's offer of an introduction, he hurried over and tapped Hays on the arm. "Tell me," he inquired, "do you think the whole thing is going to blow up?" Another time, at a dinner, he was introduced to a doctor, and opened the conversation by saying, "Doctor, I've got the funniest pain, right here in the small of my back." The doctor interrupted him politely. "I don't happen to be a doctor of medicine, I'm a doctor of sociology and economics," he said. Gordon's eagerness did not falter. "Tell me," he asked at once, intensely, "do you think Anaconda Copper is going up or down?"

Max Gordon's career has been so vivid that it might well fill a number of volumes entitled, like a boys' adventure series, *Max Gordon, the East Side Urchin, Max Gordon with the Keith-Orpheum Circuit, Max Gordon on Broadway,* and *Max*

Gordon, the President's Friend. Gordon the East Side urchin is now a frequent guest at lunch or dinner in the White House with the President and Mrs. Roosevelt, whom he met through James A. Farley, once something of an urchin himself. The Roosevelts like him, probably because he is as natural with them as he is with, say, Groucho Marx or any of his other cronies. "I never saw a reason to be afraid of a man, whether a President or a Pullman porter," Gordon says. A few weeks before the 1940 election, he dined at the White House with some fifteen or twenty other guests and was seated on Mrs. Roosevelt's left. "Mrs. Roosevelt," he asked, when she turned graciously to talk to him, "did you hear the gag about the two acrobats outside the Palace Theatre? One says to the other, 'You gonna vote for Roosevelt?' and the other one says, 'What's the matter with the guy that's in there?' " Mrs. Roosevelt liked this story so much ("It killed her," Gordon relates simply) that she called to her husband down the length of the table, "Franklin, you must hear this!" and made him repeat it. Gordon voted for Willkie. He is full of surprises like that.

Max Gordon the President's friend is candid about Max Gordon the East Side urchin, though he sometimes worries faintly for fear his own start in life may sound so humble as to appear pretentious. "I was born in poverty at 59 Goerck Street in the slums of New York, and my father was a pants-presser in a sweatshop," he will tell you, adding hastily, "but don't think I'm saying this just to sound important." Max's name was originally Salpeter, and his family included ten people—his father and mother, himself, two older brothers named Cliff and Dave, and five sisters. When Max was eight, the Salpeters moved to a flat on Lewis Street, where all ten of them lived in four rooms. Max went to Public School 88, a couple of blocks away. Mr. Salpeter was ambitious for his children, and one evening, reading the paper that Jan Kubelik, the violinist, had received $1,000 for one concert, he laid the paper on his knee and shook his head sorrowfully at Cliff, his eldest. "And to think," he said, "how I begged you to take violin lessons." On Saturdays, when he brought his weekly wages of $11 home and laid the money on the table, he would sometimes look severely at his sons and say, "I hope I live to see the day when *you* will be making eleven dollars a week." Gordon, who has occasionally made a thousand times that amount weekly, regrets that his father did not live to see the day, but he thinks it might have worried him anyway. In 1930, after his first big hit, *Three's a Crowd,* had opened, Max took some *Variety* clippings giving the show's weekly grosses to the apartment he had leased for his mother on the upper West Side and showed them to her. Mrs. Salpeter read the clippings gravely and said, "Tell me one thing, Max. Is it honest?"

The Salpeter boys discovered the theater when they were still in short pants, and sold popcorn at baseball games to get money for tickets to the neighborhood shows. Once they walked two miles to see a team called Herbert & Willy at Tony Pastor's, and couldn't get in because they were not accompanied by an adult. After that they learned to stand in line at the box office behind somebody else's mother and act as though they were with her, or, if that failed, to appeal frankly to some sympathetic grownup who would shepherd them inside and then leave them alone. When Cliff was fifteen he began to appear on amateur nights with a monologue he had worked up, and a year or so later he got a job with a burlesque show called *The Social Maids* and changed his name to Cliff Gordon. Dave also eventually went into the show business, as an agent, but with less conspicuous success than his brothers. He died nine years ago.

By 1910, Cliff Gordon had become well known in burlesque as a German-dialect comedian. He wore the conventional baggy pants and comic makeup and commented on topical events in the kind of monologue that Will Rogers was later to make more famous. Max was seventeen and a freshman at City College, but he wanted to quit his studies and follow Cliff into the theater. Cliff discouraged the idea, and even persuaded Raymond Hitchcock, whom he had come to know, to deliver a short lecture to Max on the advantages of a college education. Max listened, thinking of the letter he had written privately to one Jack Singer, owner of the Hyde & Behman burlesque shows, asking for a job. Singer took him on in a rather vague capacity, and Max joined one of the shows in Pittsburgh. His duties included announcing the Hyde & Behman features for the following week from the stage after the final curtain, and he pensively recalls his first appearance. "I walk out on the stage," Gordon relates, "and I say, 'Ladies and Gentlemen, next week's sensational attraction—' and a banana hits me right in the face."

A framed copy of a letter Gordon wrote to his family in January 1912 from the Bay Tree Hotel in Toronto now hangs on a wall of his office in the Lyceum. It reads, "My dear Folks, Enclosed please find $16. Five keep and Eleven bank. I sent home my tuxedo. Tell Papa to press it up for me. Your son Max." Max, nineteen then, was travelling with a burlesque troupe called *The Passing Parade,* of which Cliff Gordon was the star comedian. Cliff, unable to restrain his brother from a theatrical career, had found a job for him in the business end of his own outfit, and Max, settling down gratefully, had also adopted the name of Gordon. In Minneapolis *The Passing Parade* caught up with a smaller burlesque company presenting something called *Vanity Fair,* in which one Al Lewis did a comic monologue similar to Cliff Gordon's, though less impressive. Lewis revered Cliff as a big-time comedian, and when he heard one day that Cliff's brother Max was in the theater to catch a matinee of *Vanity Fair,* he hastily dug up twelve extra verses of a topical song that he had prepared as encores and, hoping to impress Max, sang all of them, doggedly reappearing twelve times in spite of an almost frantic lack of demand from the audience. After the show he invited Max to come backstage and took him to a good twenty-five-cent dinner at the Burtis House. That was the prelude to a partnership between the two men, who, as Lewis & Gordon, later produced, in association with Sam. H. Harris, such hits as *Welcome, Stranger, The Nervous Wreck, The Jazz Singer, Six-Cylinder Love, Secrets,* and *Rain.* The partnership was dissolved some years ago. Al Lewis, together with Vinton Freedley, later produced the success *Cabin in the Sky.*

In 1913, Cliff Gordon died suddenly at the age of thirty-two. Max's affection for his brother was, and is, genuinely deep, and he speaks of Cliff as "a man of infinite taste who never read a book." It was after a dazed interval following his brother's death that Max went into business with Al Lewis, who had left the stage to be a booking agent for vaudeville acts. Vaudeville, then at its height, was practically controlled by the Keith Circuit, and the spark of sentiment which often starts a long relationship in show business united Lewis & Gordon with Keith's when Max wrote to John J. Murdock, Keith's vice president and a friend of Cliff's, to tell him of Cliff's death. Murdock was grieved and, like most people in the theater, he showed his sorrow in a solid and practical way. He invited Lewis & Gordon to book their acts with the Keith Circuit. One of their first successes with Keith was a one-act play, *In the Zone,* by Eugene O'Neill, then a young and unknown playwright who asked, and was given, a fifty dollar advance on the sketch because he wanted to get married. E. F. Albee, president of the Keith Circuit, O.K.'d the advance to O'Neill. When, a few weeks later, Lewis & Gordon, drunk with power, demanded seven hundred and fifty dollars a week for an act called "Harry Green and the Cherry Tree," Albee rebelled. Gordon called on him defiantly at his office, and still remembers the details of the clash. "I am a kid from a burlesque show and I fear nobody" is the way he describes himself as he was then, adding, "Albee threw me out."

Phil Baker and Lou Holtz remember Max Gordon as the booking agent who never slept during the great days of vaudeville after the Keith Circuit merged with the Orpheum Circuit and before they had combined with a firm called Radio Pictures to become Radio-Keith-Orpheum, or R.K.O. Actors in need of a job or advice could nearly always find Gordon drinking coffee at Shulem's Restaurant on Broadway after midnight, and he would greet them all with eyebrows raised in welcome and shoulders rising too in sympathy or skepticism as they talked. One night, in 1914, the late Ben Bernie, who then had a violin-and-accordion act with Phil Baker, came to Gordon with the bad news that Baker had left the act, which was booked to open in Bridgeport the following week. "Now's your chance, Ben," Max told him. "Go on alone up there in

Bridgeport and give 'em a monologue." Bernie went on in Bridgeport, gave 'em a monologue, and was hissed off the stage halfway through it. He finished his week in Bridgeport, though, a fact which still faintly mystifies Gordon. "I guess Ben must have pulled a Masonic button on the manager," he says. Another night, in Shulem's, Lou Holtz was introduced to Gordon and told him sadly that he had been fired from almost every theater in New York. Holtz was at that time a straight singer of sentimental ballads. "Sing for me," Max suggested, and Holtz then and there delivered a number entitled "In Savannah, G. A." Next day, Gordon got him a booking at the Colonial Theatre on Broadway. "He was thrown out of there, too," Gordon relates now, shaking his head reminiscently. "He was constantly closed, that fella."

Gordon's efficiency as an agent was celebrated, but his clients often found him almost romantically absent-minded. He would call up an actor and say, "I got to see you immediately, important," and the actor would rush to meet him at whatever rendezvous he had mentioned, sometimes on a street corner. They would walk several blocks, either in silence or exchanging irrelevant chitchat, while the actor anxiously waited for the important tidings. "Well," Max would say finally, "goodbye," and he would disappear. The more thoughtful of his victims have since decided it was his preoccupation with the drama that made him act that way. Baker still insists that Max always sold Bernie & Baker to Keith-Orpheum for peanuts in order to get six hundred dollars a week for some one-act play. Gordon had a reverent crush on the theater, and other vaudeville pals now surmise that what he was dreaming about when he used to get dreamy was the day he would open a theater program and see the words "Max Gordon Presents." Gordon's ambition was partly fulfilled in 1918, when he began producing plays with Al Lewis and Sam Harris, but he did not become an independent producer until 1930, when he put on *Three's a Crowd.*

Two seasons before, Dwight Wiman and Tom Weatherly had produced *The Little Show,* starring Fred Allen, Clifton Webb, and Libby Holman, with such success that they were planning a second version for 1930. They felt, however, that it would be tempting fate to use the same three stars again, so they built *The Second Little Show* around the comedians Al Trahan and Jay C. Flippen. It was not a success.

Gordon, meanwhile, hearing that Allen, Webb, and Holman were available, called up Allen, whom he had known as a juggler in burlesque, and said, "Look, I don't know these high-toned people like Webb and Holman, but I want to do a show with the three of you." Allen was enthusiastic but candidly pointed out to Max that their combined salaries amounted to about six thousand dollars a week. Gordon got together all the money he had, borrowed some more from a bank, and engaged Howard Dietz and Arthur Schwartz to write a book and score. *Three's a Crowd* opened in October. Although the show lost money on the road after a successful New York run, and finally managed only to break even, it established Gordon as a producer of the small, smart revue built around big names. It was followed by *The Band Wagon*, with the Astaires, Frank Morgan, and Helen Broderick, and such perennial songs by Schwartz and Dietz as "Dancing in the Dark," "I Love Louisa," and "New Sun in the Sky." *The Band Wagon* made $100,000, and a good many people still think of it fondly as the greatest revue of all time. Gordon had long since discovered the stock market, and by the time *Flying Colors*, his third revue, came along, he was taking a beating. Schwartz and Dietz had written a triumphant opening number for *Flying Colors*, with the following refrain:

> Do you hear the cheering in the street?
> Here is why you're hearing all the cheering in the street:
> Max Gordon raised the mo-ney,
> Max Gordon raised the mo-ney,
> Halleluiah! Halleluiah!
> The money for another revue! *

Gordon sent for the boys one day and said, "Boys, I'm afraid the show is off. I can't raise the money." Dietz shook his head sorrowfully, but Schwartz went right to the point of his grievance. "But, Max," he protested, "what are we going to do with that *song?*" Max Gordon raised the money eventually

* Used by permission of the Copyright Owners, Harms, Inc.

and *Flying Colors* was produced with the opening number intact.

Through Max Dreyfus, the music publisher, Gordon had met Jerome Kern and had persuaded him to write the score for Gordon's first ambitious musical comedy, *The Cat and the Fiddle,* which was produced in 1931. The following year, although he had three hits to his credit (*Flying Colors* folded after a short flight), Gordon's stock market losses and his instinct for engaging the best and most expensive actors, authors, directors, and composers left him broke, and he had a nervous collapse. He likes to tell how wonderful everybody was to him then, how George Kaufman offered him fifteen hundred of the sixteen hundred dollars Kaufman had at that time, and how Harpo Marx came to see him in the hospital with his pockets stuffed with cash and strewed it over the bedspread in much the same way that he used to spill knives and forks out of his coat sleeve onto a stage. Groucho Marx gives a sympathetic description of the chapter in Gordon's life which might be called *Max Gordon and the Stock Market.* "One summer day in 1929," Groucho relates, "Max and I were playing golf in Great Neck—at least I was playing golf and Max was playing that kind of running hockey of his, hitting the ball and then running five yards to hit it again—and suddenly he said to me, strolling down the fairway and twirling his club, 'Marx, why should we work at all? Here we are playing golf and having a fine time, and I already made a profit of three thousand dollars in the market today. How long has this been going on?' " A few months later, in October, Marx's telephone rang one morning and he answered it. "Marx?" said a hollow voice. "This is Salpeter. The jig is up."

Gordon refers to himself as Salpeter only in moments of stress, seldom identifies himself by any name at all on the telephone, and never says hello or goodbye, preferring to plunge at once into what he has to say and to hang up when he has said it. The day after the opening of *My Sister Eileen* he called up Moss Hart, who was in Boston rather nervously supervising rehearsals of his play *Lady in the Dark.* "I only got one minute to talk to you, Moss, so listen and don't interrupt," Gordon said. Then he read aloud to Hart some twelve or fifteen favorable reviews of *My Sister Eileen*. "I hope your show is as good, Moss," he said and hung up. Gordon has a great affection for Hart, who is a sensitive man. When they were in Washington at the same time recently, Hart remarked that he would like to meet the President and Mrs. Roosevelt, and Gordon got Stephen Early to arrange tea with the First Lady. Tea passed off pleasantly, but as Hart and Gordon were walking down the corridor on their way out, Hart complained mildly to Gordon that he had not yet met the President. "Listen," said Max, "I can do everything, but that I can't do." At that moment a White House aide overtook them, announced that the President would like to see them, and escorted them into Mr. Roosevelt's bedroom. Hart claims that Max did all the talking while they were with the President, beginning with a resumé of the situation in the American theater today and warming up to a denunciation of certain critics who had failed to appreciate *Very Warm for May*, a Gordon production. Gordon, scoffing at this version, declares that Hart was so impressed by being in the President's bedroom that he couldn't have spoken even if no one else had said a word. "You know that old gag where one fella says about the other one, 'He went as white as my shirt,' and then he looks at his shirt and says, 'No, whiter?' Well," says Gordon, "that was Moss."

Noel Coward's *Design for Living*, which Gordon produced in New York in 1933, brought him out of his financial and physical slump and set him on the path that led to *Roberta, The Shining Hour, Dodsworth, The Great Waltz, Pride and Prejudice, Othello*, and other productions—some box-office successes, others mainly satisfying to his own genuinely fastidious taste. He had met Noel Coward in London through the simple process of going backstage after a performance of *Private Lives*, introducing himself, and telling Coward what was the matter with his third act. "Do I get the play for New York?" he then inquired. Coward had made other arrangements for *Private Lives*, but he recognized expert showmanship when he saw it, and Gordon has been identified with most of his American productions since that time. Gordon has an immense respect for Coward, to which Coward responds with affectionate breeziness. When Coward attended the first night of *Roberta* in New York, Gordon started anxiously down the aisle at intermission to ask him what he thought of the show and met him coming up for a cigarette. Coward threw his arms around Gordon enthusiastically. "Max, darling!" he cried. "It *stinks!*"

In 1921, Gordon married Mildred Bartlett, an actress whose stage name was Ray Dean. She retired before their marriage at the request of her fiancé, who has a ready explanation for his demand. "I was sitting outside her dressing room waiting for her one night for about half an hour," he says, "when all of a sudden it came over me, and I thought to myself, 'What am I, a John?' " The Gordons live quietly in a hotel in the West Fifties, and their social excitement is limited mostly to Mrs. Gordon's bridge parties (Max does not play) and the annual visit of her mother, who lives in Philadelphia. Gordon's relations with his mother-in-law are agreeable, although he wistfully insists that she has never yet said hello to him. He gets up around half past six nearly every morning and reads plays until about ten, when he goes to his office. "Max is the only man in New York," George Jessel once said, "who by nine a.m. has already been lonesome for two hours." Until his mother's death nine years ago, Max used to take a taxi to her apartment on West 116th Street every morning to have breakfast with her. He does not own a car and has never learned to drive.

Some time ago a lady interviewer asked Gordon to lunch in a restaurant and paid the check over his shocked protest, even buying him a mild cigar. Max ran into Ben Bernie later in the day and told him of this experience. "I never had such a thing happen to me before in my life," he declared. "Why, listen, thirty years ago Trixie Friganza took my brother Cliff to lunch one day and paid the check, and when Cliff came home and told Mamma about it, Mamma wouldn't speak to him for a week." Bernie replied with a suggestion. "I tell you what to do, Max," he said. "You ask this lady interviewer to lunch tomorrow, and when the check comes you turn to her and say, 'This time, my dear madam, we simply *have* to toss for it.' " Gordon instantly wired the female check-grabber and reserved a table, with flowers, at Twenty-One. By the time they sat down to lunch his mind had darted to another, ever-present problem. "All I have to say to you," he told the waiter, "is keep the potatoes away from me. I got to get into my dress suit next week for the Gridiron Dinner."

Next to his own career, Gordon's greatest interest is politics and politicians, and his love for them is as rapt and absolute as a stage-struck youth's infatuation with the theater. More than once, when a play of his is opening in Washington, he has sneaked away from the theater to sit in the gallery of the House, listening happily to a debate. Morris Ernst once remarked that Max would rather meet a congressman, a senator, or even an alderman than the most dazzlingly beautiful woman in the world. "That is only a slight exaggeration," Gordon said when he heard about it. There are few politically prominent people whom he hasn't met, and he has a talent for making them remember him. The first time he was introduced to Bernard Baruch, he thrust his chin upward and forward and pointed to a mark on it. "See that scar?" he asked Baruch. "I got that when I was ten, falling off an exercise bar in the free swimming pool and gymnasium donated to the kids on Rivington Street by your father." The dramatic quality of Gordon's approach is even more apparent in his dealings with influential men in his own line of business whenever he wants them to do a favor for a pal. One time an actor who was also an old friend mentioned to Max that he was worried because his sister's husband had just been fired from his job with R.C.A. Knowing that Gordon was friendly with David Sarnoff, the president of R.C.A., the actor said, "If you happen to see Sarnoff, Max, and if you can sort of lead up to it naturally, will you put in a good word for the boy?" Gordon replied that, as it happened, Sarnoff was having dinner with him that night at the Waldorf-Astoria. "And so are you," he said to his friend. The actor agreed after some hesitation, but urged Gordon not to bring up the question of the brother-in-law's job that night. "Leave it to me," said Max. "I won't even mention it unless it happens to come up." At eight o'clock, Gordon and his pal stood at the top of the steps outside the Empire Room to welcome Sarnoff. "Say," Gordon demanded, as Sarnoff reached the top step, "what's the idea of firing this guy's brother-in-law?" The brother-in-law was reinstated next day.

Gordon's notion of diplomacy, which is to say immediately what he has to say and to expect an answer, is refreshing to a good many people bemused by the hedging, backtracking, and doubletalk of formal diplomats in high places. Max would like to run for Congress after he has produced a few more shows. He talks about his ambition reluctantly, since he has no way of knowing that it will ever be fulfilled, but while he is dismissing it with a shrug and a shake of the head, he will pick up a pencil and a piece of paper and outline his idea about income tax after the war, for instance. Max's idea about postwar income tax is that people in the creative and precarious professions, like actors, actresses, writers, musicians, playwrights, and producers, should be given a break by the government. "They may work ten years before they make a hit and they may not have another hit for the next ten," he pointed out, "yet the tax they have to pay is based on their income at its highest point." He speaks of the olden times when poets and painters were subsidized, not soaked, with a sigh of regret that the present system offers little encouragement to creators to go on creating. If Gordon does run for Congress, this platform ought to guarantee him at least several thousand votes from the harried artists of this nation.

❁ 3 ❁

The Candor Kid:

CLARE BOOTHE

ONCE UPON A TIME, in a far country called Riverside Drive, a miracle child was born and her name was Clare Boothe. Over her cradle hovered so many good fairy godmothers that an S.R.O. sign was soon put up at the foot of the crib and a couple of witches who had drifted along just for the hell of it had to fly away and come back for the Wednesday matinee. To the infant Clare, the first good fairy gave Beauty, the second gave Wealth, the third Talent, the fourth Industriousness, and the fifth Success. The sixth good fairy flew around frowning for a while, thinking up a way to make a monkey out of the other fairies, and finally she waved her wand over the crib, and lo, each gift was doubled and tripled until the infant Clare was more shiningly endowed than any other infant in the land.

By that time it was Wednesday and the two witches were back, shrieking and bumping broomsticks and quarrelling over which curse each would put upon the babe. "I will give her Unpopularity, the distrust of her fellow men and women," the first witch asserted. "So go ahead, copycat," sneered the second witch. "I have already given her Candor, which amounts to the same thing." And the two witches dropped their gifts in a shower of stars and hisses and departed, thinking the infant Clare was sound asleep. But there they were mistaken. Clare was as wide awake as anything, and she looked thoughtfully after the vanishing harpies. "I'll fix you," she lisped.

It came to pass that the maiden Clare, growing to young

womanhood, worked harder than any maiden in the land, and she grew so increasingly beautiful that the lesser maidens invented a salutation for her, which was "Work seems to agree with you, dear." When they said that, Clare would gaze at them and reply, "You're nothing but a pack of disappointed witches, you lesser maidens, you." And the lesser maidens, observing the dangerous glow that darted from the wide blue eyes, the lightning that issued from the rosebud mouth, the rigid insult regularly delivered by means of an ethereal upward glance and a flowerlike gesture of the hand, would shake their heads and marvel. "It is like taking candor from a baby," they said.

The threat against witches is one which Clare Boothe, as a playwright and as a politician, has abundantly carried out. In her first successful play, *The Women,* she tied up her own sex crisply in cellophane and delivered it to the ashcan. *Kiss the Boys Goodbye* contributed a caricature of Southern womanhood. *Margin for Error* presented a sympathetic character in the wife of the Nazi consul, but Miss Boothe considers that this character is, like Mary Haines in *The Women* (the only other admirable woman she has depicted), a fathead. In her personal war against women perhaps her deftest weapon is the careless comment, the light and maddening dismissal. During her campaign for nomination as Congresswoman from Connecticut, in 1942, a rival Republican candidate was Miss Vivien Kellems, a manufacturer of cable grips from Westport. In a ringingly unfortunate statement to the press Miss Kellems said, "Everyone talks of Clare Boothe's sex appeal. Nobody mentions mine. But I have been working fifteen years and I couldn't have stayed that long on sex appeal. I would be very mad if anyone said I was using sex appeal." When reporters asked Miss Boothe for a retort, she remarked merely, "What's the matter with that wild-eyed little woman anyway?" Miss Kellems lost the nomination and returned to her factory and to a brief subsequent flare of notoriety as a conscientious tax objector. Miss Boothe was elected by a plurality of 6,439 votes over Leroy Downs, the Democratic incumbent. With the election won, she sighed, smiled, uttered a brief "Whew!" and took a train to Hollywood, to work out a picture contract before Congress convened in December.

In the ten months between February and December 1942, Clare Boothe travelled some 75,000 miles through Africa, India, Burma, and China as foreign correspondent for *Life*, wrote several hundred thousand words about her trip for the magazine, came home and carried on her campaign for election to Congress, made the trip to Hollywood and wrote a picture about China (which has not yet been released), and returned to Washington to take office as fresh as a rose. This program, which would have shattered almost any other woman, is an example of her remarkable capacity for getting things done. Two years earlier, as a sort of warming-up exercise, she had written *Europe in the Spring*, a book about the war, in five weeks. The speed with which she turns out her plays is so familiar to her friends that one of them, thinking up ways to kill half an hour with a companion after lunch said, "Well, if we were Clare Boothe, we could write a play." Miss Boothe is active and efficient socially as the wife of Henry R. Luce, editor in chief of *Time, Life,* and *Fortune,* and as the mistress of four homes—an apartment in the Waldorf Towers in New York, a house in Greenwich, Connecticut, a plantation in Monck's Corner, near Charleston, South Carolina, and an apartment in the Wardman Park Hotel in Washington, which her husband shares when he can. Her most widely discussed quality is her beauty, which she spends little time on, except for an occasional visit to a Du Barry Salon, where she stands on her head and does many interesting exercises. Other women writers have been fair to look on, but only to the degree that surprises people into saying, "She's very good-looking for a writer," in much the same way that a certain bird-hater once remarked of a canary, "It sings well, for a canary." Miss Boothe's looks are compelling enough to establish even a writer as a beauty. She is blonde, with a complexion that is actually pearl-like and a face that is saved from too angelic a cast by a strong, handsome nose and rather heavy, straight eyebrows. Her eyes are blue, translucent, and bland; her voice is musical; and her laughter is frequent and charming. She always looks so cool and delectable that a Frenchman, describing her, once said, "It is a beautiful façade, well constructed but without central heating."

People who know Clare Boothe well realize that the clear beauty of her face, the straight regard of her limpid eyes, and the light, high laughter with which she punctuates her conversation conceal nothing sinister. She is exactly what she seems to be—an amused, tolerant, unusually good-looking woman who has, perhaps, a blind spot in her perceptions. She writes vitriolic plays about vicious people not from any conviction that vice is wrong but because she honestly sees most people as bitches, two-timers, and phonies. Virtue neither bores nor interests her. It is simply an improbable quality that she has not yet investigated. She admits, with a schoolgirl giggle, that she finds vice more intriguing. "Intriguing" is a word she uses often, and it emphasizes the remarkable youthfulness of her manner and appearance when she talks. More than one woman, chatting with Miss Boothe, has been suddenly and strangely reminded of her boarding school days when the girls would gather to whisper and chuckle after lights-out. Miss Boothe's talk is naturally less innocent than dormitory chatter, but it has the same disarming qualities of wonder and unceasing astonishment. "Clare is the most unsophisticated darling in the world," a woman friend once warmly declared. "I mean, most of us are used to the fact that a lot of people are louses, but Clare never fails to get a kick out of it."

People who are fond of Miss Boothe consider that, for one so ingenuous, she has attracted an excessive amount of vitriol to herself. These allies are constantly being called on to defend her, and they like to tell how eagerly they respond, but sometimes their loyalty finds unfortunate expression. "Mind you, I *like* Clare," a champion will remark sincerely, "and it simply enrages me to hear people say that she dyes her hair and doesn't write her own plays." Miss Boothe doesn't dye her hair, and she does write her own plays, but those two rumors—like most rumors about her—are the kind that are difficult to deny without strengthening. The oblique support of Miss Boothe's friends is hardly less deadly than the killing attack of her enemies. At a dinner in Hollywood, at which Dorothy Parker was present, Miss Boothe's name was mentioned, and a woman friend of hers at the table found herself in the familiar, bristling position of defense. She spoke at length of Miss Boothe's generosity, of the way she often helped less gifted people with money and with letters of introduction to her own influential acquaintances, and she ended, not too happily, by declaring, "Clare Boothe is always kind to her inferiors." Mrs. Parker looked up wanly. "And where," she inquired, "does she find them?"

Mrs. Parker's disinclination for Miss Boothe is said to have sprung from the familiar but apocryphal incident of the two ladies' happening to enter a restaurant at the same time, several years ago. "Age before beauty," said Miss Boothe to Mrs. Parker, according to this tale. "And pearls before swine," Mrs. Parker replied, sweeping ahead. Probably Mrs. Parker shares the distrust felt by many writers of the sweat-and-struggle school when they hear about Miss Boothe's fine, free, glowing, and effortless gift of composition. Miss Boothe writes with a pencil on manuscript paper bound into morocco covers, and she can write anywhere at any time, with such facility that the words fairly leap past each other onto the paper. She wrote the first draft of *The Women* in three days, mostly sitting up in bed in her Towers suite at the Waldorf, wearing a pink velvet bed jacket and a blue satin bow in her hair. *The Women* was played in eighteen countries and in ten languages, and it earned about $300,000 net in royalties for Miss Boothe. Such statistics may impress the writer who spends a month or two perfecting one short story or one article that will sell for some $299,000 less than Miss Boothe has made out of *The Women,* but they do not make him love Miss Boothe. There is something dilettante and infuriating to him in the pretty picture of the Muse in spats crashing the Waldorf, and he is deaf to the redeeming fact that Miss Boothe works harder than most authors at rewriting. Max Gordon, who produced *The Women,* once said, "When one of Clare's plays goes into rehearsal, that is the time I would like to break both of Clare's wrists. You give her a suggestion about changing a line, and what does she do? She goes away for a little while and comes back with a whole new act." Voluminous production is an important feature of literature to Miss Boothe, and she has no patience with unprolific writers. Once, speaking of a noted woman poet, she said, "Why, all the fuss about her? What has she done in fifty years except produce four or five slim vols. of poetry?" Since the noted woman poet was precisely forty-three years old when the remark got back to her, it may have been the carelessly inserted phrase rather than the critical comment that caused one more coolness between Miss Boothe and a fellow member of her craft. Miss Boothe is frank about her own age; she is forty-one, and admits it. "I have never heard Clare lie about her age," one female admirer said recently to another. "Neither have I," the other agreed, and after a moment's reflection added, "How old did she tell *you* she was?"

This curious doubletalk, in which every boost is a knock, enmeshes even people who sincerely like and respect Miss Boothe. Helplessly, they find that they always have a bad word for her. It may be due to her remarkable gift for bringing out the worst in people, or it may be the result of an unacknowledged spark of envy that is apt to nag at the most unenvious when they are confronted with the spectacle of a woman who has everything, and has it all in superlatives. Scarcely any woman is bothered by another being more beautiful than herself, by a second being more talented, or by a third being more successful, but when beauty, talent, and success are all three extravagantly embodied in one woman, it is sometimes more than the girls can take. They find it hard, too, to forgive Miss Boothe's flawless ability to do almost anything. One time, at a weekend party on Long Island, the other guests were gathered around the swimming pool when Clare appeared, slim and dazzling in a white bathing suit. "Let's see you do a swan dive, dear," said one of the women nastily, thinking she had at last touched on the impossible. Miss Boothe put on her cap, made a perfect swan dive from the high board, swam the length of the pool in an expert, easy crawl, climbed out gracefully, and sat down to talk to the men. She is too intelligent to be unconscious of her own extraordinary gifts, but it is not true that she considers herself superior to other people, and she is impatient with loftiness in anyone else. A friend of the Luces who visits them often says that one of the few quarrels that ever took place in their home life occurred one evening when Luce remarked that he could not think of anybody who was mentally his superior. His wife felt that this sentiment was extreme, and argued with him hotly and in vain, bringing in the names of Einstein (who, Luce objected, is a specialist) and John Kieran (a freak, said Luce). After nine years of marriage, Luce has finally convinced his wife that he invariably means what he says, and sometimes it worries her.

Clare Boothe's most conspicuous virtue is a fine willingness to accept any challenge, and her life has been full of double dares. Christened Ann Clare, she was the only daughter of an obscure couple who at the time of her birth were living in a flat on upper Riverside Drive. Her mother, Ann Snyder, was a pretty daughter of Bavarian immigrants and had been a chorus girl in one or two musical comedies before her marriage to William Boothe. Boothe was a minister's son, an amateur violinist, and an executive of the Boothe Piano Company in New York. Through her father, Clare is distantly related to the Maryland Booths, the family which included Edwin and John Wilkes Booth. After John Wilkes Booth assassinated Lincoln, the Maryland Booths added an "e" to their name in an effort to dissociate themselves from the murderer. Through this relationship, Clare Boothe is probably eligible to such societies as the Ark and Dove and the D.A.R., but she has not yet got around to applying for membership. Until now, Miss Boothe's connection with the Maryland Booths has been little more than another poisoned dart in the winged exchange that goes on between Clare and almost all other women. Not long ago, Miss Boothe, speaking of the happy and wildly fertile marriage of a friend who was then expecting her fifth child, said lightly, "That marriage is what you might call an *enceinte cordiale*." When this crack was dutifully reported to the busy wife and mother, she murmured, "Ah yes, Clare Wilkes Boothe."

When Clare was eight, William Boothe wearied of the piano

business and left his family to be a professional violinist, announcing himself, when he could get a job in music halls or restaurants, as Billy Boothe, the Irish Fiddler. He never resumed formal relations with his wife and daughter, and Mrs. Boothe eventually divorced him, some time before his death in California thirteen years ago. After the departure of the Irish Fiddler, money was scarce, and Clare and her mother went to live with a friend of Mrs. Boothe's, an actress who had a two-room flat on Columbus Avenue. Miss Boothe now speaks of those days with a musing expression and a dramatist's forcefulness. She will describe to you vividly the garbage cans that cluttered the hallway and the night a mouse got in her bed and she ran screaming from her cubbyhole of a bedroom into the next room, which her mother shared with their hostess. It is certainly true that Clare and her mother had almost no money until Mrs. Boothe, reading an article about Mary Pickford one day, glanced at her daughter's golden hair and sweet, cerulean gaze and decided that what Mary Pickford could do, Clare could do. The decision eventually became a motto which has shaped Clare Boothe's whole life, although the name of Mary Pickford has been replaced at intervals by Mrs. Cornelius Vanderbilt's, say, by George Bernard Shaw's, and perhaps by Daniel Webster's or William Pitt's. Through her theatrical friends, Mrs. Boothe got Clare a job as understudy to Mary Pickford, who was then starring in *A Good Little Devil* under the direction of David Belasco, and also succeeded in having her tested for a part in a movie starring Viola Dana, which was being made at Fort Lee, New Jersey. Clare never played Mary Pickford's role in *A Good Little Devil,* but in the light of what happened at Fort Lee, it might have been interesting if she had. The movie test required Viola Dana and Clare Boothe, representing two orphans, to stand together hand in hand and register anxiety, fright, fear, and finally horror. When the camera began to grind, Viola Dana went into her act. Tears trembled from her dewy eyes, her lips quivered, her childish hands curved in alarm and then pushed at the air as though repelling some loathsome thing. Throughout this performance, Clare surveyed Miss Dana with a dead pan, her arms folded, her eyes critical. She was fired, but later returned for a child's part in a Marie Doro picture and also appeared briefly on Broadway in a play called *The Dummy,* starring Ernest Truex. Her stage name was Joyce Fair.

No woman is more triumphant than the mother of a successful child actress, and the mother of a child actress who has not quite made good is apt to be correspondingly depressed. As Clare's career wavered, Mrs. Boothe came to a quick decision. She had heard that you could bring up a child in Europe economically and in a manner worthy of one connected with the Maryland Booths, whose traditions of gentility she cherished. With what money she had, she gambled in stocks on a tip from a friend and made about $2,000. In 1913, she and Clare, who was ten, sailed for France. For the next year the two led the frugal lives of impoverished gentlewomen, in a small hotel in Paris. The war and the fact that their capital was dwindling drove them back to America in 1914, and soon Mrs. Boothe fell ill and was removed to a hospital in Greenwich for an emergency operation. The surgeon who attended her was Dr. A. E. Austin, a local physician, and a year or so after her recovery Mrs. Boothe married him. The couple took up housekeeping in Sound Beach, and Clare was placed in the Castle School in Tarrytown. Until then, her only formal schooling had been a year at St. Mary's school in Garden City, since her mother was too proud to send her to public school in New York and not prosperous enough to afford private establishments. At St. Mary's, Clare formed her first friendship with another girl, Elizabeth ("Buff") Cobb, Irvin Cobb's daughter, and she also learned her first lesson in womanly warfare. A boy had asked Buff to go to a prom at his military school, and Buff, who was—and is—dark-haired and vivacious, told him lightly that she would let him know. In the meantime, the boy, to make sure of a good-looking date, asked Clare to go if Buff couldn't. It appears that Buff waited too long to give him his answer, so he took Clare. Buff then wrote Clare a letter that said in part, "You are a cold, scheming, unscrupulous woman," and the rift between them lasted for some ten years, until one day on the beach at Southampton, after Clare had married her first husband, George Brokaw, and Buff had married Frank Chapman, the baritone, the girls happened to come out of adjoining bathhouses at the same time. Each was carrying a wet bathing suit and a wet towel. "Clare, darling!" Buff cried, and "Buff, darling!" cried Clare. "What was that row about anyway?" Buff demanded. "I wouldn't know," said Clare, and they tearfully flung their wet suits and towels around each other's shoulders and made up then and there. They have remained good friends, and several years ago, between their respective divorces and remarriages (Buff is now Mrs. Cobb Rogers), they travelled through Europe and part of Africa together. The trip was a success, with only an occasional breath of friction, caused by the fact that Buff likes to leave books and other belongings cozily flung around a room or a ship's cabin, while Clare is so passionately neat that she cannot abide even an ashtray out of place.

After Clare graduated from the Castle School, she went to live in Sound Beach with her mother and stepfather, but she soon rebelled against suburban life, and with a fairly dramatic gesture. With ten dollars she had saved, she ran away to New York, took a room in a boarding house, and got a job at Dennison's, making nut cups and bonbon holders out of frilled paper at a salary of eighteen dollars a week. The child actress Joyce Fair had long been forgotten, but Clare found a certain drama in pseudonyms; as a factory girl, she worked under the name of Jacqueline Tanner. Toward the end of her second month at Dennison's an attack of appendicitis obliged her to go home to Sound Beach—somewhat to her relief, she now admits. While she was recovering from the appendix operation, she decided that she wanted to be an actress again. Mrs. Austin, who had settled nicely into the role of a Sound Beach matron, was opposed to that notion, but she finally agreed to let Clare take lessons at Clare Tree Major's School of the Theatre in New York.

Mrs. Major now speaks proudly of Miss Boothe as a former pupil, but their relations were not always so placid. When Clare entered the school, she was apple-cheeked and plump, with long, fair hair, and Mrs. Major, who apparently liked her pupils to do things the hard way, kept putting a black wig on her and telling her to be a geisha girl. To Clare, who had a logical mind, this seemed freakishly bad casting, and her annoyance reached its climax on the day of the students' first public performance. On that occasion each pupil was called onto the stage, before an audience of distinguished guests and professional critics, and told to draw a slip of paper from a bowl. The pupil was to read aloud, and then act out, whatever assignment was written on the slip of paper. Most of the pupils drew simple tasks, such as "You have just been told that your lover has been killed" or "You are a girl receiving a proposal of marriage which you gently decline." When Clare saw her assignment, however, she was stunned. "You are a cave man," it read, "and your whelps are starving. You go out and slaughter an animal for food, drag the carcass home, and you and your family eat it." Baffled but game, Clare squared her elbows, planted her feet wide apart, twisted her pretty face into a savage snarl, and, rocking from side to side in a bloodthirsty manner, uttered a piercing growl. The audience collapsed into helpless laughter, and Clare, dropping the cave man role, announced clearly, "This whole thing is unreasonable," and walked off the stage. Miss Boothe sometimes tells about this incident these days, and when she does, she likes to act out the cave man, crouching, swaying, and growling. She can do it pretty well, now.

After this performance, Mrs. Major intimated to Clare that the acting laurels of the Boothe family had better rest with Edwin and John Wilkes, and, in 1919, Clare took a trip to Europe with her mother and Dr. Austin, who wanted to study plastic surgery, which had come into prominence as a result of the war. The late Mrs. O. H. P. Belmont was a fellow passenger on the return voyage to America, and she took such a fancy to Clare that, back in New York, she encouraged her in fashionable pursuits, which included going to church to hear Dr. Harry Emerson Fosdick preach. One Sunday, after service, the James Stewart Cushmans introduced George T. Brokaw to Miss Boothe. George Brokaw had inherited a fortune from his father, Isaac Vail Brokaw, one of the founders of the men's clothing firm of Brokaw Brothers. He and Clare Boothe were married on August 10, 1923, when she was twenty years old and he was forty-three. Clare's mother was pleased by the marriage, and from that time took a quiet pride in her daughter's increasing social brilliance. Mrs. Austin died in a motor accident six years ago. Dr. Austin, who now lives in Greenwich, served a term in Congress, from 1938 to 1940, as representative from Connecticut—the office his stepdaughter was to hold later.

People who met young Mrs. Brokaw at the time of her marriage have since described her as naïve and, in a way, winsome. "She wore flowers in her hair when nobody else did, if you know what I mean," one woman says, "and she was always saying she wanted to have six babies." One child, Ann, was born of the marriage. Last year Ann, aged nineteen, was killed in an automobile crash on her way back to college after a Christmas vacation spent with her mother. Recalling the tragic and strangely identical deaths of her mother and her daughter, other women are less inclined to envy Miss Boothe these days.

The Brokaws lived in the Brokaw town house, on Fifth Avenue at the corner of Seventy-ninth Street—a gloomy mansion which the bride tried to enliven by a series of dinner parties and masquerade balls. Her efforts were hampered by the fact that she baffled the women she came to know in her new role of Fifth Avenue matron. They were simple, goodhearted society women, intent upon the business of life, which was, for them, home, servants, children, entertaining, and keeping abreast of other people's business. They discovered with concern that Mrs. Brokaw was not interested in the details of housekeeping or of cuisine. They will tell you that in the Brokaw house neither was of the best. Mrs. Brokaw had a way of speaking, too, which puzzled these ladies. A witty feminine dinner guest, for example, who had prattled entertainingly at the table, felt less than rewarded when Clare said to her later, in a tone of incredulous surprise, "Darling, you were really *amusing* tonight!" Women could not decide whether such a crack was naïve or somehow double-edged. It's a good guess that it was naïve, and that Miss Boothe eventually allowed her comments to be interpreted as murderous in much the same way that a comedienne, seeing that a fumbled line pleases an audience, keeps it in the act.

Her marriage to Brokaw ended in divorce in 1929, and she received a settlement of $425,000. She returned to New York from Reno, rich, independent, and insecure. As Mrs. Boothe Brokaw, she had an uncertain social standing, few intimate friends, and nothing special to do. Brokaw soon married a Miss Frances Seymour, who is now Mrs. Henry Fonda of Hollywood; he died in 1935. In 1929, with her five-year-old daughter, of whom she had part-time custody, a governess, and three servants, Clare Boothe Brokaw moved into a penthouse apartment on Beekman Place. She had sometimes thought she would like to write, but she had completed only two one-act plays, which were never presented; one was called *The Lily Maid* and the other was a grim sketch about a man in prison. Her main connection with playwrighting was a photograph of George Bernard Shaw, whom she had not met, which she kept reverently on her dressing table. Miss Boothe likes to tell about her eventual meeting with Shaw in 1939, when she had gone to London with her husband, Henry Luce, for the opening of *The Women.* Impressed by the fact that Shaw had consented to see her, and remembering his picture on the dressing table at home, she said breathlessly, "Oh, Mr. Shaw, if it weren't for you I wouldn't *be* here!" Shaw said "Oh," and then, nodding understandingly, added, "Let me see what was your dear mother's name?" What pleased Miss Boothe even more was the postcard Shaw sent her a few days later. "Kindest regards to you and Mr. Boothe," he had written on it.

At a dinner party in 1930, Mrs. Brokaw (as she was then still known) sat next to the late Condé Nast. She confided to him that she was restless and bored, and asked him to give her a job on one of his magazines. Nast told her cordially to come and see him in his office sometime. She turned up the next morning at nine-thirty, half an hour before Nast himself arrived, and announced to Mrs. Edna Woolman Chase, the editor of *Vogue,* that Nast had hired her. Mrs. Chase accordingly put her to work writing captions for fashion photographs in *Vogue.* It was a job which was to lead to a career dizzily divided into three epochs, in which she shone successively as a magazine editor and literary hostess, as a playwright, and as a political crusader, but at the time it bored her slightly and left her simmering with unused vitality. By a coincidence, another blonde who was later to become famous was also simmering in 1930. This was Dorothy Thompson, who, living rustically that year on a farm in Vermont with her husband, Sinclair Lewis, was busy with housewifely duties and the care of her infant son, but was privately chafing because she had a number of things to say to the American public and had not yet found a column in which to say them. Miss Boothe and Miss Thompson had not met in 1930. Ten years later, Miss Boothe, the playwright, and Miss Thompson, the columnist, together supplied the feminine and feline interest to the dark, momentous presidential campaign of 1940.

If that campaign can be said to have had its lightsome side, surely it was furnished by these two blonde Valkyries rampant on the prows of opposing ships of state, both articulate, both utterly sincere. Even now, when the battle is long over, the details are fearsome in retrospect. Miss Boothe's decision to campaign for Willkie was largely inspired, or at least crystallized, by Dorothy Thompson's public announcement in October 1940 that she had changed her mind about the election and would support Roosevelt instead of Willkie. Ten days after Miss Thompson published this resolve, Miss Boothe made her first political speech at a "Work with Willkie" rally. The speech was called *An Answer to Dorothy Thompson,* and in it Miss Boothe spoke of Miss Thompson's "mounting hysteria," her "anxiety neurosis," and her "acute fear." "Fear," she went on to say, "is an *emotional* and not an intellectual reaction to a problem. Fear distils adrenalin into the blood, the victim sweats, her breath comes fast, her nostrils dilate, her pulse races, her breast heaves, and heaves, and she begins to babble incoherently. But worst of all, the blood leaves her head, and her brain ceases to function normally. I say 'her'," Miss Boothe added diplomatically, "because the doctors tell me that a highly sensitive woman is much more likely to get into this pathetic condition than a man." Later in the same speech, Miss Boothe commented as follows on Miss Thompson's visit, the preceding May, to the Maginot Line, which Miss Boothe had already visited in April:

> I was the first American woman to be taken on an official conducted tour to the Maginot Line. Dorothy Thompson was the second—and last. . . . Now, it seems that when Miss Thompson went to the Maginot, she had been less circumspect but much more natural in her behavior than I. The guns were firing. . . . Down in the gun turret they loaded the great "seventy-five." They found the range in German ranks . . . *Un! Deux! Trois!*—and Miss Thompson herself pulled the gunlevers! Three times they loaded. Three shells they fired. "This," she said, "is for Hitler. And this is for Goering, and this is for Goebbels!" . . . I am sure no column Miss Thompson has ever written gave her the profound emotional release or intellectual satisfaction those three personally fired shells into German ranks gave.

Later she referred to Miss Thompson as "The Molly Pitcher of the Maginot Line."

To these bouquets, Miss Thompson replied, in a broadcast:

> Miss Boothe is the Body by Fisher in this campaign. She is the Brenda Frazier of the Great Crusade. She has torn herself loose from the Stork Club to serve her country in this serious hour. She has everything—everything to pull in the orders. The Powers-model face that you see on the magazines; the recommendations of Lady Whosis and Ethyl Montgomery-Bangs. . . . Clare is the Snob Copy in this campaign. But she is also Fear Copy. They usually go together, my friends. Snobbery is the result of fearing that one may not be with the "best people." Well, Clare, the other night, tried to scare me to death. She described my symptoms minutely. . . . Thanks, Clare, but my pulse is normal, my blood pressure a hundred and twenty, and there is nothing wrong with my eyesight, either. I have met you before, Clare, in various costumes and under various hats. . . . I have met the ladies of café society who save nations in their time of crisis, and I have visited the nations they have saved.

Miss Thompson was wrong about at least one thing. Miss Boothe hardly ever goes to the Stork Club. Even now that public life has claimed her, she and her husband like to spend evenings at home (whichever home they may manage to meet in) whenever they can. Mr. Luce reads aloud to his wife while she does needlepoint. She recently made for Luce's office a needlepoint tablecover, six feet long and embellished with the names of all his magazines and the names of all her plays. Mostly, Luce reads detective stories to her, but sometimes he will read aloud the manuscript of whatever play she is working on. He is a deliberate reader, pausing often between words, and Miss Boothe finds this practice helpful. "If I can stand the dialogue slowed up like that," she says, "I know it must be good."

When Miss Boothe announced her candidacy for Congress, two years after her brush with Dorothy Thompson, Miss Thompson, ever a bundle of surprises, marched into print with the statement that she would support the fair contendant, her erstwhile foe. "Curiously enough," Miss Thompson told reporters, "I am for Clare Boothe Luce for the same basic reason that I was for the President. The reason is a simple one. I believe that she knows more about world affairs than the other candidate, and I believe that some knowledge of world affairs is absolutely indispensable for members of Congress." In a way that was even more curious than Miss Thompson evidently felt her own reasoning to be, Miss Boothe's interest in world affairs won her the nomination and possibly the election, and at the same time deprived her in a backhanded fashion of a still dearer dream. What she really wanted to do, in 1942, was to go on being a foreign correspondent, a career she had successfully begun by making two trips for *Life*—one to China and the Philippines in 1941, and the other to Egypt and the Far East the following year. This career was suddenly denied to her in the spring of 1942 by the whims of fate and the State Department. As she couldn't be a foreign correspondent, Miss Boothe stifled her disappointment and ran for Congress instead. She has always been a girl who, if she can't have a present off the middle bough of the Christmas tree, is content with the star at the top.

In May, Miss Boothe, home from her second voyage as a *Life* correspondent, began to impress a good many of her influential Republican neighbors in Greenwich with her accounts of what she had seen and the conclusions she had

have been startled into a certain thoughtfulness by being thrown out of a Frenchman's house; anyone with a viewpoint less inverted might have recognized Mme Pomaret simply as a Frenchwoman and a hostess antagonized by a too-rapid and too-personal questioning from a stranger. But Miss Boothe has the gift of genuinely forgiving the people who disagree with her, and instantly forgetting them. When her hosts and hostesses in the Far East turned out to be as captious and mistaken as Mme Pomaret, Miss Boothe sighed for their blindness and accepted the nomination for Congress. It was time, she felt, that she stopped wasting precious moments trying to talk to tired or reluctant individuals. It was high time she began to address the nation.

Clare Boothe, as the author of *The Women, Kiss the Boys Goodbye,* and *Margin for Error,* entered Congress with the reputation of being "the most beautiful living playwright" —a title bestowed on her by people who, contemplating the rare combination of her comeliness and her talent, felt understandably that they were in the presence of something uncanny, like a horse that can count up to ten. Miss Boothe's beauty was never known to dim throughout the gruelling strain of rehearsals, tryouts, rewriting, and other headaches of show business, which drives most playwrights into dark corners with aspirin tablets. Several years ago, before *The Women* went into rehearsal, she asked the members of the cast to come to her apartment in the Waldorf Towers one afternoon to hear her read the play. Margalo Gillmore, Ilka Chase, Betty Lawford, and the other actresses who had been engaged for the show assembled in the suite on the thirty-sixth floor which Miss Boothe occupies with her husband. A butler served sherry, and presently Miss Boothe appeared, wearing a Bergdorf Goodman house coat and a pink ribbon bow in her hair. She looked divine. "Now!" she said, in a friendly way, after greetings had been exchanged, and handed each of her guests a pencil and a paper pad. "For you to make notes and suggestions," she explained, settling down in a chair by the window and opening the manuscript. The girls, accustomed to hearing plays read on a bare stage by a haggard author under a single, harsh electric bulb, stared in fascination. "It was exactly," one of them said later, "as though we were at a house party, playing pencil-and-paper games after dinner." The play ran for eighty-two weeks in New York, and gave some members of its cast the most profitable jobs they had ever had, but their principal recollections of it are still that first reading and the subsequent daily vision of Miss Boothe arriving at rehearsals with her blonde hair freshly done, her nails newly manicured, and her lovely face serene.

The impact of Miss Boothe's physical perfection upon the world of toil was evident as long ago as 1930, when she went to work for *Vogue*. She was still Mrs. Boothe Brokaw, she was twenty-seven years old, and she had, through a settlement by her former husband, an income of some twenty-five thousand dollars a year. *Vogue* paid her thirty-five dollars a week for writing picture captions and doing other editorial chores. The Condé Nast Publications, which then included *Vogue*, *Vanity Fair*, *House & Garden*, and the *American Golfer*, occupied a floor in the Graybar Building on Lexington Avenue. *Vanity Fair* was housed in three semi-partitioned rooms at the head of a long corridor leading from the elevators and the reception room to the spacious and scented purlieus of *Vogue*, so anyone bound for the *Vogue* offices had to pass by the doors of *Vanity Fair*. Most of the ladies on *Vogue* were married, and so many of them were pregnant so much of the time that certain assistant editors of *Vanity Fair* took to leaving the office doors open and making bets on the condition of the next *Vogue* editor to appear. Accustomed to a long procession of maternity dresses, the *Vanity Fair* speculators got a jolt the first morning Mrs. Brokaw arrived to report for work at *Vogue*. She was slim and airy-footed in a simple gray frock with touches of white at the throat and wrists, and the light from a window at the end of the hall celestially illumined her face and hair. "Geez, what was that?" a *Vanity Fair* editor murmured as she passed.

After a few months on *Vogue*, Mrs. Brokaw became an assistant editor of *Vanity Fair* at forty dollars a week, and also began to write a series of satirical sketches about Park Avenue types, which were published first in the magazine and later as a book called *Stuffed Shirts.* In the next two years, she reached ten thousand dollars a year and the position of managing editor, succeeding the late Donald Freeman, who died in 1933. From the beginning, she showed an astonishing capacity for work and a beautiful disregard for obstacles. The magazine had the thrifty habit of buying, for a small sum, the republication rights of short fiction pieces by French authors and having them translated into English in the office. The woman editor who had been doing the translating left to get married shortly after Mrs. Brokaw's arrival, and Freeman asked Mrs. Brokaw if she knew French. Although she had spent a year in Paris when she was ten, her French was limited to school book phrases. Nevertheless, she regarded Freeman blandly. "Certainly I know French," she said. She took the stories home at night and translated them with the aid of a French-English dictionary. One time, when she decided that she wanted a secretary who was working for one of the other editors, her method of getting her was equally unobtrusive and efficient. She offered the girl a large increase in salary, said she would pay the increase out of her own pocket, and, after everything was arranged, simply announced to the other editor that there had been a switch in secretaries and that the other editor would now have the secretary who had worked for Mrs. Brokaw. There is no malice in this kind of wide gesture, which is still habitual with Miss Boothe; she merely goes after what she wants with such directness that any obstacle, intangible or human, ceases to exist for her. Mrs. Brokaw was well liked by the stenographers and secretaries in the office, who spoke of her as being very democratic. She often asked them to dinner with other guests at her penthouse apartment on Beekman Place, and knowing that one or two lived in Brooklyn, she would tell them not to bother dressing. When they arrived for the dinner party, wearing their office clothes, they would find that Mrs. Brokaw tactfully had not dressed either; generally she was wearing a simple hostess gown made of gold lamé.

Mrs. Brokaw's parties were mainly literary for a time, and her apartment, a place of mirrored walls and terraces, was full of people like George Jean Nathan, the late T. R. Smith of the publishing firm of Boni & Liveright, and Ernest Boyd, the bearded Irish essayist. In 1932, however, her interest shifted to politics when Condé Nast, deciding that *Vanity Fair* was too frivolous, engaged John Franklin Carter, Jr., who was then employed in the State Department in Washington, and Henry Pringle, the writer, as part-time editorial advisers to inject a sterner note into the magazine. Under the pen name of Jay Franklin, Carter wrote several political articles, including one called *Wanted: A New Party*. This was a kind of pep talk to American youth, suggesting that they demand a new political order of things, or, in the phrase Carter thought up for it, a New Deal. Carter later contributed this slogan to President Roosevelt's Brain Trust, of which he eventually became a member. Among the *Vanity Fair* readers who were stirred by Carter's notion of a new deal were Mrs. Harrison Williams and Mrs. James Forrestal, the wife of the present Secretary of the Navy, and with financial and emotional backing from these two and from Mrs. Brokaw, the organization, christened the New Nationalist Party, opened a one-secretary office a few doors down the hall from *Vanity Fair*. Nobody who was connected with it remembers its platform clearly now, but it was such a lively organization for a while that strangers crowded into the office, clamoring to join. One of them said his name was Howard Scott. Mr. Scott's ideas, upon examination, turned out to conflict with those of the party, and he said crossly, "Very well, I'll found my own party." He went off in a huff and founded Technocracy.

Before the Roosevelt-Hoover campaign of 1932, the New Nationalist Party delegated Mrs. Brokaw to go to the Democratic National Convention in Chicago and try to win recruits to the New Nationalists, and sent Mrs. Williams to the Republican Convention, also in Chicago, for the same purpose. "The No. 2 company of *Joan of Arc*," a male sub-editor of *Vanity Fair* skeptically remarked of the lady crusaders. "I presume the girls are having their swords forged at Cartier's?" Mrs. Williams ran into opposition from those practiced opposers Mrs. Alice Longworth and Mrs. Ruth Pratt, and dismally wired Carter that she couldn't do a thing with the Republican Party. Mrs. Brokaw also failed to win any recruits to New Nationalism, but she did get to know Bernard Baruch and other important figures, and she began to develop a love of prominent people and a gift of absorbing factual information from them.

Her friends are familiar with her habit, at a dinner party, for example, of gazing speculatively around the table and silently deciding who is worth talking to. If she is not seated near that person (usually a man), she will seek him out afterward and give him what one hostess has described as the full treatment. This consists of asking him endless questions about whatever subject temporarily interests her and about which he is informed. She is a good listener if the talk seems valuable to her, but aimless or desultory conversation bores her, and she has little time for anyone who, in the course of a chat, cannot give her at least one big, important fact.

The New Nationalist Party quietly dissolved after the fiasco at the Conventions, and Mrs. Brokaw spent the next year or so mainly in a futile campaign to turn *Vanity Fair* into a picture magazine, writing voluminous memoranda on the subject to Nast, its publisher, and Frank Crowninshield, its editor. In 1934, she resigned from *Vanity Fair*, two years before it merged with *Vogue*, and set about becoming a free-lance writer. Her book, *Stuffed Shirts*, had already been published and she had sold to a Hollywood picture company, for $1,500, a two-page movie scenario which she dictated one day at her office during a spare half hour. Although she was not well known as a writer, she attacked the business of free lancing with characteristic confidence. Generally, a writer who has not been asked to contribute anything to any particular magazine sets out by writing a piece and then submitting it to one or more publications, until, with luck, it is accepted. Mrs. Brokaw proceeded differently. She would have her secretary telephone an editor and ask him to come for cocktails to her Beekman Place apartment on a certain day. Sometimes it was an editor who had not met Mrs. Brokaw, occasionally it was one who had been introduced to her vaguely. In either case, editors being mostly simple men, he would feel rather pleased at being asked to one of Mrs. Brokaw's parties, which generally included only the more celebrated political, literary, and social personages. When he arrived at the apartment on the appointed day, he would find himself the only guest, and Mrs. Brokaw, after giving him a cocktail, would inform him that she had a little time on her hands and thought it might be fun to dash off some articles for his magazine.

In 1934, Paul Block engaged her to write a column for his chain of newspapers. The column, entitled *This World of Ours,* also appeared in Hearst's *New York American* for a few weeks, but certain editors of that paper soon persuaded Hearst to give it up. Mrs. Brokaw was sending her articles from Europe at the time, and when the *American* cabled the news of the cancellation to her, she replied blithely, by cable, that she was much relieved. This airiness considerably puzzled the Hearst editors, who had been encouraged to revere the master and speak to him softly. Mrs. Brokaw has declined many requests to write a newspaper column since she became Miss Boothe. The only one she attempted was called *Here the Gavel Fell,* a chatty report of Congressional doings which she wrote without pay for a while in 1943 for the *Roundup,* a service men's weekly published overseas. The column was withdrawn by order of the War Department on the ground that it contained the writer's views on controversial political subjects and had no place in an Army publication—a decision which considerably depressed and bewildered Miss Boothe.

In 1935, when Mrs. Brokaw's first play, *Abide with Me,* was presented at the Ritz Theatre in New York, the most puzzled man in the publishing business, however, was Henry R. Luce, whom she married two days after the play opened and twenty-eight days before it closed. The attitude of the critics and public toward the failure of *Abide with Me* was a striking example of the curious pleasure people seem to take in any disaster that overtakes the beautiful and socially conspicuous Clare Boothe. The dramatic critics were not content with merely pulverizing the play; they also ganged up happily on Miss Boothe for having had the temerity to take a bow after the last act. Luce, about to marry the lovely playwright, was faced with the twin spectres of his love and his editorial integrity, and *Time*'s dramatic critic rewrote his review of *Abide with Me* seven times before he arrived at a successful compromise between tact and reason. Today Miss Boothe, fortified by the later triumphs of *The Women, Kiss the Boys Goodbye,* and *Margin for Error,* cheerfully expands that story. "Harry," she says, "brought me the original copy of *Time*'s review and said, 'Darling, it was a bad play and I think this notice is too gentle. See what you can do with it.' " She rewrote it then and there, using a good many forthright words, like "lousy" and "stinking," and Luce carefully read what she had written. "It won't do," he said, speaking kindly, like an editor. "No play is *that* bad." The review which was finally published in *Time* was about two hundred words long, and was the combined work of Luce, Miss Boothe, and *Time*'s dramatic critic, an anonymous toiler. Referring to Marsden, the sadistic drunkard of the play, and to its other characters, it read in part, "They all have good reasons for shooting him. In the middle of the last act someone finally does. This event brings relief from much tedious psychiatry and gratifies those spectators who like melodrama."

Although Miss Boothe now speaks musically and with a good deal of tinkling laughter about the debacle of her first play, it left such a wound that she has never since been to one of her own opening nights in New York. She either spends those evenings with her husband in their Waldorf Towers apartment or at another play, or else she goes to a movie. The night *Margin for Error* opened, she saw the Marx Brothers in *Room Service*. Her book *Europe in the Spring* recounts a conversation at a dinner party in Rome between herself and the late Count Ciano, who told her he had once written a play, which was booed by the critics. "After that I understood Count Ciano very well indeed," Miss Boothe writes, "and why he was at once so indifferent and good-natured in the face of the bitterest personal attacks on him in the foreign press. When your first play (which is as precious and personal and tender and tremulously sacred to a budding author as a boy's first declaration of love) has been greeted with the loud derisive whoops and hollers—the savage, blood-curdling Indian yells of those master scalpers, the critical fraternity—well, no poisoned shaft has ever after any power to penetrate or inflame. Public life, with all its attendant censure, has no horrors for a man who—however grievous his theatrical sin—has once been taken naked over the live coals by a group of professional theater critics." Miss Boothe's analysis of the late Italian Foreign Minister has been disapproved of by some readers of her book as being sketchy, but as a person, if not always as an author, Miss Boothe has a way of coming out on top, and she triumphed prettily in the end over the critics who had cast stones at *Abide with Me.* During the 1940 Presidential campaign, she made speeches supporting Willkie so fast and so often she sometimes didn't know exactly where she was to speak next, even though every day her secretary gave her a typed engagement list and also gave the chauffeur a similar list. One night a Willkie rally was held in a theater, and it was not until Miss Boothe came out on the stage to address the audience, that she recognized the place as the Ritz, the scene of her first, calamitous opening night. Taking this discovery in her stride, Miss Boothe spoke so eloquently of Willkie that the audience interrupted her several times with laughter, cheers, and applause. At the end of the speech, the audience applauded and applauded, and Miss Boothe bowed and bowed. "I think I took an extra bow that night, just for the hell of it," she said afterward.

Clare Boothe was well known as Mrs. Boothe Brokaw, but she became famous as Miss Boothe only after her marriage to Henry Luce, a man who had already made quite a name for himself as the editor of *Time* and *Fortune.* Miss Boothe unconsciously explains this by relating that she sat up in bed one night and said, "Harry, I think I'll write a play about women without any men in it," and Harry encouragingly said, "Why not?" *The Women* and Mrs. Luce's fame as Clare Boothe were the results. Miss Boothe's first meeting with Luce occurred at a dinner party at the Thayer Hobsons' in 1933, when she was still called Mrs. Brokaw, and it was a rather hostile encounter. Three years earlier she had written the caption for a photograph of Luce in *Vanity Fair* on the page headed "We Nominate for the Hall of Fame." It read, "Henry Luce, because he originated the news-magazine idea; because at the age of 32 he is the successful editor and publisher of *Time* and *Fortune* magazines; because he was born in China; because he was once a humble newspaper reporter for the Chicago *Daily News;* and lastly because he claims that he has no other interest outside of his work and that his work fills his waking hours." As Luce, presumably attracted by Mrs. Brokaw's blonde beauty, came and sat beside her on a couch, she instantly opened up on him about the magazine business. She talked sensibly on the subject for some twenty minutes, and when she at length paused for breath, Luce drew out his watch, looked at it briefly, and said, "Twelve-fifteen. I must be going," and left. Mrs. Brokaw rather indignantly forgot him for several weeks, and then, when they happened to meet at another dinner, she coldly answered "Yes" or "No" to everything he said to her. At the end of that evening he gave her a favorable glance and said, "I think you are the woman I am going to marry." They were married a couple of years later, in Old Greenwich, seven weeks after Luce's divorce from his first wife became final.

The marriage had an agitating effect upon certain *Time* and *Fortune* editors, who, having followed the former Mrs. Brokaw's career on *Vanity Fair,* feared that she might descend on *Time* and *Fortune* with some campaign or other, or just with her own ideas about editing a magazine. A rumor also got around, considerably astonishing Condé Nast, that Luce was planning to buy the expiring *Vanity Fair* from Nast and give it to his bride as a wedding present, to do what she liked with. None of these things came to pass, and the new Mrs. Luce concerned herself with her husband's business on only one occasion during the next few years. This was in 1936, when he came home one day to Greenwich, where they were living at the time, and told her that he had just paid $85,000 for *Life,* the comic magazine, because he wanted its name for a picture weekly he was preparing to publish. "Eighty-five thousand dollars seems a lot of money for the name of a magazine everybody is sick and tired of," Mrs. Luce remarked. "Wait a minute." She disappeared briefly, and came back with the files of her memoranda to Condé Nast during the years she had been on *Vanity Fair*. One twelve-page memorandum, dated 1933, began, "Mr. Nast: My spies tell me that *Life* can be bought for $20,000. Why not buy it for the name and turn it into a picture magazine?" Although the tardiness of this discovery apparently cost Luce $65,000, he still enjoys the coincidence, and frequently speaks of it as weird.

To describe Clare Boothe as a Congresswoman or as a playwright is as elusive a task as describing a pretty girl at a party. She looks lovely, she has a fine time, and she is a great success. Her confidence is unbounded, and it is cheering to her fellow workers, who mistake it for optimism—always a more engaging quality than confidence, especially to theater people. When *The Women* was trying out in Philadelphia before its New York opening, Max Gordon, its producer, and George Kaufman, who owned part of the play, sat after the first performance with their heads in their hands. The third-act curtain was wrong. They broke the news to Miss Boothe, who, they remember, was wearing a little black thing of a hat and looked marvellous, and the three of them talked it over until two in the morning. Miss Boothe nodded agreeably to everything they said and went back to the hotel where they were all staying. The next day at noon Kaufman was haggardly descending in the hotel elevator when Miss Boothe got on at her floor. She was wearing a beige frock and a hat with a feather, and she was beautiful. "You look fresh as a daisy," Kaufman said, peevishly. Miss Boothe smiled and waved a manuscript at him. "I feel fine," she said. "I'm just taking a new third act to Max." Kaufman sometimes mentions this when people bring up the once-popular suspicion that he wrote most of *The Women*. "Listen," he says darkly in this connection, "if I had written *The Women*, why would I want to sign it Clare Boothe?" Kaufman did make many suggestions about the construction and direction of the play, one of them being to put back the kitchen scene in the second act, after Miss Boothe had taken it out at Gordon's request.

Clare Boothe's plays are not generally popular with dramatic critics—possibly because critics are perfectionists who feel that her success has been too flashy, too easy; also, perhaps, because most critics are men, and men, being born admirers of women, are often horrified by the meanness, malice, and really shocking vulgarity of Miss Boothe's female characters. To quote from the dialogue of *The Women,* they are all, almost without exception, "dirty little trollops," "double-crossing little squirts," and "Park Avenue pushovers," and they tell each other so with accompanying hair-pulling and kicks in the shins, to the vast amusement of metropolitan audiences. Out of all the eighteen countries in which *The Women* was produced, it failed only in France, a country in which nobody understood it, since, while Frenchwomen may behave virtuously or loosely, they always behave properly, according to the wishes of their men and the customs of the country. Boothe dialogue has a good deal of wit, but it is the wit of farce rather than comedy, and sometimes it is even somewhat heavy-handed. In *Kiss the Boys Goodbye,* the radical columnist, Madison Breed, crossing the stage to take a swim in the pool, says to Maimie, the negro maidservant, "I'll bet the pool's full of scum again," and Maimie replies, "Nawsuh, Comrade, you ain't been in yet." Certain literati in the audiences at *Kiss the Boys Goodbye,* joyfully decided that Breed was intended as a caricature of the late Heywood Broun, and that the character "Top" Rumson, the polo player in the same play, was modelled after Jock Whitney. Half the fun in Miss Boothe's plays lies, for a knowledgeable audience, in identifying the characters with people of the playwright's acquaintance, but Miss Boothe denies that there is anything in the identifications. After *Kiss the Boys* opened, she went so far as to state, in interviews and in a preface to the published version of the play, that Cindy Lou Bethany, its heroine, was not merely a girl but also a symbol of Southern fascism. "This play was meant to be a political allegory about Fascism in America," Miss Boothe wrote somewhat wistfully in her preface, which is some five thousand words long. "But everywhere it has been taken for a parody of Hollywood's search for Scarlett O'Hara." (A pardonable mistake on the part of

her blinds by the simple device of throwing out corn as bait. This is considered unsporting, but no one has ever complained about it. "What would be the use?" one thwarted hunter said. "With her logical mind, she'd probably just say, 'Well, why don't the other people throw out corn, too?' " The Luces are apparently unconscious of the neighbors' comments. Moving among her miles of camellias, and looking rather like one, Miss Boothe, when in residence, visits the servants' quarters daily, bringing the Negro babies cod liver oil, which their mothers refer to as conjur' medicine and later pour into the friendly earth. The Negroes call Henry Luce "Boss," but in spite of gentle corrections from their mistress, who would like to be called Mrs. Luce around her home, they address her firmly as Miz Lewis. Luce's nickname for his wife is Mike.

The Luces think of themselves as simple people, and when they travel together on a train or in a plane, they while away the journey by playing word games invented by themselves. (Example: I know Mr. and Mrs. Pen and their son, a flower. Answer: John Quill.) To each other, they talk a language that sometimes sounds strange to unaccustomed ears. Miss Boothe has absorbed from her husband some of *Time*'s prose style, and she says things like "No nitwit he" when she wants to describe an intelligent man. Luce has partially adopted his wife's more dramatic form of expression. In 1940, when she had been in Europe several weeks getting material for *Europe in the Spring,* she sent Luce a cable urging him to come over, and ending with "The curtain is about to go up on the greatest show the world has ever seen." Luce joined her in Brussels the day before the Nazis bombed the city. At dawn, when the bombardment began, he woke her up by shaking her shoulder. "The curtain has gone up," he said. Occasionally, when some of Miss Boothe's political or theatrical friends drop in late at night, the opening door reveals Luce, a dark and nervous gnome, scurrying off to bed before the merrymakers can close in on him. Miss Boothe accepts this calmly. "Harry has gone to bed," she tells her guests. She doesn't mind sitting up late, drinking hot milk and talking, and no matter what time she gets to bed, she is generally up around seven-thirty the next morning. Two or three years before Miss Boothe had thought of running for Congress, the tranquillity of the Luces' routine was disturbed by a persistent rumor that Luce had political ambitions and would, in fact, like to be president of the United States. Miss Boothe was so anxious to deny this story that she sometimes mentioned it at gatherings before anyone else did, and the legend she thus helped to build had a curious sequel one night in the summer of 1940 when the Luces went to dine with friends. It was a dinner party of six—the host and hostess, Mr. and Mrs. Luce, and another couple, whom Miss Boothe had met once or twice. During dinner the host remarked that what this country needed was a businessman in the White House. The man sitting next to Miss Boothe quietly agreed, but Luce said nothing, and Miss Boothe spoke up, suspecting that something was afoot. "Such as who?" she demanded, instantly adding, "I hope nobody here is going to bring up that ridiculous idea of Harry being president of the United States! Why on earth would Harry Luce want to be president? Why should Harry, or any other businessman, give up a good business just to be a bad president?" These queries were lost in a sudden flurry of polite chatter on another subject, and on the way home Luce explained to his wife, with a few groans, what he had neglected to tell her beforehand. There *was* a definite political plan behind the dinner party, he said, but it was not concerned with making him president. Miss Boothe then learned that during her absence in Europe, Russell Davenport, their host of the evening, had been up to some colorful political activities. She had known, of course, that the other man at the table, who had agreed with Davenport about the White House needing a businessman, was Wendell Willkie, but it had not occurred to her to think of him in any way except as president of Commonwealth & Southern.

In Congress, Miss Boothe has exhibited all of her uniquely blended qualities of energy, charm, sincerity, and debonair tactlessness. She is a hard worker, bursting with ideas and fearless about expressing them. A few quibblers point out that she follows each of her new inspirations so dauntlessly, in fact, that she is never even hampered by any previous stand she may have taken on the question involved. This, they fret, does not make for consistency. Her well-wishers are equally troubled by her gift for the ill-considered wisecrack and the forthright and hapless gesture. The coined word, "globaloney," which she thought up for her attack upon Vice-President Wallace, seemed cheap even to her admirers and a sorry way of spoiling an interesting, if possibly impractical, speech on postwar freedom of the air. Perhaps the sorriest result of the "globaloney" speech was the barrage of bad gags it inspired from other leaders of the people, notably from Mayor La Guardia, who surely reached some kind of depth when he retorted, "No place for Isol-hash on the United Nations menu, Clare!" Undeterred, Miss Boothe flourished her next play on words in a sharp reproof of Assistant Secretary of State Berle, whom she charged with arousing "a mischievous political 'hurly-berle' which might cause misunderstanding between ourselves and our allies." It is not in her to resist a pun, brilliant or otherwise.

Sometimes it seems as though Miss Boothe, like the horse in the story, just doesn't *give* a damn. Although she represents a district of Connecticut that includes Danbury, the center of the hat manufacturing industry, she has appeared long and doggedly in public without a hat. In spite of her expert knowledge of the potential wrath of women, especially writing women, she has treated the Washington newspaper girls with a combination of indifference and phony sweetness that would outrage a milkmaid of three. Her gesture to the President himself seemed worse than incongruous in a woman as socially experienced as Miss Boothe. In reply to a traditional White House invitation to a reception for freshmen members of Congress, she sent a letter—to the President and to the newspapers simultaneously—saying, in part, "Sure of military victory as this Congress is, we are not complacent about the war effort. Indeed we are very much perturbed. There has been transferred to Congress, as if by swift contagion, the people's long-delayed fury against the swollen and wasteful Washington bureaucracies that have burgeoned through the years." Miss Boothe's reason for sending the letter is simple. "It was the only way I could reach the President's ear," she explained to a puzzled friend. "That invitation gave me my first chance to speak to him directly—wouldn't I have been a fool to ignore it?" Mr. Roosevelt, who is no more foolish than Miss Boothe is, had his secretary, Stephen Early, reply with an assurance that the White House evening would be purely social, non-political, and in no way world-shaking. When Miss Boothe finally reached the President, at the reception, his only remark to her scarcely encouraged a discussion of world affairs. As probably everybody knows by now, what the President said to Miss Boothe that evening was just, "How's Henry?"

Such airy dismissals resemble Miss Boothe's own maneuvers, and they must be irritating to her now that she genuinely wants to get into toe-to-toe combat with important people about important things. Even the tributes that come her way carry an occasional sting. When Congress re-convened after a recent recess, another member who had often belittled Miss Boothe in print and heckled her on the floor of the House stopped at her table in the Senate restaurant one lunch time, and said that he was prepared to withdraw any unfavorable remarks he had made about her in the past because he had lately become convinced of her hold on the American public. Miss Boothe gave him the shadow of a bow. "Yes, sir," the Senator continued amiably, "when you first came to Congress, Miss Boothe, my wife and daughter were very much against it. But now—well, the first question they asked me when I got off the train at home was about you. They said, 'Tell us, Daddy, is it true that Clare Boothe wears bows in her hair?' "

4

Hi-yo, Platinum!

MOSS HART

In May 1943, an Army bomber took Moss Hart on a tour of airfields and Army camps in search of material for *Winged Victory*, his play about the Air Forces, which was presented in New York six months later for the benefit of the Army Emergency Relief. Probably no bomber ever bore aloft a playwright more buoyantly successful or one more bowed down with care. Hart is thirty-nine years old, wealthy, attractive, and beloved by his friends. With George S. Kaufman he has written such popular plays as *The Man Who Came to Dinner*, *You Can't Take It With You*, and *Once in a Lifetime*. With Irving Berlin he wrote *Face the Music* and *As Thousands Cheer*. In a spell of depression following these triumphs, during which he daily consulted a psychiatrist about his troubles, he thought up the idea of *Lady in the Dark*, which he wrote alone, in loneliness. *Lady in the Dark* ran one hundred weeks in New York and on tour, was bought by Paramount Pictures for $285,000, and earned its author almost $300,000 in royalties. Altogether, Hart has made over a million dollars in fourteen years of writing plays.

Hart is successful, but he is also haunted. Sprinkling systems installed in theaters in case of fire remain correctly dry throughout days of rehearsal and then insanely turn themselves on the minute he steps under them. Little people who have never been identified have come in the dead of night and carved crosses and the word "Beware!" on his apartment door and even on the foot of his bed. A peaceable fellow himself, he has nevertheless apparently been chosen as a kind of practice ground for imps. One evening not long ago he was sitting at a table in Lindy's with Oscar Levant and a few other companions. Levant, a heckler who does not like to see another man finish a story, kept interrupting Hart, who was trying to tell one. Hart's inclination is to move away from quarrels or any other violence, and when Levant's badgering grew macabre Moss finally said, white-lipped, "Very well, Oscar, I yield the floor to you." He then excused himself from the table, strode with dignity from the restaurant into the street, and walked straight into a crazed Italian who happened to be stabbing another Italian in the throat.

George Kaufman, who collaborated with Hart for thirteen years, is still interested by the way Moss's life has always ignored the ups and downs of the average man and has leapt instead along empyrean summits at a sort of courteous, perplexed gallop. Kaufman puts it simply, saying merely that Hart is unique. He is the only man Kaufman knows, for instance, who will decline an invitation to dinner because he has to be at the dentist's at that hour. When Hart goes to the dentist's, he goes for the day and sometimes spends the evening there as well. He has frequently arrived at eleven o'clock in the morning and stayed until nine at night. Once he was there from 11 a.m. until two the next morning. Rightly thinking that none of his friends would believe him, he turned up at the Kaufman's apartment next day with an affidavit signed by three dentists who had worked on him in shifts, testifying that he had spent fifteen hours in the chair. Kaufman thinks that this endurance is due to Hart's passion for getting things over with and to the unique character of his dental ailments. "Moss doesn't just have cavities and fillings like the rest of us," Kaufman says. "When *he* needs a dentist it's because he has a couple of teeth growing out of his elbow or his knee, or something."

Hart has an electric toothbrush, the kind that whirls when you shove it into a wall plug. He takes a straightforward pleasure in the diversions money can buy, and until the war he bought all he could find. Generally he made his purchases in pairs, one for his New York apartment and the other for a farm he has in New Hope, Pennsylvania. In this way he has come to own (in the plural) air-conditioning units, television sets, Capehart radio-phonographs with remote-control attachments for piping the music from room to room or from tennis court to swimming pool, recording machines, color cameras, sun lamps, and eight monogrammed cribbage boards. His other possessions include over one hundred pipes, some elephant tusks, a collection of star sapphires, a pair of red doeskin slacks marked down to a hundred dollars at an Abercrombie & Fitch sale, a bucketful of gold gadgets from Cartier's, and a complete cowboy outfit, which he bought on a trip West for about one thousand dollars. It was Kaufman who, viewing him for the first time in this costly rig, murmured, "Hi-yo, Platinum!"

Nobody minds Hart's enthusiasm for riches, partly because it is wide-eyed and candid and partly because his simple delight blends so interestingly with the mildly satanic cast of his face that he manages to look, most of the time, like Mephistopheles peering up a chimney for Santa Claus. Hart is a tall man, sparsely built and full of eager gestures, with a hairline and eyebrows so curved and winged, in the Mephistophelean fashion, that they threaten continually to carry him aloft. In contrast to his soaring and devilish look, his manner is confiding, even cozy. He will speak so starkly to friends of his poverty-ridden childhood in Coney Island that his listeners glow with sympathy, even after they have discovered that he never lived in Coney Island. He did live for a while in Sea Gate, not far from Coney, and the toughest skeptic understands his dramatic perceptiveness in substituting Coney Island for Sea Gate because Coney Island sounds so much worse. Without any added gloom, his childhood and early youth were grim enough to explain why he now likes to stroll into Cartier's and buy baubles.

Moss's father, an English Jew named Barnett Hart, emigrated from London to New York, married a Miss Solomon, an English girl whom he met here, and set up a newsstand and stationery store in the Bronx. He was a cigar maker by trade and would set up a newsstand somewhere whenever he couldn't get a job in a cigar factory. As Moss remembers it, his father had a newsstand more often than not. Moss was born on East 103rd Street, in a railroad flat over his father's newsstand

and stationery shop. To help out the family finances, he left public school when he was in the eighth grade, at the age of twelve, and went to work as errand boy for A. L. Levenson's Music Store, a local concern. Two years later he got a job as stockroom boy and messenger for the National Cloak & Suit Co., in the garment district around Twenty-third Street. Although the Harts were poor, they were lively theatergoers and Moss was always one of the family party in gallery seats at matinées. He has a younger brother, Bernard, who also developed an early taste for the drama and is now a successful stage manager.

The Hart boys' mother died about seven years ago and took with her the great family mystery and possibly its solution. This was the celebrated bogey of the crosses on the door. From the time Moss was six and Bernie an infant, a crude cross would appear spasmodically on the door of the Harts' flat, apparently cut with a knife, and with the warning "Beware!" scratched above or below it. Sometimes the doorbell or the name plate over the Harts' buzzer in the entrance would be ripped out. These things happened too often to be dismissed as a neighborhood prank, and at length the elder Hart went to the police, accompanied by the landlord, who was getting pretty tired of having to repair the fixtures. A policeman was put on guard for a while, but nothing happened while he was there. As soon as he left, the cross and the warning reappeared. The Harts moved to Bensonhurst when Moss was about nineteen, and the crosses and the warnings followed them. The crosses and the warnings pursued them for more than twenty-five years wherever they moved—from the Bronx to Bensonhurst, from Bensonhurst to Sea Gate, from Sea Gate to New York, from New York to California. As Moss prospered and installed himself and his family in appropriate surroundings, the crosses loomed successively on the doors of a hotel suite, a Park Avenue apartment, a bungalow in upper New York State, and a house in Beverly Hills. One night, in New York, Moss came home and found the symbols carved on the foot of his bed; his family had been sitting in the next room all evening. He engaged private detectives, who kept watch twenty-four hours a day, collected twenty-four dollars a day, and reported nothing. The Harts knew of no one who would want to persecute them, and they began, in a nervous, half-joking way, to suspect one another. About six years ago, or perhaps longer, the business of the crosses and the warnings suddenly stopped. Moss and his father and brother are not positive that it ended precisely with the death of Mrs. Hart, and they wouldn't know exactly what to make of it if it had. They have never found any explanation.

The three men live separately these days, although they are on terms of vast affection. Barnett Hart is seventy-nine and vigorous, and spends most of each year in Miami, where he wears white suits and a yachting cap and is widely known as the Commodore. The Commodore's hobby is writing songs, and he has composed a ballad to celebrate each of Moss's plays. These anthems, of which he writes both words and music, are entitled "George Washington Slept Here," "Lady in the Dark," "The Man Who Came to Dinner," and so on. The chorus of the last starts off, "The man who came to dinner, what a man! What a man!" For his father's birthday last year, Moss thought up the idea of having Irving Berlin publish one of the Commodore's songs, and for this purpose he brought Berlin and the Commodore together to confer about the musical arrangement. At the first suggestion from Berlin, the Commodore patted him on the shoulder and said, "Now listen, boy, you tend to your song writing and I'll tend to mine."

When Moss was sixteen and working for the National Cloak & Suit Co., he had a glamorous friend, an office boy to Augustus Pitou, the theatrical producer. Pitou was known as the Road King because of his great success with touring companies, notably with an outfit called the Henry Duffy Players. He lasted as the Road King until some fatal impulse led him, in the twenties, to turn down a play Henry Duffy's wife had written. Mrs. Duffy was Anne Nichols and the play was, of course, *Abie's Irish Rose*. One day in 1921, during his lunch hour, Moss Hart walked uptown to Pitou's office, on Forty-second Street, to see his friend the office boy, and learned that he had quit his job that morning. Moss went to work for Pitou that afternoon and never returned to the garment center.

He had learned to type with two fingers when he was ten, on a broken-down typewriter a cousin had given him, and soon his duties with Pitou came to include taking the boss's dictation (with two fingers on a typewriter) and reading plays. In 1923, Pitou was looking for a vehicle for Fisk O'Hara, an Irish tenor whom he had under contract, and Moss, laboring through a pile of manuscripts at home one night, decided to try writing a play. He wrote the first act of a romance, which he called *The Beloved Bandit,* signed it Robert Arnold Conrad (a pseudonym devised from the first names of three old schoolmates), and submitted it to Pitou a few days later as the work of a friend.

Pitou read the first act and enthusiastically demanded to see the rest. Moss worked all that night and delivered the second act in the morning and the last act three days later.

"Get this Conrad. I want to sign him up," Pitou ordered when he had finished reading.

"Well," said Moss, inventing wildly, "Mr. Conrad is a very busy man. He's a lawyer and he works all day. I don't know if I can get hold of him—"

"Take a letter," said Pitou. He then dictated the first of a series of letters to Conrad, all of which Moss wrote down and later privately tore up. He says now that he dared not tell the truth for fear Pitou, discovering that he was dictating long daily appeals to a mythical playwright, would feel foolish and fire him. When Conrad failed to answer any of the letters or to show up for an appointment Hart had wretchedly promised to make, Pitou finally said one day, "Get your hat, Moss. We'll go to this fellow's office." In the elevator, Hart said desperately, "Mr. Pitou, I have a confession to make. *I* am Robert Arnold Conrad."

Hart declares that Pitou's expression scarcely changed; he just got out of the elevator at the ground floor and led Moss into the next elevator going up. It was only when he handed Hart a contract and a pen that he spoke his first words.

"Now, Mossie," he said, "when an author writes his first play, he doesn't get the regular royalties."

The Beloved Bandit, which was also known for a time as *The Hold-Up Man,* ran six weeks in Chicago and lost $45,000.

Hart continued to work in Pitou's office for about six months, receiving fifteen dollars a week as office boy-secretary, and seventy-five dollars a week as a playwright until the show closed; after that he just got the fifteen dollars. This experience so depressed him that he did not write another play for two years. His second one, *Panic,* was the story of a father and son, vaguely based on the Douglas Fairbankses, and was produced by Bela Blau in a summer theater but was never put on in New York. *Panic* came in handy some five weeks later, however, when Max Gordon asked Hart to adapt the book for his Viennese spectacle, *The Great Waltz,* which was the story of the Strausses, father and son. Hart dusted off his early drama and *Panic,* with certain changes, became *The Great Waltz.*

One day while Hart was still fretting in the Pitou office, a friend of his who was directing an amateur theatrical group at the Labor Temple, on Fourteenth Street, fell ill and asked Moss to pinch-hit for him at putting on a play. During rehearsals Hart met a man who ran a summer vacation paradise in Pennsylvania called Camp Utopia and who was looking for some new social directors. Hart left Pitou and for the next three years spent his summers as a social director at various camps and his winters as a paid director of amateur groups at the Labor Temple and at Y.M.H.A. clubhouses in New York, Brooklyn, and Newark. Both of these occupations have been steppingstones for a good many New York boys; Richard Rodgers and the late Lorenz Hart, the songwriters, used to direct amateur theatricals, and Edward Chodorov, the author of *Kind Lady, Those Endearing Young Charms,* and *Decision,* helped conduct social activities at Camp Utopia at the same time that Hart was there. Arthur Kober, who dramatized a social camp a few years ago in *Having Wonderful Time,* is regarded by veterans like Chodorov and Hart as an amiable dilettante who drifted about in canoes at one camp or another but never worked in any.

A social director has charge of camp waiters (mostly college boys from N.Y.U. and Columbia), leads games and outings, and dances with wallflowers among the stenographers and lady shipping clerks who come up to spend their two weeks' vacation. Chodorov remembers that at Camp Utopia Hart was popular, romantic-looking, and a great hand at vamping on a guitar and singing the songs of that summer. On rainy days, he also read palms and gave lessons in tap dancing. In a burst of artistic zeal Camp Utopia put on a production of O'Neill's *The Emperor Jones,* with Chodorov as Jones and Hart as Smithers, the overseer. According to Chodorov, Moss kicked like a horse at the approach of grease paint and was terrified until the moment he set foot on the stage. "From that second, he became the complete ham," Chodorov says affectionately. "When he got back to New York, they couldn't keep him off the stage at the Y.M.H.A. He'd play anything. One night he played Aubrey Piper in *The Show-Off* at eight-thirty and then hurried over to another clubhouse and played Oswald in Ibsen's *Ghosts* at eleven." Hart still loves acting and he has appeared in two of his own plays—the West Coast production of *Once in a Lifetime,* in which he played Lawrence Vail, the playwright, while George Kaufman was moodily acting the same role in New York; and the Bucks County Playhouse production of *The Man Who Came to Dinner,* with Kaufman as the Man and Hart in the Noel Coward part. Candid witnesses of these occasions say that Hart underplays to the point of pitching his voice in a monotone that makes him sound like some kind of Chinese actor. The Bucks County *Man Who Came to Dinner* was not an ideal setting for any actor given to underplaying, since the part of Harpo Marx in that company was played by Harpo himself. Harpo, a loving friend to both Kaufman and Hart but an elf nevertheless, carried a pocketful of candles and his cane with the automobile horn attachment and appeared wildly in corners during the play, eating candles and honking his cane throughout most of his pals' speeches.

Hart's recollections of his career as a social director are mainly poignant. One summer he thriftily asked his camp director to hold back his salary, amounting to several hundred dollars, for safekeeping and to give it to him all at once at the end of the season. A few days before camp closed, the director disappeared with the money. Another summer, lacking the white flannels and cummerbunds necessary to a social director, especially in the evenings, Moss appealed to his camp director, who told him to go to Geller's haberdashery on Eighth Avenue before camp opened, buy what he needed, and charge it to him. Moss dizzily bought flannels, sports jackets, slacks, and scarves and went to camp to await the arrival of his wardrobe. It never came, the merchant having looked up the camp director's credit rating in the meantime. Moss spent the rest of that summer acting out a painful, prolonged, and gallant gag. He found some trunks containing costumes for charades and pageants and thenceforth appeared at dinner every night in a different guise, as a gypsy, a Colonial gentleman, or whatever else the trunks afforded, gaily explaining that he had thought of it as a good way to pep up the evenings.

In the winters, commuting on the subway from Sea Gate to his Y.M.H.A. groups, Hart had taken to reading *Variety*, especially the Hollywood section. In 1929, he began working in his spare time on *Once in a Lifetime.* He sent the completed play to an agent, who sent it to Sam H. Harris. Harris read the manuscript in Palm Beach, where he was spending a few weeks with Irving Berlin, and wired Hart's agent that he would produce the play as a musical comedy with songs by Berlin. To this offer Moss replied, "Tell Mr. Harris I have written a play, not a musical comedy." Harris, impressed by Hart's retort as well as by his manuscript, agreed to produce the play with a few changes and suggested George S. Kaufman as collaborator. Kaufman was already well known. He had written several successful plays with Marc Connelly, among them *Dulcy, To the Ladies, Merton of the Movies,* and *Beggar on Horseback;* he was co-author with Edna Ferber of *The Royal Family,* and he had written *The Butter and Egg Man* alone. Hart entered into the collaboration with reverence and delight, but he cannily continued to direct amateur groups in his spare time. These groups charged a small admission to their performances, to take care of expenses, but they had no money left over to pay out in royalties. Moss contrived to give the customers good shows and at the same time to avoid any foolish expense in royalties by putting on Broadway successes with a change of title as a sop to the copyright conventions.

The Trial of Mary Dugan was produced, for instance, as *What Price Justice?*, and *What Price Glory?* was presented as *No Retreat*. Hart did not tell Kaufman until some years afterward that, while the two men were working on *Once in a Lifetime*, Moss was also presenting *Beggar on Horseback* somewhere downtown, royalty-free, under the somewhat different title *Dreams Are Not for Sale*.

People who have read Hart's original manuscript of *Once in a Lifetime* say that it was not very different in plot and dialogue from the final version. "Of course, no play has ever exactly suffered from George's lapidary work," one observer has put it. Kaufman himself thought so well of Hart's play that he insisted that the contract with Harris give Hart sixty per cent of the author's royalties from the production and—an even greater boon—top billing. The programs and advertisements of the play read "By Moss Hart and George S. Kaufman." In spite of the happy business relations between the collaborators, their first few meetings were social failures. Hart worried himself into a frenzy because he could scarcely help noticing that Kaufman, his idol, visibly winced at his approach. Hart would bravely breeze in to work with outstretched hand, and Kaufman would shrink away. *Once in a Lifetime* had been running for months before Hart discovered that Kaufman had been shrinking all that time, not from Moss, but from the stench of the five-cent cigars which Moss, as a newly arrived playwright and man of the world, saw fit to smoke. Hart smokes a pipe these days. For the first year and a half of their collaboration, Hart called Kaufman "Mr. Kaufman" and Kaufman, a reticent man, called Hart "Er." They have since become companionable and relaxed. When they write a play together, Kaufman usually sits at the typewriter or lies down on the floor and picks lint off the carpet while Hart paces. If they hit on a line or a situation that amuses them, they laugh uproariously. Sometimes they turn out only four pages a day, occasionally they write an act in that time. They worked six months on the revisions of *Once in a Lifetime*, and it took them the same length of time to write *The Man Who Came to Dinner*. They finished *You Can't Take It With You*, on the other hand, in five weeks.

Both Kaufman and Hart have a nervous attitude toward actors, whom they look upon as dreamers. When they had decided that they needed Monty Woolley for the Alexander Woollcott role in *The Man Who Came to Dinner,* they wanted to surprise Woolley, who at that time was playing obscure bits in Hollywood, and called him on the telephone to offer him the part. Owing to the difference in time the call woke Woolley at noon. "What do you mean by waking me up in the middle of the night with your corny jokes?" he shouted wrathfully, and hung up. Kaufman and Hart completed the deal through an agent, and took a simple pleasure in the knowledge that Woolley had to pay the agent ten per cent of his salary for the run of the play.

Winged Victory, Moss Hart's first successful serious play, did as much for Hart psychologically as it accomplished practically for the Air Forces or the Army Emergency Relief. Until then, Hart's success with satirical comedies had probably caused him more anguish than any of the other problems that beset him. His was the woe of the expert who does one thing superbly well and is never allowed to do anything else. During his collaboration with Kaufman both men were driven by the Pagliaccio deep in every humorist to write three serious plays—*Merrily We Roll Along* (a study of the disintegration of a man because of too much prosperity), *The Fabulous Invalid* (a study of the decay of the theater), and *The American Way* (a study of the slow dissolution of audiences and profits). Each one was a resounding flop, *The American Way* going so far as to lose sixty thousand dollars in a theater holding four thousand persons, most of whom stayed away. Herman Mankiewicz, a Hollywood wit, once described *Merrily We Roll Along* to a friend as follows: "It's about this playwright who writes a play and it's a big success, and then he writes another play and *that's* a big success, all his plays are big successes, and all the actresses in them are in love with him, and he has a yacht and a beautiful home in the country and a beautiful wife and two beautiful children, and he makes a million dollars. Now the problem the play propounds is this," Mankiewicz concluded, "how did the poor son of a bitch ever get into that situation?"

After critics and customers alike besought Kaufman and Hart to stick to comedy, they realized that they were better at writing comedy than tragedy and more adept at handling cockeyed characters than at propounding treatises. Kaufman was philosophical about it, but Hart was still bothered by the feeling, common to many writers these days, that he ought to be writing about some aspects of the war. When, last year, General Henry H. (Hap) Arnold commissioned him to write the Air Forces show and suggested the research tour in the bomber, Hart, who has a nervous stomach and is habitually airsick, welcomed the discomfort and even danger the assignment promised. "The first thing they did," he told friends when he got back from the bomber tour, his face lighting at the recollection, "was to set up a table, typewriter, and chair in the bomb-bay, strap a parachute on me, zoom a couple of thousand miles straight up in the air, and say to me, 'So, go ahead, write the play.' " Hart did not write *Winged Victory* in the bomb-bay, but he made so many notes that he was able to complete the play in a few weeks at his farm in Bucks County. He also directed the production and helped engage the cast of three hundred Air Forces men, most of whom had never appeared on a stage. Another source of gratification to Hart is the fact that *Winged Victory*, which he wrote and staged without pay, left him considerably poorer than he had been in some time.

Hart's most crowded hour was probably the period in 1930 between the dress rehearsal of *Once in a Lifetime* and the morning after the opening. Coming away from the dress rehearsal haggard and worried, he ran into Sam Harris, who took him to his office for a drink. "You needn't worry, you've got a great show with a wonderful plot," Harris assured him, and then, putting his elbows on his desk, he proceeded to reassure him by telling him the wonderful plot, word for word. "It's about these three fellas who go to Hollywood," he began, and went on to describe to Hart all three acts of *Once in a Lifetime*. Toward dawn the two men left the office and Hart headed for a subway station to take a train home to Sea Gate. Harris reminded him that he would have to be back for another rehearsal at eleven that morning and urged him to get some sleep at a hotel in town. When Hart insisted that he had to get home, Harris correctly surmised that he hadn't the price of a hotel room, and, taking a bill from his pocket, he shoved it at Moss and left him. The bill was a one-hundred-dollar note. Like an arrow from a bow, Moss sped to the Astor, took a suite, and ordered up a big breakfast, a barber, a manicurist, and a valet. "I spent sixty dollars that morning between six o'clock and ten-thirty," he recalls comfortably.

After the opening that night, Moss again stayed up until dawn to read the reviews of the play, which were ecstatic. When he had read them all, he went out and sneered at a subway station and then took a taxi to Sea Gate. There he told his father, mother, and brother to put on their hats and leave everything else behind, and brought them all grandly to New York, to the Ansonia Hotel, where he rented a large apartment with a circular living-room in one of the turrets. The Harts never again saw the furniture, clothes, and other belongings they had abandoned in Sea Gate and never gave them a second thought. Moss summoned an interior decorator, the first of a bevy which has come to float after him as inevitably as motes after a sunbeam, and the decorator transformed the turret apartment into an impressive affair of red velvet, gilt, and carved Spanish furniture. Moss's room had three sets of curtains at each window—glass curtains, silk draperies over them, and brocaded hangings over both. "I never had any curtains when I was poor, so I thought I'd like to have plenty," Moss would explain to interested visitors. His taste has gentled into a fondness for the Victorian style, which he likes to have decorators reproduce around him with the speed of a Buck Rogers in the Twenty-fifth Century. His admiration for Alban Conway, who decorated his present apartment on East Sixty-fifth Street, began with Conway's prompt action in rescuing Moss from a welter of ostrich plumes and indoor rock gardens into which another decorator, rashly engaged, had plunged him. After Hart had dwelt miserably for weeks among these mistakes, wondering how to hide them, Conway took most of them one evening and buried them in an excavation the New York Steam Corporation had considerately dug in the street outside. Hart was so grateful that, in addition to his check for the new decorating job, he gave Conway a gold wrist watch inscribed "With appreciation."

Hart's passion for speedy accomplishment has literally caused a forest to appear almost overnight on a bare hilltop on his place in New Hope. He had thirty-five hundred pine trees transplanted to the hill at a cost of over five thousand dollars. No man to wait for the growth of saplings, he also imported one hundred and thirty-nine twenty-year-old elms, maples, and other shade trees to his lawn for the sum of twenty-eight thousand dollars. "When Moss plants a tree, he sits down under it and waits five minutes for it to give shade," his brother Bernard once remarked. Another comment, which gained a certain fame but has never been traced to an authentic source, is supposedly that of the cynical guest who, on being shown Hart's ready-made forest, murmured, "Well, it just goes to show you what God could do if he had money." The New Hope place is run by Raymond, a caretaker, and Charles, a butler who also works at the apartment in town. Charles and Raymond are convivial folk, and Hart treats them as friends to a degree that sometimes rattles his other cronies. Charles and Raymond play croquet, backgammon, and bridge with Hart's guests. One Bucks County matron, settled at a bridge table after dinner at Moss's, glanced curiously at the face of her partner, wondering where she had seen him before, only to realize with a start that he was the man who had served her soup.

About six years ago, things were going so well with Hart that he fell into a state of profound gloom and consulted a psychiatrist about himself. Much as he likes speed, the swiftness with which he had attained wealth and fame sometimes made him nervous. Two of his early trips to Europe provide an example of the change that had come over him. In 1930, on his first trip abroad, he met Cole Porter and dined at Porter's house in Paris; he gasped at Elsie de Wolfe's green hair and stammered over Elsa Maxwell's motherly grilling, and when the ladies left the table after dinner he trotted along with them, never having heard of that custom. In 1935, only five years later, he scarcely thought twice about calling up Porter one day in New York and saying casually, "What do you say we take a trip around the world and write a show?" The result of the telephone call and the trip was *Jubilee!* a musical comedy kidding the King and Queen of England. Hart admired the bored irreverence of the Porter crowd, but he is basically a conventional man, and learning to reverse all his values, as they did, was something of a strain. Occasionally he felt that he was getting a little too smart, and his old friends further depressed him by heartily agreeing with this opinion. Now in his sixth year of psychiatry, Hart says he thinks he can see the end. His friends declare that he is a new man, and no one can deny that psychiatry, or something, has enabled him to write three plays alone, independent of any collaborator.

Everybody always wants to see a bachelor who is happy that way get married, and Hart's friends have been no exception to this rule. They have long pointed out that it was time he settled down—a suggestion that finally forced him to declare that he could not marry because he was mourning the death of his only passion, a schoolteacher whom he had loved years before. Months afterward, Beatrice Kaufman, in a heart-to-heart chat with Moss, mentioned the schoolteacher and Moss stared at her in astonishment. "You didn't *believe* that stuff, did you?" he said. He is still unmarried. He is a courtly and popular escort, and so many personable young women have glanced off him so harmlessly that a certain thoughtful observer, seeing him enter a restaurant one night with an actress who shall here be called Miss Blank, murmured, "Here comes Moss Hart and the future Miss Blank."

Hart will always have his sorrows. Before his thirty-eighth birthday placed him beyond the military age limit last year, he tried to get a commission in the Navy, and was rejected because of insufficient education. He sat around feeling ignorant and rebuffed for a whole morning after he got the notice. What finally consoled him a little was the recollection that he was scheduled, that same day, to deliver a lecture on the drama at Columbia.

❀ 5 ❀

Miss Lily of New Orleans:

LILLIAN HELLMAN

A GOOD WAY to annoy Lillian Hellman, if you happen to be someone who wants to annoy Lillian Hellman, is to call her a woman playwright. This simple descriptive term, applied to Miss Hellman, author of *The Children's Hour, The Little Foxes, Watch on the Rhine,* and *The Searching Wind,* sends her into a strange rage, often interesting because, although it may be accompanied by a stamping of the feet, it is not without a cool, unanswerable logic. Being called a woman playwright bores and exasperates her for the same reason, she explains, that a man who writes plays would be bored and exasperated by being continually called a man playwright. Her admirers argue that few people could tell, anyway, whether her plays are written by a man or a woman, since they are all distinguished by the kind of intellectual indignation that must be sexless. This is honest tribute, but Miss Hellman has suffered from such praise. People who meet her for the first time are apt to come away murmuring in astonishment, "She's sort of cute, isn't she?" and interviewers who find her in a hostess gown write dazed pieces about her feminine draperies and fail to disclose much else about her. There has been one notable exception among the interviewers. After Miss Hellman's first success, *The Children's Hour,* in 1934, a feature-writer for a New York paper called on her and apparently surprised her in a tailored suit and a crisp mood. "She's the kind of girl who can take the tops off bottles with her teeth!" this analyst wrote enthusiastically afterward.

Actually, Lillian Hellman is neither cute nor tough. For a woman with militant undercurrents, her surface behavior is more often mild than not, and she is genuinely feminine to a degree that borders engagingly on the wacky. Although her writing is sure and pointed, she has no geographical sense of direction whatever, and last summer, after she had got lost twice in one week on the 130-acre farm in Pleasantville, New York, where she has lived for the past six years, Dashiell Hammett, an old and solicitous friend, undertook to teach her how to take her bearings. "Look," he said, pointing, "that's north. When you face north"—he grasped her by the shoulders and pointed her north—"east is on your right hand, west on your left, and south behind you." He then drew a little map indicating that the house was east of the chicken farm, west of the woods, and so on. Next day, Miss Hellman got lost for three hours. "You told me," she said accusingly to Hammett when he found her in the woods, "that north was in front of me, so naturally I followed my left hand from where I was facing." Her approach to scientific phenomena is equally baffled and baffling. One evening, Herman Shumlin, who has produced all of Miss Hellman's plays, happened to remark that heat rises. Miss Hellman thought that over, and suddenly glowed with the light of reasonable argument. "If that's true," she said, "why doesn't your hand get burned worse if you hold it a foot above a radiator than it does if you put it right on top?" There is nothing coy about Miss Hellman's helplessness in the face of geography and physics. Defeated by them, she dismisses them with a word, generally of four letters.

Lillian Hellman's face and appearance are not well known to the public in spite of her three hit plays, the Drama Critics Circle Award for 1941 to her *Watch on the Rhine,* and the various pictures she has written or adapted for Hollywood—*Dead End, The Dark Angel, These Three* (a movie version of *The Children's Hour*), *The Little Foxes,* from her stage play of that name, and *The North Star.* She is five feet three inches tall, and slim, with reddish hair, a fine, aquiline nose, and a level, humorous mouth. When she is in repose or talking business, her nose and mouth give her a fleeting and curious resemblance to the familiar Gilbert Stuart portrait of George Washington. Her voice is flexible and interesting, and her hands, feet, and legs amply reward the candid pleasure she takes in them. She likes clothes and is so sensitive to them that the right or wrong dress has been known to produce a momentary success or disaster in her social career.

A week or so after the opening of *The Little Foxes,* she was invited to dine with Mr. and Mrs. Henry Luce at their Waldorf Towers apartment. Mrs. Luce is famous as Clare Boothe, a woman who would just as soon be called a woman playwright. Another guest was Dorothy Thompson, the columnist and firebrand. After dinner the ladies, leaving the men to their cigars and brandies, fluttered to Mrs. Luce's powder room, and a conversation sprang up between the hostess and Miss Thompson about a remark Dorothy Parker had made to Somerset Maugham when she had met him a week or so before. "I am a great admirer of your style," Mr. Maugham had said to Mrs. Parker, and Mrs. Parker had replied, "Thank you, Mr. Maugham. I have always admired you because you have no style." This, a true compliment from one discriminating writer to another, was construed by Mmes Luce and Thompson as a deadly insult to a dean of English letters. Miss Hellman, whose best woman friend is Dorothy Parker, listened in silence as long as she could and then mistakenly tried to explain to the two what Mrs. Parker had meant. They stared at her and, it is said by other witnesses, giggled. A few minutes later, in the drawing room, they approached her in tandem, so to speak, drawing up chairs to the couch where she rather miserably sat.

"We're going to *heckle* you, Miss Hellman," said Mrs. Luce archly. At this, Miss Hellman simply got up and fled blindly back to the bathroom. "Ordinarily, I might have coped with those—ah—beauties," she says now. The reason she was routed, it seems, was that they were sleek in satin and she, that night, was wearing an expensive error in yellow organdie, threaded with black velvet ribbon tied in girlish bows at the throat and wrists.

Revenge is sweet, especially when it's on Dorothy Thompson, and such an opportunity is not given to many women. A few weeks after the dinner party, however, Miss Thompson telephoned Miss Hellman. Metro-Goldwyn-Mayer had made motions toward buying Miss Thompson's play about refugees,

Another Sun, which had run eight days in New York in 1940, on condition that Miss Hellman adapt it for pictures, and they had sent it to her to read. Miss Hellman, studying the manuscript, found that Miss Thompson, in a welter of nostalgia for the old Germany, had flung into the dialogue a good many *gemütlich* phrases in the mother tongue. When Miss Thompson called up about the play, she was ready for her. "I suggest first that you translate it from the German," she said coldly. Nothing ever came of this incipient collaboration.

Lillian Hellman, at thirty-nine, is the youngest successful woman playwright, or woman successfully writing plays, in the United States, and therefore probably in the world. She was born in New Orleans and was cared for as a child by a Negro mammy—two facts that have embarrassed certain playgoers and critics, who denounced her Negro characters in *The Little Foxes* as being artificial and overdrawn. Her father, Max Hellman, was a prosperous shoe merchant with a store on Canal Street in New Orleans; her mother had been Julia Newhouse of Alabama. Mrs. Hellman died nine years ago. Mr. Hellman, living with a gusto his daughter has inherited, has retired from business and spends most of his time playing pinochle with cronies in Atlantic City. He confesses a mild amazement but practically no awe when he thinks how his little girl has grown up to be a famous playwright.

When Lillian was five, a partner of her father's absconded with the company's funds, and Max Hellman came to New York with his wife and only child to start over again as a travelling salesman for a clothing firm. For many years afterward, Lillian spent her summers in New Orleans, visiting her aunts or her grandmother. In New York, the Hellman family lived on West Ninety-fifth Street near the River, and from this base Lillian soon established a widening circle of activities. America entered the first World War when she was twelve, and in an excess of patriotism she and a friend named Helen Schiff took to trailing people who they thought looked like German spies. Long-haired fellows carrying brief cases or violin cases (handy for holding machine guns and bombs) were especially suspect, and once the girls chased two men ten blocks and reported them to a police sergeant, who, after considerable trouble, discovered them to be a professor of Greek from Hunter College and a second violinist from the Palace Theatre. Lillian and Helen had a stooge, a timid blonde who was detailed to eavesdrop on conversations of suspects and report them to the two head spy-catchers. Her reports were dull and her superiors grew bored. "It's got to be more *interesting!*" Lillian exclaimed one day, and she and Helen then twisted the stooge's arm until she managed to think up something worth hearing. A version of this incident appeared in *The Children's Hour*, but Miss Hellman says that she did not remember it consciously while she was writing the play.

When Lillian was fourteen her budding taste for sitting in a chatty group around a table led to her first open rebellion. A boy in his second year at Columbia asked her to go to a fencing match with him and another boy and girl, and after the match the four repaired to Constantine's ice-cream parlor on upper Broadway. The Columbia student was nineteen, the other girl and her beau were at least seventeen, and Lillian, irked by her own youth and her father's order to be home by eleven, brooded herself into a state of defiance and stayed out until after midnight. The stern reception she got when she did turn up further inflamed her, and next day she left home for good, with seventy-five cents in her pocket. She spent an agreeable afternoon a couple of miles to the south, talking to strangers and eating candy, but by nine o'clock that night most of her money and her spirits were gone, and she called up the Columbia sophomore with her last nickel. "I have left home," she told him romantically. "Come and look after me." Columbia came all right, but Lillian was depressed to note that instead of looking gallant and protective, he looked protective and very bored. He took her home and shoved her in the door, and Lillian reluctantly entered, to find her mother in tears from grief and worry. "Are you all right, my baby?" she kept saying, and this gave the wanderer an idea. She assumed a frail look, waited for a pause, and announced, "Mother, I have heart trouble."

When Lillian entered Wadleigh High School in 1922, her dramatic instinct easily surpassed that of the dramatic coach, who carelessly gave her the role of the villainess in a school play, *Mrs. Gorringe's Necklace.* This character actually had few lines to speak, but at Lillian's final exit the night of the play the door stuck and she couldn't get off the stage. Pleased by the happy circumstance, she returned calmly to the panic-stricken members of the cast, who were grouped about a drawing-room set and, arranging herself on a sofa, proceeded to invent a dazzling scene, which fattened up her own part by a number of showy remarks and lasted a good five minutes after the stricken coach had got the door unstuck and started to wave wildly at her from the wings. Lillian appeared in no more plays, but she soon got around to writing a column for the school paper. The column was called *It Seems to Me, Jr.*, and, since it appeared before either Heywood Broun or Lillian Hellman had become the people's friend, it was light, chatty, and without social significance.

Miss Hellman has been called a Communist almost as often as she has been called a woman playwright, and her political viewpoint is about the only thing toward which she has a regrettable tendency to be coy. Pinned down to a statement of her allegiances, she says vaguely that she would like to be a liberal if she could tell, these days, exactly what the hell a liberal is. Reminded of Dorothy Thompson's crack in her 1940 valentine column, which suggested "To the Communist Party of America—*The Little Foxes*," Miss Hellman says candidly, "I stuck my neck out there." Miss Thompson's reproof was inspired by the row, familiar along Broadway, between Miss Hellman and Tallulah Bankhead over the benefit performance of *The Little Foxes*, which Miss Bankhead, the star of the play, proposed to give for Finnish relief. Miss Hellman, backed up by Herman Shumlin, producer of the play, objected on the ground that Miss Bankhead and the cast had refused, some months earlier, to play a benefit Miss Hellman had asked them to give for the Spanish Loyalists. "And besides," Miss Hellman added, cannily, as it turned out, "I don't believe in that fine, lovable little Republic of Finland that everybody gets so weepy about. I've been there, and it looks like a pro-Nazi little republic to me." The battle, gentled along by Richard Maney, Shumlin's press agent, got into the headlines, and public sympathy was with Miss Bankhead, since Finland was then being attacked by Russia. People reasoned that Miss Hellman, being opposed to aiding Finnish relief, must be a Red. The knowing ones pointed out that she had been in Russia and in Spain in 1937 and had published pieces about her trip in the *New Masses* and the *New Republic*. Miss Hellman now says mildly that she submitted the pieces first to several slick magazines, which turned them down. The detached biographer, looking through the record, will find that the longest and most heartfelt of these articles was called *A Bleached Lady* and was a semi-fictional piece about a Spanish woman refugee who, noticing that an American lady traveller's hair had begun to turn dark at the roots, recommended a friend who ran a hairdressing shop in Madrid and had a skillful hand with *teinturerie*, if she was still alive.

People who know Lillian Hellman well say that what some theorists consider her Communist tendency is actually more a violent anti-Fascism and an equally strong instinct to fight for the little people who can't fight for themselves. She is a woman who hates to see anybody pushed around, they say. Miss Hellman agrees with this explanation, but she is an arguer at heart. Once, in her presence, a friend of hers set out to prove to a heckler that Lillian was not even sympathetic to the Communists, and gave a number of convincing reasons. "Isn't that true, Lillian?" the friend said, turning to her rather breathlessly. "Well . . ." said Miss Hellman.

The easy riches of the 1920's, of which she had no share, may partly explain her curiously split social attitude, which combines a sensible fondness for money with a violent dislike for people who wallow in it. Graduating from Wadleigh High, she entered N.Y.U., where her reaction to culture seems to have been entirely normal. She admired Lewis Carroll and Dante and thought of writing a biography of the latter, but got no farther than a line in her notebook stating, "Dante is okay." Graduated from N.Y.U., she took a course in journalism at Columbia, as an indirect result of which she was engaged to write several one- and two-column book reviews for the Sunday *Tribune*, at about $4.70 a column. In the middle twenties, still living with her family, she worked at a series of jobs—as a reader for Horace Liveright, the publisher, as a play-reader for Anne Nichols, who was then trying to find a worthy successor to *Abie's Irish Rose,* and as a press agent for something called *The Bunk of 1926.* Through her theatrical contacts she came to know Herman Shumlin and Arthur Kober, who shared an office in the Selwyn Theatre Building and worked, as general manager and press agent respectively, for Jed Harris, the most fabulous producer of that period. In 1925, Miss Hellman married Kober. Kober later became a successful Hollywood writer and author of the play *Having Wonderful Time.*

Divorce ended the marriage in 1932, but it did not affect Kober's attachment to Miss Hellman. A man whose cherubic appearance conceals hell's own inner turmoil, he was probably the first to appreciate her great common sense and capacity for shouldering burdens, and certainly the last to want to give them up entirely. His friends (and Lillian's) grew accustomed to the familiar sight of Arthur seated in a dim corner of some *boîte* mentally wrestling with himself in an effort to get along without Lillian's advice about a new play, a new apartment, or whatever was torturing him. It was always a losing battle. Whenever Kober returned to New York from Hollywood and began looking at furnished apartments to sublease, he would say to the occupant, "May I bring my friend to see it?" The householder, expecting another man, would naturally consent, and soon Kober would reappear with his ex-wife, whom he nervously introduced as "my friend." Miss Hellman would then inspect closets, stove, plumbing, and other important details, and finally state her opinion to the startled tenant. "It stinks," she would say agreeably more often than not. When Kober eventually decided to remarry, four years ago, he brought his fiancée for Lillian to see, in the most natural way in the world, and Miss Hellman was so pleased with the prospective Mrs. Kober that she stood up with the bride and groom at the wedding as matron of honor.

By 1933, Herman Shumlin had become a successful producer with *Grand Hotel* and *The Last Mile,* and Miss Hellman went to work for him as a reader. She had written one play, *Dear Queen,* in collaboration with Louis Kronenberger, now dramatic critic of *PM*, but it was never produced, chiefly, Miss Hellman thinks, because she and Kronenberger had a hilarious time writing it. As writers keep on sorrowfully finding out, the kind of writing that entertains its authors is generally not the kind that entertains the public. One night, at a party at Ira Gershwin's, she said to Shumlin, "What would you think of a play about a couple of schoolteachers accused of being Lesbians by a brat pupil?" "I wouldn't waste any time on it," he answered kindly. Miss Hellman had already spent several months on such a play, and after she had spent six or eight more, she laid the manuscript on Shumlin's desk. "Here's that play I mentioned," she said. "Oh," said Shumlin, "all right, I'll read it." Miss Hellman said, "When?" Shumlin said, "Now." Miss Hellman said, "I'll wait." She sat down in a corner of the office and appeared to read a magazine while Shumlin read *The Children's Hour*. He made three comments: "Swell!" at the end of the first act, "I hope it keeps up" at the end of the second, and "I'll produce it" when he had finished the third. Miss Hellman looked at him in astonishment. "You really mean that?" she demanded. This has been her invariable remark each time Shumlin has eagerly agreed to produce a play of hers, and it is often followed by the dour prophecy "Well, this is *one* play you'll lose your shirt on." Her confidence in her own work is unaffectedly shaky, in strange contrast to her almost reckless poise in private life.

Miss Hellman had fifty dollars in the bank the day Shumlin first read *The Children's Hour,* and made about $125,000 out of the play, which ran twenty-one months in New York, another year on the road, and was produced in London and in Paris. Its tours, although not its publicity, were frequently interrupted by censors, who objected to the theme. Once, in Chicago, a test performance was given for the local censor, a lady, who brought a woman friend. In the middle of the scene in which one teacher confesses her illicit love for the other and goes offstage to commit suicide, the censor, who had been silent throughout the performance, turned to her friend, and Shumlin and Miss Hellman, sitting tensely in the row behind, leaned forward anxiously to listen to what she might have to say. "I like that suit she's wearing," the lady censor said. *The Children's Hour* was officially banned in Chicago, but it was put on there anyway by the Actors' Company, a high-spirited group of amateurs.

In 1936, Miss Hellman turned out a drama about labor called *Days to Come,* a harrowing flop. On the opening night, as the play's doom became increasingly clear, Miss Hellman plodded from her seat in the last row to the door of the theater and dispatched the doorman with a ten-dollar bill for a quart of brandy. When he came back with it, she retired to the lonely box office and took several deep, consoling drinks. A few minutes later a form of death attacked her. No amount of failure or brandy could account for the way she felt, she thought dimly, trying to unclench a clammy fist. As her fingers slowly loosened, the change the doorman had returned to her from the ten-dollar bill fell from her hand; it was $9.06. The effect of the ninety-four-cent brandy was not lessened by the party Ralph Ingersoll, now editor-on-leave of *PM,* gave for Miss Hellman after the show that night. It was grisly, like all festivals after a failure. Dashiell Hammett, apparently choosing frankness as the best policy, sat down beside Miss Hellman and told her that in his opinion the play was terrible. "But when you read it," she reminded him desperately, "you said you thought it was the best play you'd ever read." Hammett rose and called for his hat and coat. "I have changed my mind," he said coldly and left.

Although Miss Hellman's next play, *The Little Foxes,* established her as a sure-fire playwright (if there is such a thing), she continued to give each manuscript to friends to read and trembled each time for their decisions. She takes criticism uncomplainingly and writes so many drafts of every play—from four to as many as ten—that the script that finally goes into rehearsal seldom requires any change. She finished the first version of *The Little Foxes* in the summer of 1937, in a cottage she had taken on an island off South Norwalk, and gave it to Hammett, who happened to be a weekend guest. Writing about the South she knew, she had evidently been carried away in the first draft into composing lengthy dialogues of a local color between the two Negro servants in the play. Hammett read it in bed Sunday night and left for town in a cowardly fashion before his hostess was up next morning, leaving the manuscript and a note. "Missy write blackamoor chitchat. Missy better stop writing blackamoor chitchat," the note said. Miss Hellman went for a grim swim after she read this and, she says now, thought of drowning herself. That afternoon, however, she started work on a new version. It took her ten months of writing and rewriting to complete *The Little Foxes,* and as long, or longer, to write each of her other plays.

Her notebooks for a play are monumental, running to two or three volumes of four or five hundred typed, single-spaced pages each, containing data on contemporary history, local customs, factual anecdotes, political aspects, celebrities of the time, and long lists of likely names for characters. In one of her notebooks for *Watch on the Rhine,* three pages are filled with German first and last names—Kathe, Werner, Maxl, Pilar, Willy; Lange, Brech, Reger, Unruh, Rochow, and so on—all of which she studied and discarded before she decided to name the German, played by Paul Lukas, Kurt Mueller, and his wife, played by Mady Christians, Sara. Other pages carry details of the age, life, and background of the characters before their entrance into the play. Frequently there are notes like "What was he doing in Germany? Scientist? Trade Union Movement? Maybe China? What was going on 1920–1932? Maybe they have only been here about 6 months? What was he doing here?" All of this research, in which Miss Hellman is assisted by one secretary, is the usual task of a careful writer, but even in the case of a careful writer it is uncommon to find notes that could be expanded, as the notes for *Watch on the Rhine* could be, into a detailed and accurate history of a period covering twenty-five years. Miss Hellman leaves the direction of her plays to Shumlin, but her thirst for perfection sometimes leads her to wander into a theater during a play's run and take a look at the performance. When *The Little Foxes* was playing to capacity in New York, she appeared silently one night and made the following notes in pencil on a program: "Sound over air system. No thank you from Collinge too quick. Dingle—no looks to audience. Bankhead cuts in on important lines. Don't clutch Horace. Leo—you too cute." These flaws were corrected before the next performance.

Miss Hellman works at a typewriter perched on a rickety table that, in search of solitude, she drags around from one room to another of her Pleasantville house, which is generally full of guests. Not long ago, with a job to do, she posted the following notice outside the room where she was working:

> This room is used for work
> Do not enter without knocking
> After you knock, wait for an answer
> If you get no answer, go away and don't come back
> This means everybody
> This means you
> This means night or day
>
> By order of the Hellman-Military-Commission-for-Playwrights.
>
> Court-martialling will take place in the barn, and your trial will not be a fair one.
>
> The Christmas Court-martialling has now taken place.
>
> Among those:
>
> Herman Shumlin, Former *régisseur.*
> A Mr. X, former insurance man.
> Miss Sylvia Hermann, aged three, former daughter of a farmer.
> Miss Nora, former dog.
> Mr. Samuel Dashiell Hammett, former eccentric.
> Mr. Arthur Kober, former itinerant sweet-singer.
> Mr. Louis Kronenberger, born in Cincinnati, lynched by me.
> Emmy Kronenberger, wife to Kronenberger, died with him.
> Mr. Felix Anderson, former butler.
> Irene Robinson, former cook and very pretty.
>
> Note: Mr. Max Bernard Hellman, father, is a most constant offender. His age has saved him. This sentimentality may not continue.

When posted warnings fail to keep visitors out, Miss Hellman comes into town, rents an apartment in a quiet street, and writes there, doing her own housework and cooking. She is a fine, resourceful cook, specializing in crab gumbo and other New Orleans dishes, and skillful at turning even a domestic annoyance into a *plat de résistance.* Last summer the lake on her Pleasantville place was invaded by snapping turtles, and Miss Hellman, burned up because this threatened to spoil her swimming, sharply ordered her farmer to set traps and deliver all the turtles he caught to the kitchen door. Then she made a superior soup out of them. She has a gourmet's interest in food and will bedevil any hostess who serves her a new and succulent dish until she has got the recipe for it. The food in her own house is beautifully cooked and served, under her fairly gloating direction, by Irene and Felix. Irene is a woman of such exceptional tact that it is a source of wonder to her employer. Not long ago she asked Miss Hellman, politely and rather deviously, to tell Felix to wash the living-room windows for the party. "What party?" inquired Miss Hellman, who had not planned any. No special party, Irene said, going on to explain that Felix was simply the type of man who works better with a definite object in view. Miss Hellman especially admires Irene's way with people because she knows that her own tactfulness is often less than consummate. In 1940, for example, she went to Philadelphia to cover the Republican Presidential Convention for *PM.* In a hotel lobby one day she ran into Thomas E. Dewey, an acquaintance of hers. "Hello!" she said to him cordially. "You going to be here all week?" After Dewey had wanly passed on, a friend who was with Miss Hellman gazed at her and said, "Look, dear. The poor guy just hopes to get nominated. Remember?"

Like most independent women, Lillian Hellman has more men friends than girl friends. A few of these men, with Miss Hellman, form a solid, affectionate group whose friendship for one another is never disturbed by the fact that most of the men have, at some time, been in love with Lillian. Miss Hellman presides over the brotherhood like an exceptionally maternal Maintenon. Her house is permanently open to the boys, and they like to go there and stay for weeks, perhaps, taking their work with them and often turning out a book, a play, a set of editorial memorandums, or a production schedule for the new season. She is a good hostess, casual and entertaining, and her advice about business and artistic problems is sure to be either wise enough or just screwy enough to be exactly right. Among the headaches she has shared is *PM*, which she helped Ralph Ingersoll formulate. She was one of its original stockholders—"mainly," she explains, "because I lent them some money to pay the electric-light and telephone bills once or twice when they were broke, and got paid back in stock." She also thought up the name *PM* after a series of conferences during which Ingersoll kept doggedly insisting that the paper be called simply *Newspaper*, on the peculiar theory that people habitually walk up to a newsstand and say, "Give me a newspaper." She was concerned because Dashiell Hammett didn't write a new book after *The Thin Man*, eleven years ago, and she was warmly proud of him when he enlisted as a private in the Army in 1942, and went overseas. When Herman Shumlin needs relaxation, she goes on fishing trips with him and his admiration for her increases because, he says, she always knows what every goddam fish is planning at the other end of the line. She likes to gamble with men for manly stakes and once won twelve thousand dollars in an evening at *chemin de fer*. She ordered two ambulances for the Spanish Loyalists next morning, lost the twelve thousand dollars in another game that night, but bought the ambulances anyway.

In spite of Miss Hellman's liking for masculine company, she has none of the phony impatience with her own sex so often affected by female literary celebrities. She is fond of a number of women and likes to send them unexpected and interesting presents, half a *prosciutto* ham or a silver bowl for mixing New Orleans *café diable*. She is not above loud and bitter complaint if she doesn't get enough presents in return. A week before her birthday last year, she sent a telegram to some twelve or fifteen friends. "A birthday present for Lillian Hellman is a blow against Fascism," it suggested. When the friends came through nobly with gifts, Miss Hellman wept frank and grateful tears. Although she is subject to attacks of sentiment, her aspect is not always tender. "When Lillian gets mad," Dorothy Parker will tell you in her soft, deprecating voice, "I regret to say she screams." This talent for making a noise is partly responsible for Miss Hellman's success in Hollywood, notably with Sam Goldwyn, who is no whisperer.

In 1935, Mrs. Parker and Miss Hellman were among the leaders of a group of Hollywood writers who wanted to revive the moribund Screen Writers' Guild and were therefore enthusiastic about the proposed Wagner Act, which guaranteed collective bargaining and the right to strike. One day the two ladies called on Goldwyn. "Sam," said Miss Hellman, "why don't you come out in favor of the Screen Writers' Guild and help us revive it? You would be the first producer to do it, and it would give you tremendous distinction." "That's right, Sam," added Mrs. Parker, who does not always speak in epigrams. Goldwyn thought it over, and finally replied, "I can't do it, girls. I can't come out in favor of the Screen Writers' Guild, but I tell you what I *will* do for you. I will definitely," he said with a ringing sincerity, "come out against the Wagner Act." Miss Hellman's screams echoed through Hollywood then, but by the time she got back to New York, a few weeks later, they had dwindled to a murmur far more deadly. One night, Charles MacArthur said to her, "A fine thing, you twenty-five-hundred-a-week Hollywood writers wanting to strike for more pay." The truth was that Miss Hellman and the other supporters of the Guild felt they had been fighting for the little people again, the anonymous forty-dollar-a-week writers, and she suspected that MacArthur knew that. Although she has a gentlemanly quality of never being rude to anyone unintentionally, she can sometimes hit below the belt. "Let me see," she said to him idly. "You used to write for pictures, too, once, didn't you? Whatever became of you?" The Wagner Act was passed in 1935, and the Screen Writers' Guild was reestablished shortly afterward. Miss Hellman's standing with Goldwyn, which is exalted, antedates those events, however, by at least a year. Some people say it goes back to the time she made *The Children's Hour* into a good, uncensorable movie, *These Three,* by replacing the Lesbian theme with the simple triangle; others, including Dashiell Hammett, maintain that her success with Goldwyn springs from a mutual gift they have for causing people to vanish by not looking at them. "When Sam doesn't look at you, you cease to exist," Hammett explains. "Lillian solves that by just not looking at *him.*" Miss Hellman's contract with Goldwyn pays her thirty-five hundred dollars a week for as many weeks as she wants to work, whenever she wants to.

From this cushioned ease, she worries harder than ever about the hope and doom of the world these days. Once or twice lately she has quoted T. S. Eliot's lines from *The Hollow Men:*

> This is the way the world ends
> Not with a bang but a whimper.

She will repeat them in conversation, looking thoughtful and faraway. But she never stays dreamy long. Her zest for living soon recalls her to the realities of food, clothes, friends, work, war, enemies, love, hate, and indignation, and when she returns to them it is not with a whimper but a bang.

❁ 6 ❁

Veni, Vidi, Vicky:

HELEN HAYES

PEOPLE WHO WANT to describe a woman of the theater who is exceptionally pleasant and agreeable in private life often use the somewhat curious phrase "You'd never know she was an actress." By this they mean, presumably, that she is genuine, unaffected, and lacking in the languors and the fancy frame of mind displayed by some of the showier stars. No comment has ever pursued an actress more regularly or with more reason than this one has come to haunt Helen Hayes. It depresses her a little because she has heard so many people, waiting around the stage door or seeing her for the first time at parties murmur, "Is *that* Helen Hayes?" with what seems to her to be disappointment, and she suspects them of adding offhandedly that you would never know she was an actress. During a performance of *Victoria Regina,* one of her most famous roles, an old gentleman in the audience unconsciously gave her an inverted version of "Is *that* Helen Hayes?" that shook her. In her startling makeup as the aged Queen, Miss Hayes was well into her scene with John Brown at Balmoral Castle when this old man, who had been moving uneasily in his seat in the fourth row, nudged his companion and, pointing to the stage, demanded in tones clearly audible across the footlights, "Who is that woman?" The lady who was with him whispered something, apparently telling him that it was Helen Hayes, and the old man raised his voice to a note of indignant disbelief. "Nonsense!" he said loudly, and during the rest of the Balmoral scene he kept shifting around in his seat, shuffling his feet, and muttering "Nonsense!" thunderously at intervals. He must have left, Miss

Hayes thinks, before she was trundled on in a wheel chair for the Diamond Jubilee, or else that spectacle threw him into a paralyzed silence; at any rate, he was not heard from then. It bothers her sometimes to reflect that, whether she appears as herself in a sweater and skirt or as an aged queen in a jet bonnet, she is always met by incredulous exclamations from people who expect her to look different.

Off the stage, Helen Hayes is small, humorous, quiet, and attractive as a rather thin, pleasant child might be attractive. She is not strikingly beautiful, and actors who have worked with her believe that this has something to do with her being a good actress. "Take Ina Claire," they say. "She's wonderful, all hair and figure and personality, but she's always Ina Claire. Lynn Fontanne the same way. Helen has no glamour—her face is just a face that reflects things—but how she can *give* a character!" In this statement, the word "give" is accompanied by a clenching and curving of the hand and a sharp jerk upward. In her personal contacts, Miss Hayes is, unlike most actresses, a good listener, with the flattering habit of paying attention to each word that is said to her as though it might be the last she would ever hear, and she carries this quality with her onto the stage. Bit players in the cast of *Victoria Regina* who had perhaps one sentence to address to the Queen will tell you that she turned as eagerly to listen to it on the nine-hundred-and-sixty-ninth, and last, performance as she had done on the opening night. This was not as spontaneous as it sounds; she did it deliberately, to keep a tired company on its toes, as the conductor of an orchestra pulls music from his men by an intent glance at the right moment. Of the last weeks of *Victoria Regina* Miss Hayes says now, "I felt as though I were playing it under water."

The physical fatigue of playing Victoria began to affect her when the play had run for almost two hundred performances, and it was praise from a colleague that almost defeated her then. She had asked Gilbert Miller, the producer of the play, to lunch with her at the Algonquin for the purpose of pleading with him to close the show in May for a couple of months so as to give her a little rest, and she had, by a colorful account of her own exhaustion, brought him almost to the point of consenting, when Glenn Anders, the actor, came over to the table and, after placing a reverent kiss upon the Hayes brow, addressed Miller intensely. "God bless this great little trouper!" he said. "Do you know what she said to me when I went to see her backstage? She said, 'Glenn, I love this play so much I never get tired acting it. I could willingly go on playing Victoria as long as anybody wants to come and see it.'" Here Anders gazed emotionally at Miss Hayes, and Miller gazed emotionally at Anders. "Thank you, Glenn," he murmured, "thank you very, very much indeed." Miss Hayes' comment was briefer; she stared at Anders and said simply, "You louse."

Although she now freely accuses Anders of prolonging the New York run by a couple of weeks, *Victoria Regina* did lay off in June 1936. It reopened the following August, and when it finally closed in Pittsburgh in January 1939, it had played one hundred and twenty-three weeks in New York and on a coast-to-coast tour of forty-five cities, doing a gross business of over three million dollars. In all but two of the cities included in the tour, the play broke the local box-office record—a record which, in every city, had been held by Miss Hayes' earlier tour in *Mary of Scotland*. Broadway columnists, who like the heady feeling of being able to bestow titles on people, have been busy trying to decide whether Helen Hayes or Katharine Cornell is actually the First Lady of the American Theater. Whatever the chatter-writers finally conclude—and neither actress feels more than a mild interest in the controversy—it is undeniable that both Miss Hayes and Miss Cornell have tremendous drawing power on the road and that they have done more than anyone else in recent years to keep the theater alive throughout the country.

As Victoria, Miss Hayes succeeded in cutting down the time required for the makeup change that transformed her into the aged Queen from twenty minutes on opening night in New York to eight minutes in the final months of the run. Her fingers came to be so tired from applying the difficult makeup that they ached regularly every Saturday night, but this physical discomfort was less disturbing than the mental blankness brought upon her by almost three years of having people ask her what she put in her cheeks to puff them out like Queen Victoria's. To one interviewer in the Middle West who posed this question, Helen was goaded into replying, "Oh, nuts!" It seems to her just a further example of the barrenness of the whole topic that the reporter hurried back to his paper and disclosed to a startled public that Helen Hayes put nuts in her cheeks so as to look like the late Queen.

"The only person I can remember who came back to see me and didn't ask me what I put in my checks," she says, "was Toscanini. I guess he just didn't care." It was no false sense of theatrics that kept her from revealing how she had copied Victoria's facial contours, nor was it any command of the publicity department, although everybody concerned realized that the mystery made fine publicity. Miss Hayes felt simply that the audience should be more concerned with Victoria as she was able to portray her than with the tricks by which she did it. She had, too, an obscure fear that if the truth were printed about her facial buildup, audiences might concentrate on it unhealthily, as people sometimes stare at a cross-eyed man without wanting to, and—worse than that—might fall to airing their knowledge during a performance.

The truth is that sometimes she used one thing, sometimes another. First she had her dentist make two gutta-percha supports to be slipped inside her cheeks; she was obliged to discard them after a few performances because they pressed so hard against her gums that they made her mouth sore. Charles Laughton then suggested half an apple in each cheek and Miss Hayes tried that for a while, but the apple, though tasty, softened up too quickly and she found herself inadvertently swallowing her disguise. She thought up the final solution herself, and for the rest of the run she used two wads of absorbent cotton moistened with a liquid antiseptic. Nothing as simple as cotton occurred to her audiences, and nothing kept them from wondering audibly how she managed to look like Victoria.

During her scenes as Queen Victoria in her dotage, Miss Hayes heard everything from "It's peach pits," which, from an obscure row in the orchestra, sounds like hissing, to "It's half an apple," which, slowly spoken, is apt to sound like a well-considered yawn. One audience gave her a genuine inspiration for the role of Victoria. The play required the Queen in her last years to laugh often, chiefly at the philosophic wisecracks of John Brown, and Miss Hayes was obliged to create, or imitate, an old woman's laugh. She knew that most old women laugh eagerly but with physical difficulty, that laughter in the very old is a strong surge of merriment in a body too frail to express it. On opening night she was still dissatisfied with the way Victoria laughed when she was seventy. The second night, during the scene in which the Queen, as a bride, watches her husband shaving, she happened to look across the footlights and saw an old lady having a fine time in the first row. Her laughter came in short, hard chuckles from the deep folds of her black silk, and after each spasm she gasped, wiped her eyes with her handkerchief, and settled back in her seat, sighing pleasurably. From that time Victoria's laugh was the laugh of the ancient playgoer in Row A.

Miss Hayes' own laughter is a fine thing to hear. She laughs easily, throwing her head back and letting the sound of her amusement run out of her like water from a tap, and she has a devious and unexpected humor. She laughs at gags such as the one about the man who had claustrophobia so bad that he couldn't wear a double-breasted suit, and she is agreeable, if less uproarious, when confronted with the wit of her husband, Charles MacArthur. MacArthur is the playwright and scenarist who is also prominent as a merry-andrew, and his sense of comedy is more robust than his wife's. One New Year's Eve in Philadelphia an audience stirred by the final scene of *Victoria Regina,* in which the feeble Queen welcomes her family and subjects to her Diamond Jubilee, was abruptly jerked from its mood of reverence when Victoria, at the second curtain call, pulled a red tin horn from the wrappings of her wheel chair and blew a gaudy blast on it. Later someone asked Miss Hayes what had prompted her to do it. "Charlie thought it would be funny," she explained.

Helen Hayes was not born with the high aspirations and devotion to a calling that begin to make some geniuses uncomfortable early in life. Her family background was only dimly theatrical. A great-great-aunt, Catherine Hayes, was a singer, known professionally as the Erin Swan, who had sung Irish ballads for the Forty-Niners in lumber camps and mining towns in the West. Helen's mother, whose maiden name was also Catherine Hayes, had spent one dizzy week in her own youth as the feminine lead in a stock-company production of *Damon and Pythias* in her home town, Washington, D. C. She had abandoned the theater after that flourish partly because of incurable stage fright and partly because of the melancholy discovery that the quality in her which her fellow-actors and the company director seemed to admire above her acting talent was the fact that she could sit on her hair. She married Francis V. Brown, who was manager of road salesmen for the N. Auth Provision Co., a wholesale butcher concern in Washington that dealt principally in pork products. After Helen was born, Mrs. Brown sought to inspire her daughter with her own love of the theater, and as Helen grew older, Mr. Brown would often come home from a comfortable atmosphere of spareribs and pork chops to find his wife classically parading the living room, intoning mellow passages from the poets with appropriate gestures, while Helen drifted along behind, dutifully imitating her. To people who ask Mrs. Brown nowadays whether she hoped that her daughter would grow up to be a great actress, she replies simply, "Doesn't everybody?" She qualifies this by saying that she never explicitly planned a stage career for Helen, but that as soon as she realized her daughter was a born actress, she encouraged her talent in every possible way. This is what most mothers of actresses say, and it is a reasonable statement once you have conceded to actresses' mothers the ability to recognize a born actress at sight.

Helen's childish antics, which her mother now likes to recall, seem little more than the usual doings of an intelligent child, but Mrs. Brown had the gift, strong in all mothers whose daughters eventually become actresses, of seeing only the dramatic and the unique qualities in her daughter and of taking care that the right people saw them as well. The showmanship displayed by a woman with a child she believes to be talented is something that almost any professional impresario can only envy. She knows instinctively how to invade managers' offices with bared fangs or with a pantherlike glide, according to the situation—and instinct tells her, too, that the child must always be pushed ahead of her, never pulled along behind. Fathers have little to do with these preliminaries. Perhaps they never sharply visualize their daughters as grown-up and famous, or it may be that they are too busy making a living for the family to do much dreaming about the future. Whatever the season, most fathers of successful actresses seem to have lost touch with their daughters at an early date. Mothers, on the other hand, are women, as a songwriter once insisted, and another cynic has said that all women are actresses whether they work on the stage or off. Possibly it is a love of vicarious drama that keeps an actress's mother always with her, hand in glove and sometimes tooth and nail.

Mrs. Brown's approach to a career for Helen was unusually peaceful. When Helen was six, her dancing class gave a recital; Mrs. Brown rushed around in a fury buying false curls and materials for a costume, spent hours teaching her daughter the then celebrated Gibson Girl walk, and Helen's impersonation of Annabelle Whitford, the Ziegfeld Gibson Girl of that period (around 1907), was the hit of the show. A guest in the audience that day, possibly scouting for talent, was Lew Fields, of Weber & Fields, who were then playing Washington. Mr. Fields sent a note to the head of the dancing school saying that if Helen Hayes Brown's mother should ever consider a stage career for her daughter, he would like to see her about it. Mrs. Brown thought the note gracious, but Helen's success that afternoon had naturally started her mother's mind working on a career for her daughter similar to Bernhardt's or Modjeska's, and the idea of Weber and Fields was a comedown. She dismissed it and accepted instead an offer that presently came from the Columbia Players, a Washington stock company which more nearly approached her notion of art in the theater. Next year, with the Columbia Players, Helen appeared in *The Prince Chap* and as Little Lord Fauntleroy. In both productions she knew everybody's part as thoroughly as her own and enjoyed prompting any member of the cast who so much as hesitated, in a voice that was clearly heard as far as the tenth row of the orchestra. She also displayed a gift for ad-libbing that was sometimes enough to frighten adult actors. One scene in *Little Lord Fauntleroy* required Fauntleroy to pull a red bandanna from his pocket and show it to his grandfather, the old Earl, and most of the dialogue depended on this gesture. At one performance the property man forgot to put the bandanna in the pocket, and when Helen reached for it, it was not there. "Well," she said distinctly, and without a perceptible pause, "I must have left it in my room. I'll just go and get it." And she strolled off the stage, leaving the old Earl in a spot that would make any actor shudder. Inspirations like this convinced Helen's mother that her child was truly destined to be a star, and before Helen was eight, Mrs. Brown had persuaded her husband to advance living expenses for herself and her daughter in New York. Mr. Brown was bewildered by the giddy turn affairs were taking, but he was helpless before the invasion of art into his home. He agreed to supply thirty-five dollars a week for a limited number of weeks.

In New York, Mrs. Brown remembered the offer from Lew Fields, but what she wanted for Helen was still something grander than association with a couple of Dutch comedians. She loftily kept Helen away from the Weber & Fields office, somewhat in the frame of mind of a man who holds the Koh-i-noor in his hand passing a hockshop, and when the financial time limit was up before she had found Helen a job, she sadly bought railroad tickets home to Washington on a train leaving the next day. That night, in the rooming house where they were living, a fellow-boarder to whom Mrs. Brown had lightly mentioned Fields's interest in Helen said, "You're crazy not to see Fields before you go. Suppose you don't want musical comedy for Helen. Fields has the Shuberts in the hollow of his hand, and the Shuberts produce plays." The next morning, Mrs. Brown, a little nervous about train time, called at the Weber & Fields office with Helen. She was kept waiting in an anteroom while Fields escorted one highly scented beauty after another from his private office to the elevator, turning upon Helen and her mother each time a stare of blank un-recognition. When the door of the private office opened for the fifth time and Lotta Faust, a famous theatrical siren of that day, breezed out on Fields' arm, Mrs. Brown took Helen's hand and got up to go. In the corridor, where Fields had tenderly placed La Faust in a descending elevator, Mrs. Brown, with a last weary gesture, pushed Helen around so that she stood about eye to eye with his lowest waistcoat button. "Do you remember this child, the one who impersonated Annabelle Whitford in Washington?" she said rapidly. Fields stared and beamed. "Come right in!" he said.

Helen and her mother took the train for Washington that day, but it was only to carry the tidings to Helen's father that Helen had been given a contract at fifty dollars a week to play the part of Mime, a little Dutch girl, in the Weber & Fields production of *Old Dutch,* and that rehearsals were to start almost immediately. Mrs. Brown and her daughter never went back to Washington to live. Helen played a full season in *Old Dutch* and remained with Weber & Fields three years longer, until she was twelve. Long before that, Mr. Brown had retired into the obscurity that waits for actresses' fathers, and his disappearance was punctuated by his wife's decision to drop the "Brown" from Helen's name. Mrs. Brown lives now in an attractive apartment full of canaries on East End Avenue in New York; she is a small, gay woman, known as Brownie to Miss Hayes' friends, and her voice and mannerisms are startlingly like her daughter's. Mr. Brown retired from the meat business some years ago and lives comfortably in a house Helen bought for him on Chesapeake Bay. He goes to Washington when Helen opens there in a new play, and once in a while he is one of the invited guests at parties given for his daughter. At these fetes, he is a medium-sized, unobtrusive figure, listening quietly while the other guests rave about Helen Hayes. Mr. Brown has never found a graceful way of telling them who he is. From the time Helen was eight, she and her mother trouped hardily through most of the United States, including some in the Far West which were still considerably wild and primitive. In 1917 Helen played *Pollyanna* in a little Western town to an audience that consisted chiefly of cowhands from neighboring ranches. All of them carried guns and wore spurs, and they were men who liked to express themselves simply, but Helen was not prepared for the candor with which they greeted the play. In one scene, Pollyanna, the Glad Girl, was carried onto the stage with both legs broken after she had been run over by a heedless motorist, and she then flung her arms out to the audience and cried, "I'm so glad, glad, *glad* it happened! For after all you have to *lose* your legs to *really love* them!" At this point, every performance, the cowhands would break down and sob like little children.

As other children are kept from the lowdown on Santa Claus and the stork, Helen, in her youth, was protected by her mother from the facts about dramatic critics. When she was thirteen and her opening performance with John Drew in *The Prodigal Husband* inspired praise in the papers next day, Mr. Drew called to Helen from his dressing room on the second night as she and her mother were passing the door and began to compliment her on the reviews. Mrs. Brown marched into the dressing room and slammed the door behind her, shutting Helen out in the hall. "My daughter," she told Mr. Drew fiercely, "does not know that dramatic critics exist." Whether or not Helen had any suspicions on the subject, it was not until she was eighteen and made her first big hit, in *Dear Brutus* with William Gillette, that Mrs. Brown took all the papers into her daughter's room next morning and turned them over to her without a word. It required a national calamity to bring about Helen's success in *Dear Brutus*. She was playing in Booth Tarkington's *Penrod*, under the management of George Tyler, when a telegram from the Charles Frohman office offered her the role of the daughter in *Dear Brutus* opposite Gillette. Tyler refused to release Helen from *Penrod*, and Mrs. Brown likes to relate what happened to Mr. Tyler then. "The hand of God," she says, "sent an epidemic of influenza to New York and the Board of Health closed every theater that children were likely to attend." *Penrod* shut down, and Tyler's misfortune set Helen free to act with Gillette under Frohman management, which was a step up.

Helen returned to Tyler the following year, 1919, to appear

in *Clarence* with Alfred Lunt, and in the next five years, under various managements, became established as an ingénue in such plays as *Bab, a Sub-Deb,* based on the stories by Mary Roberts Rinehart; *To the Ladies,* by George Kaufman and Marc Connelly; *We Moderns,* by Israel Zangwill, and *Dancing Mothers,* an Edgar Selwyn play.

In the summer of 1925 Helen and her mother rented a house at Syosset. Two other actresses came to spend the summer with her; one was June Walker, who was then about to go into rehearsals for the Theatre Guild production of *The Glass Slipper,* and was considerably more important in the theater than Helen; the other was Halcyon Hargreaves, a schoolmate of Helen's in the days when she had intermittently attended the Convent of the Sacred Heart in Washington. Helen bought an automobile and is still remembered around Syosset as one of the most remarkable drivers ever to frequent those parts; she was all right as long as she could go ahead, but when she had to stop or back up, she stripped the gears every time. On the rare occasions when she drives a car these days her conduct behind a steering wheel continues to be interesting, consisting mainly of warnings wildly shrieked to pedestrians and motorists to get out of the way if they know what's good for them. Among the lighthearted incidents of the Syosset summer was the casualty to June Walker, who sat on a bee; Helen drove her violently all over the county looking for a middle-aged doctor, since June had forcefully declared that she was not going to let any young man treat her for this wound. They finally found a gray-bearded physician, who took the case in his stride.

Attracted by the glamour of the theater that hung over the Hayes house, the beaux of the neighborhood came courting in droves, and few were more arresting than one Colonel Lloyd C. Griscom, who had been United States Ambassador to Italy and to Brazil and who further spoke of himself in conversation as a writer, a painter, a playwright, and a soldier. As a distinguished man of affairs who owned a yacht, Colonel Griscom was encouraged by Mrs. Brown to visit the house, and he fascinated the girls, chiefly because he had a way of persuading them to pose for his water-color sketches until they dropped from exhaustion, upon which crisis he would take them out to recuperate aboard his yacht and keep them out until they got seasick. Griscom, a widower with children, was also a Quaker, and it was his young son who made a thoughtful remark the first time he saw the yacht. He said it didn't seem to be big enough. "Where is thee going to put all the actresses?" he inquired of his father.

In spite of her professional success and the attentions of Syosset swains, Helen Hayes remained socially detached, silent in the presence of strangers, and worried about her own simplicity of appearance. Her mental unease was the worse that summer because she was, for the first time, painfully concerned with being attractive to a certain man. In the spring she had gone to a cocktail party in New York at the studio of Neysa McMein, whom she had come to know slightly. Miss McMein was the tawny artist and illustrator whose love of celebrities made her salon one of the dizziest phenomena of all the mad twenties, and Miss Hayes, who knew almost no one there, sat uncomfortably in a corner while quips were tossed around like confetti.

One of the guests that day was Charles MacArthur, a Chicago newspaperman who had come to live in New York and who was temporarily serving literature by turning out highly improbable articles for Hearst's *American Weekly*. MacArthur wandered over to Miss Hayes and offered her some peanuts out of a paper bag. She thanked him and took a handful, and MacArthur then made the remark that has since become a shining goal for romantic young men to aim at. "I wish they were emeralds," he said. MacArthur now wishes that he could hear the last of this crack and says rather peevishly that he never suspected Helen was the type who would go around repeating it. His objection to it is that it has a whimsical charm, and his reputation for whimsical charm is one of the things that he is fighting against these days, now that he is an Army major stationed in Washington. His gallantry at the McMein party struck Miss Hayes starry-eyed, though, and soon MacArthur became a frequent weekend guest at the house in Syosset, generally arriving without a toothbrush or pajamas but full of winning ways which plainly failed to fascinate Mrs. Brown. Not only was Charlie a newspaperman, she pointed out to her daughter, and so presumably irresponsible, but he already had a wife. His wife was one Carol Frink, a motion-picture critic on a Chicago newspaper, from whom he was separated but not divorced. To Helen, however, who had worked hard all her life, MacArthur's easy charm and his casual way of doing things that attracted attention were irresistible.

In 1925, when she opened in Shaw's *Caesar and Cleopatra,* Charlie missed the first night but promised to drop around soon and catch the show. Every night after that Miss Hayes would hurry out onto the stage before the performance began and look through the peephole in the curtain to see if he was there. One night Helen Westley, who was in the cast, asked her what she was looking for and Miss Hayes said that she was looking for the man she loved, who had promised to come to the play. "Call him up and tell him to come," advised Miss Westley briskly. "Oh, I couldn't do that!" Miss Hayes protested. "Why not?" said Miss Westley. "With me, I keep calling them up until they move."

Not long ago Miss Hayes told this story in MacArthur's presence and he glanced at her thoughtfully. "Does my charm still hold for you, dear?" he asked. "Well," said his wife peacefully, "I'm still looking for you most of the time."

Miss Hayes and MacArthur were married in 1928, after a deadly series of obstructions. Two years earlier, in Chicago, Miss Frink had filed suit for divorce against MacArthur, but shortly after the success of *Lulu Belle,* which he wrote in collaboration with Edward Sheldon, she had dropped the proceedings. Through his lawyers, MacArthur then made a financial arrangement with her, filed a countersuit for divorce, and received his decree. After he began courting Miss Hayes, Miss Frink claimed that the decree had been fraudulently obtained and threatened to get out an injunction preventing his remarrying. In addition to this headache, Helen's mother and some of her friends were still skeptical of MacArthur as a husband, although he had by 1928 earned a solid reputation as a playwright with *Lulu Belle* and *The Front Page,* the last written with Ben Hecht and running successfully at the time of the marriage. Mrs. Brown subsequently became friendly with Charlie and sometimes speaks of him affectionately as "that devil."

Ben Hecht was on Charlie's side in the problem of his marriage to Miss Hayes, and when MacArthur and Miss Hayes decided that the best idea would be to get married quietly before Miss Frink could proceed to any more stirring activities, Hecht told them that Horace Liveright, the publisher, had said that T. R. Smith, his assistant, knew of a former city magistrate who could, with dignity, arrange a marriage without any publicity. On an August day in 1928, MacArthur hired a car and with the late Alexander Woollcott, another ally, as best man, he and Miss Hayes drove to the office of Charles A. Oberwager, a lawyer, where Magistrate Mark Rudich was to marry them. After they had waited some forty minutes in an anteroom, a number of men carrying notebooks, cameras, and flashlights arrived, and Oberwager came out of an inner office, saying, "You may proceed, Mr. Rudich. The press is here." MacArthur then offered to paste Oberwager in the jaw, but was restrained by the reporters, and the marriage took place somewhat tensely. For Helen Hayes, it was a strange wedding to the man who was the trademark for Prince Charming, but she had no time to mourn its lack of romance. She was playing in *Coquette* then, and she had to get back to the theater in time for the evening performance.

From the time of their marriage, Miss Hayes and MacArthur have been pursued by picturesque situations that have resulted in some fairly gruesome publicity. Even their honeymoon, during a ten-day vacation Miss Hayes managed to get from *Coquette* several weeks after the wedding, was touched with the macabre. On the boat to Bermuda, a friendly couple introduced themselves as Mr. and Mrs. Conway; Conway was one of the editors of *Variety*. Late one night in the Bermuda hotel where the Conways and the MacArthurs were staying, Mrs. Conway knocked frantically on the MacArthurs' door with the hysterical tidings that her husband had just dropped dead. The local authorities insisted on an inquest, at which Helen and Charlie were required to testify, and although the coroner's verdict simply enough stated that heart disease was the cause of death, the inquest occupied most of the wedding trip, and the MacArthurs' sentimental journey ended with bringing Conway's body and his prostrate wife back to New York. MacArthur now refers to this incident the way a scenario-writer would refer to a scene in a movie; he calls it "the Death."

The following year, a clash between the cast of *Coquette* and Jed Harris, the producer, struck the front pages with such force that it is still familiar to most people, a good many of whom have the facts wrong. The popular version is that Miss Hayes, who was going to have a baby, claimed through her lawyer that her pregnancy was an act of God and that she could not therefore fulfill her contract with Harris, which called for a six-week tour in *Coquette*. What actually happened was that Miss Hayes, after two weeks of the tour, told Harris that the impending birth of her child would not allow her to finish the tour, and Harris decided to close the show rather than replace its star with another actress. The members of the cast, informed of this plan, claimed that six weeks' salary was due them by right of contract. Before an arbitration board appointed by the Actors' Equity Association, the late Joseph P. Bickerton, junior, Harris's lawyer, quoted the clause in Equity contracts stating that actors are not entitled to salaries "if the company cannot perform because of fire, accident, strikes, riot, act of God," and so on, and argued that the birth of a baby was an act of God. Harris was required by the board to settle with the actors by paying them an extra two weeks' salary, but it was too late to prevent ribald journalists all over the country from hailing the MacArthur child as "the act-of-God baby." Mary MacArthur, who is now fourteen, has grown up without any painful knowledge of the skirmish. She is attractive, blonde, and about three inches taller than her mother. She knows that one of Helen Hayes's first parts in the theater was Little Lord Fauntleroy and that she was obliged, in the play, to call her mother "Dearest" with a dead pan, but this subject is not often referred to between Mary and her mother except when they discuss the names MacArthur would like to give to the new French poodles he wants to buy. He would like to call them

Fauntleroy and Dearest. Mary calls her mother Mommy, and so does the MacArthurs' seven-year-old son Jamie, an endearing child who has a way of appearing out of a lilac bush when you least expect to see him. "Jamie is like some woodland thing," Miss Hayes remarked, one day when he turned up silently at her side as she was passing a hedge. The fifth member of the MacArthur family is Charles, a seven-year-old English boy, who is living with them for the duration.

Miss Hayes's latest, and worst, bout with the press occurred about ten years ago when Carol Frink, MacArthur's former wife, from whom he had been divorced in 1926, sued her for one hundred thousand dollars on the ground that Miss Hayes had alienated MacArthur's affections while he was still married to Miss Frink. Charlie, who by that time was writing for the movies and had enough Hollywood money to withstand almost any affliction, was in favor of settling the case out of court to spare his wife the unpleasantness. Miss Hayes pointed out that Miss Frink was mistaken, and that for the sake of the MacArthur home and Mary MacArthur, the mistake had better be proved in public. For the hearing, which took place in Chicago in 1935, MacArthur flew East from Hollywood, and Miss Hayes went out from New York. With Carol Frink, they made a curious trio in the Chicago courtroom: Miss Frink, full-blown and unafraid, carefully dressed in a new summer ensemble; Helen Hayes, patient and incredulous, in a plain dress and a plain straw hat; and MacArthur, angry and scared, as a man might well be at the prospect of hearing tales of his own devastating behavior in the early 1920's. Letters from Charlie to Carol signed "Charliecums" and other embarrassing diminutives were read aloud in court. Miss Frink, after describing how gay a companion MacArthur had been when he married her and the romantic circumstance of his proposal to her in the Old Mill at Coney Island, looked across the courtroom at him and pensively remarked to reporters later that Charlie was losing his hair and getting fat. "I wouldn't take him now," she said, "if he came in a box of Cracker Jack." The hearing lasted three days, at the end of which time the court was convinced that MacArthur had been long separated from his wife before he met

Miss Hayes, that they had been divorced two years before he and Miss Hayes were married, and that the plaintiff had no case. Miss Frink withdrew the suit on the advice of her lawyers and was ordered to pay court fees amounting to one hundred dollars. Painful as it was for Charlie and Miss Hayes, she is thankful that she had this situation out with Charlie's ex-wife. Miss Frink has made no further comment.

When Miss Hayes is playing in New York, she commutes by car or by bus between the theater and the house she and her husband bought eleven years ago in Nyack. Set back slightly from the street, with grounds in the rear sloping down to a swimming pool and to the river beyond, the house is Victorian in style and decoration; artificial flowers under glass stand on the fireplace mantels, crystal chandeliers are reflected in wide gilt-framed mirrors, and on a small table in the living room a plaster cast of Helen's hands holds an old-fashioned nosegay of real flowers in a paper frill. The décor was not inspired by *Victoria Regina;* Miss Hayes has always liked the Victorian period and she furnished her house in that style two years before she had heard of Housman's play. In the basement beneath this elegance, the bar, MacArthur's domain, lurks like some carefully planned hell. Obscurely lighted and approached by a winding staircase, this apartment has wall benches covered in the MacArthur tartan, a dour arrangement in two shades of dark green. A couple of standing lamps with red glass-domed shades illuminate a photograph of the late King Edward VII (unautographed, MacArthur will proudly point out) and a poster advertising the unparalleled feat of Blondin, who "will walk backwards on a rope over Niagara, heavily chained with his feet in large baskets." On the mantel there is a clock with chimes, waterfall, and bird's nest containing a father and a mother bird peering stonily at their little one, which has fallen out of the nest into the torrent below. A shooting gallery behind the bar is not yet completed, owing to a difference of opinion between the MacArthurs. The idea is that you stand across the room, aim, and fire, being careful not to break any bottles, and MacArthur thought it would be a fine jest to line up likenesses of well-known dramatic critics to shoot at. Miss Hayes protested that critics had always been very nice to *her*, and MacArthur has now reconciled himself to a quieter notion. He plans a jungle scene, wtih a large ape prowling slowly back and forth as the target. Radio music in this den comes from behind a vast canvas of a reclining nude hung on one wall and flanked by potted palms; at the foot of the staircase stands a statue of a lady eternally transfixed in a diving pose and wearing long marble underwear ribbed and scalloped in a lifelike manner; and in the adjoining bathroom there are all kinds of tricks, of course. MacArthur's attitude toward callers who are introduced to these caprices for the first time is a curious blend of watchfulness and hope, like a man telling a funny story he thinks you may have heard before. He follows the visitor around and waits for the laughs as anxiously as Ed Wynn with a new comical hat. Miss Hayes, to whom it is all pretty familiar, generally sits with one foot under her on the MacArthur tartan and drinks Kalak water.

Even when the Major is home on leave, the MacArthurs rarely go out in Nyack, and they have each found a social excuse that is surefire on the telephone against the most pressing invitations: Helen, who may be feeling in radiant health, simply says that she is sick in bed, and Charlie, speaking in precise and almost offensively sober accents, will explain that as for him, he is far too drunk to go anywhere. They have found these statements unanswerable. Helen spends a good deal of time at home knitting complicated garments for Jamie or sometimes just sitting side by side with him and looking into space. She and Jamie are both great ones, she says, for sitting and looking into space. In the evenings, Charlie likes to play old Scotch airs on a silver clarinet he won from Arthur Hopkins on a bet that a play called *Salvation,* by himself and Sidney Howard, would be a failure. His wife finds his tunes mournful, "but then, I am a mournful man," says Charles. In the daytime, Miss Hayes sometimes puts on roller skates and, with Mary, skates down to the village and along the sidewalks, where she attracts little attention from the passers-by. Nyack people are accustomed to colorful neighbors and it takes more than an actress on skates to raise their eyebrows.

Beginning with Oom the Omnipotent, who founded his colony of Yoga students there, the local pixies now include one mild-mannered woman who patrols the village streets wearing white robes and a crown of gold and pausing at each crossing to blow heartily on a gilt trumpet; and another lady, an animal-lover, who drives a horse and buggy around town on cold days with the horse wearing two pairs of pants.

Dressed for the street in Nyack or New York, Miss Hayes looks young and casual, rather like the pictures of college girls in rotogravure fashion sections. She is indifferent to fashion, however, and will tell you complacently that a dramatic critic once spoke of her as the worst-dressed actress on the American stage, and that Elsa Maxwell contradicted him, saying, "It isn't that Helen dresses badly, she simply doesn't dress at all." Twice the blandishments of her husband and friends have got her into Hattie Carnegie's, and she solved both crises by pointing to the dress Miss Carnegie was wearing and saying, "I'll have that one." One day she came out of the stage entrance after a matinee of *Victoria Regina* wearing a rather shabby fur coat and heard a woman say to the man she was with, "There's Helen Hayes!" The man stared and said, "Looking like that? It couldn't be!" The next day, Miss Hayes, in a spasm of duty to a public which expects her to look dazzling off the stage, called up Jaeckel's and talked to them seriously about a sable coat. The coat, as the Jaeckels dreamed of it, was to cost fifteen thousand dollars, and it seemed to Miss Hayes that such a gesture ought to satisfy almost anybody. "Besides," she says characteristically now, "I figured that if I had on a fifteen-thousand-dollar sable coat, I could wear any old sweater and skirt I liked underneath." Leaving the theater that afternoon after the matinee, she passed the Durand-Ruel Galleries and saw a Renoir in the window priced at around fifteen thousand dollars. The Renoir now hangs in the house at Nyack, and the Jaeckels, if they are the emotional kind, are still weeping into their sables.

Except for knowing where she wants to spend it, Helen Hayes is not shrewd about money, and her finances are handled by Leland Hayward, who acts as agent for her and for MacArthur. During *Victoria Regina* and her later engagement in *Harriet,* her salary was sent to Hayward every week after an amount varying from thirty-five to fifty dollars had been deducted by Harry Essex, the company manager, for weekly expenses, including Kleenex, cold cream, cigarettes, and other incidentals. The allowance was advanced bit by bit by Essex with many protests; he says he could never be sure that Miss Hayes would not hand it all to some pal with a hard-luck story. She has an honest respect for cash, though, and it pleased her to be able to treat Mr. Essex airily when he came around with the weekly dole one time last fall. "I don't believe I will be needing that pittance," said Miss Hayes loftily. "I have a little money of my own." And she waved in his face a check for three thousand dollars that had been paid directly to her for a radio broadcast. Her generosity is not limited to gifts of money. A year or so ago, broadcasting on a program sponsored by a manufacturer of silverware, she received in addition to her regular payment a showy chest of the sponsor's table silver; it drifted around the Nyack house for a week or so until Miss Hayes got the idea of giving it to Ruth Gordon, a good friend of hers, who had just moved into a new apartment. She dispatched it with an affectionate note to Ruth, and was disconcerted to get it right back next day; at least, it looked like the same chest of silver. It turned out that Miss Gordon, appearing on the same radio program a week after Miss Hayes, had been similarly rewarded and had thought it would be nice to give *her* chest of silver to Helen. The two gifts crossed, and between them the girls have more table silver than they care to think about.

In the theater, Miss Hayes works on a straight salary basis and has more than once refused offers of a share in a play's profits. One reason is that she has no desire for money in any larger quantities than she needs to live comfortably, to buy a painting once in a while or a willow tree for the grounds in Nyack, and her salary is enough to take care of that. Another, more poignant reason is that the more money she makes, the more she has to pay to the government in income tax. The government has, even before the war, annually taken more than one-third of her earnings in the theater alone, and fifty per cent of what she made when she worked in plays and in pictures as well. In 1938 she refused an offer of eighty-five thousand dollars to make another picture in Hollywood, partly because she did not want to go to Hollywood but mainly because too much of the eighty-five thousand dollars would have gone for taxes. Actors, actresses, and writers suffer more from the pressure of income tax than people in ordinary businesses do, because prosperity in the theater and in the writing business is uncertain and often brief. An actress may go through several seasons of failures before she hits on a successful play, and a writer may work for years barely making a living before he writes a best-seller; but when success and money finally come, the government makes no allowance for the unprofitable years. Nor does it practically recognize the comparative brevity of a star's career. One year Miss Hayes' lawyers asked for a five-per-cent reduction in her income tax on the ground of depreciation; actresses, he argued, depreciate as surely as buildings and machinery do, and he went on to build up a picture that vividly suggested the slow dissolution of Miss Hayes, like a sand castle at flood tide. The Department of Internal Revenue was unimpressed, and Miss Hayes paid.

Things like that give Miss Hayes a panicky feeling about money, and she worries sometimes when her husband gives way to one of his expensive impulses. Charlie has been known, for instance, to lay out a great sum on a pool table for the nursery, maintaining that a pool table not only makes for conviviality but is also a fine thing for babies to hang onto when they are learning to walk; and he is forever settling down with a telephone on his stomach for a half-hour's comfortable chat with some friend in California at the usual rates of $6.25 for three minutes. When his wife reminds him that such indulgences come high, Charlie is elaborately indignant. "Is it my own money I'm spending or is it not?" he demands. It is his own money he is spending.

The transformation of Helen Hayes from an ingénue into a dramatic actress of power and prestige came about largely through one of those accidents of the theater which allow producers, a harassed lot, to do most of their worrying in limousines. The failure of a play called *Young Blood* in the spring of 1926 left Miss Hayes with five hundred dollars and no job at a time of year when few new plays were being put on. With her mother, she decided to take her first trip to Europe, where the five hundred might last longer than it would in New York. When she returned one day from booking passage on a tourist-rate boat, her mother told her that William A. Brady had been telephoning all afternoon and wanted her to play Barrie's *What Every Woman Knows* for four weeks at the Bijou Theatre. Miss Hayes reluctantly gave up the idea of going abroad, and *What Every Woman Knows* ran for nearly a year in New York, followed by a profitable tour, mostly because audiences that had grown accustomed to seeing Miss Hayes in ingénue roles (she had played even Cleopatra as a flapper) were impressed by the wisdom and tenderness of her portrayal of Maggie Shand, the little Scotch wife in the Barrie play.

Many actresses preserve their energies for their work by insisting on the kind of personal peace that comes from having everything at home happen the way they want it to, but Miss Hayes' career in the theater, mostly a matter of simple appeal until *Coquette,* seems to have profited since then from a private life that has been less than tranquil. Probably her most important professional step was the decision to play *Victoria Regina*—a conclusion she came to in the bathroom of her house at Nyack. Max Gordon wanted her to do a dramatic version of *Pride and Prejudice,* and she had almost decided in favor of it when one evening she picked up Laurence Housman's book of short plays about Queen Victoria, which Gilbert Miller had sent to her several weeks before. When she had read a few pages, she became so interested in it that she took it into the bathroom with her for greater privacy and locked the door. She studies most of her parts in her bathroom, which is large enough for pacing and brooding. The next day she sent her regrets to Mr. Gordon and telephoned Mr. Miller that she would like to do the Housman play. Her three years as Victoria brought Miss Hayes into contact with several members of European royal families descended from the late Queen. The former Queen of Spain, a granddaughter of Victoria, saw a matinee of the play in New York and was so struck by the star's resemblance to her grandmother that she told reporters she had been obliged to go right back to her apartment after the performance and sit quite still for a long time. During a summer layoff of the play, Helen and Charles were staying at a house near Salzburg when the late Duke of Kent, another guest, arrived late one night and sent an equerry to the MacArthurs' room to say that His Royal Highness was anxious to meet Miss Hayes and would be glad if she and her husband would join him downstairs for a drink. This amounted to a command, but Miss Hayes had gone to bed, and when Miss Hayes is in bed for the night nothing except the next morning gets her out of it. "You go down," she said to Charlie, and added, "If any dukes want to see me, let 'em come here." A few minutes later she heard footsteps chummily approaching the door, and Charlie breezed in with the Duke. Miss Hayes was lying with the blankets pulled up to her chin, her hair tumbled, and her face covered with cold cream. She still holds this against Charlie, but she is able to look on the bright side. "At least I didn't have to curtsy," she says. The incident she likes to remember during that trip was meeting, in London, the Dowager Marchioness of Milford Haven, whose father was Louis IV, Grand Duke of Hesse, and whose mother was Princess Alice, Queen Victoria's daughter. "Please tell me something I haven't been sure of," Miss Hayes asked the Marchioness. "Queen Victoria's mother was a German princess—did Victoria speak with an accent when she was Queen of England?" The Marchioness raised her hands in astonishment. "Ach, no!" she said. "She het no more eggzent den you or me!"

The tour of *Victoria Regina* is considered the most successful any play has had since the movies drove the theater out of the majority of American cities, but it was not without its mishaps. In Los Angeles, the opening night—a glittering affair attended by crowds of Hollywood celebrities—coincided with a convention of the Knights of Columbus; some hundreds of these revellers stood outside the theater to watch the stars arrive in a blaze of floodlights and, when the doors had closed on the last of them, lightheartedly returned to their own pleasures, which happened to be shooting off firecrackers on the curb. They kept it up during most of the performance, but it had a happy result in the end; the second night nearly everybody came back to find out what the people on the stage had been saying, and it was almost as brilliant an occasion as the first. In Toledo, one Saturday night, Charles Francis, who played Lord Melbourne, wanted to make a midnight train to spend Sunday with relatives nearby, and his anxiety made him absent-minded. In the middle of his scene alone with Miss Hayes, she was startled to hear him say, "Your Majesty, have you ever heard the story of the monk who was vouchsafed a vision?" This was no part of the play, being a speech which had been cut in rehearsal months earlier, but Miss Hayes took the cue and proceeded calmly with the uncut version. "Why no, Lord Melbourne, pray tell it me," she said. Mr. Francis helplessly told it all while Miss Hayes sat back inwardly shaken with a wild mirth at the spectacle of a man who was trying to catch a train hopelessly involved in telling a long story that he need never have started. Such situations do not ruffle her when she is acting, but off the stage she is inclined to be helpless in unexpected ways. She has, for instance, no sense of direction and has regularly lost money betting nickels against other members of the cast who prophesy that she will turn the wrong way when she steps out of the stage door. They like to watch her walk confidently up the alley toward, say, a brick wall, and then to murmur indulgently, "Where do you think you're going, dear?" On trains, during the tour of *Victoria Regina,* Harry Essex generally pinned a typewritten slip of paper outside the men's room, where he knew Helen would be sure to see it repeatedly. "The ladies' room is at the *other* end of the car," it read.

One thing Miss Hayes is sure of is that she will make no more motion pictures; her experiences in Hollywood have considerably baffled her. In 1931, the urgent pleas of Metro-Goldwyn-Mayer took her there to make *The Sin of Madelon Claudet*, for which Charles MacArthur had written the script. Miss Hayes, finding herself awash in a sea of incredibly beautiful women who were always behaving picturesquely, was once more overcome by her old feeling of drabness, and was depressed to learn that the studio felt the same way about her. Press agents and makeup men assailed her with publicity buildups and false eyelashes, and when she declined both, they shrugged sadly and forgot her. In the projection room, when she went to see the rushes, or completed scenes, of *Madelon Claudet,* Miss Hayes sat dejectedly in a corner while executives in nearby seats gloomily smoked cigars and left afterward without speaking to her. The night the picture opened in Hollywood, Helen and Charlie avoided the theater and fled to some friends who had rented a house at Santa Barbara. Long after midnight, as they sat on the terrace, someone who had traced them there telephoned the news that the audience was still applauding and calling for Helen Hayes, and that the picture was the sensation of the year. A few minutes later telegrams began to arrive from excited executives. "You are the greatest actress in the world" was about the most moderate of these messages. Miss Hayes, astonished, decided then and there on what seemed to her a gesture appropriate to Hollywood. "Ah me, Hollywood!" she sighed, and jumped into the swimming pool with her clothes on.

Helen Hayes received the Motion Picture Academy Award of 1931 for *Madelon Claudet* and followed it by a widely praised performance as the young nurse in *A Farewell to Arms.* But the creed of moving-picture producers is a simple one; with them, an actor who plays gangsters well must play gangsters forever, an actor who is good as a detective is cast as a detective all his life. Now that Helen Hayes has triumphantly played Queen Victoria and the aging Harriet Beecher Stowe, Hollywood understands that she knows how to play old ladies, and she has had some striking picture offers. One came from Mervyn Le Roy, who wanted her to play the role of Granny in a picture based on a story by William Faulkner. Miss Hayes protested mildly that she was tired of playing an old woman and would like to do a contrasting part for a change, and Le Roy then demonstrated that Hollywood, too, can be flexible. "O.K.," he said at once, "in the picture we'll make Granny young."

❁ 7 ❁

The Wise Lived Yesterday:

COLE PORTER

At a party recently, an attractive woman in her thirties was dancing with a young man who in his working hours plays an oboe in a swing octet. The orchestra drifted into a Cole Porter tune, and the woman closed her eyes reminiscently as she followed the familiar words:

> Like the beat, beat, beat of the tom-tom
> When the jungle shadows fall,
> Like the tick, tick tock of the stately clock
> As it stands against the wall,
> Like the drip, drip, drip of the raindrops
> When the summer show'r is through,
> So a voice within me keeps repeating
> You, you, you . . .
> Night and da-ay . . .*

The woman hummed softly with the chorus.

"Yeah," said the oboe player. "Wouldn't you think that guy Porter would have the *initiative* to get off that one goddam note?"

Some of the swing boys are inclined to pout at Porter's musical tricks as compared to their own; others revere him, believing that the calculated monotony of some of his songs is a smoother stunt than any that has yet come out of swing. Neither reaction seems to affect Porter's popularity or to confine him to any particular period of songwriting. He wrote his first hit, "An Old-Fashioned Garden," in 1917, and one of his later ones, "Make It Another Old-Fashioned, Please,"

* Used by permission of the Copyright Owners, Harms, Inc.

twenty-three years afterward, for *Panama Hattie.* The way Porter kept abreast of the phrase "old-fashioned"—from a nosegay to a national institution—is one indication of his agility in marching with the trend. His relation with the public has been a timeless one, unconnected with the calendar except in the number of emotional careers his songs have punctuated. Mention "Begin the Beguine," "What Is This Thing Called Love?" "In the Still of the Night," "I Get a Kick Out of You," "I've Got You Under My Skin" to almost any affectionate and not too repulsive woman, and she is likely to murmur dreamily, "Yes, that was 1936," or "That was that year in the south of France." Generally she is not referring to the year the song was published.

Cole Porter produces this sentimental dynamite methodically, working with charts. The charts, occupying the top of his piano along with a litter of cigarette cartons, throat tablets, and Kleenex, indicate the musical plan of whatever show he is working on and help him to pace the show by writing a comedy number after a romantic song, a fast number after a slow one. Porter's headquarters in New York is a three-room suite on the forty-first floor of the Waldorf Towers—a kind of streamlined Mecca where a tide of agents, actors, arrangers, managers, and fascinated friends is regulated, but seldom stemmed by Miss Margaret Moore, Porter's secretary, and by his valet. Miss Moore's telephone rings constantly with urgent messages from Elsa Maxwell, William Rhinelander Stewart, Clifton Webb, and other of the boss's cronies, all of whom must communicate with him through his secretary. Porter has not answered a telephone in years. The living room, where he works, has, besides the piano, a radio-phonograph so huge that Porter, who is not very tall, has to stand on his toes to see the machinery in the top of it. A card table holding bottles, glasses, and a cocktail-shaker stands in one corner of the room, and some two hundred phonograph records are stacked indiscriminately on a long table against one wall. Behind the records is a row of dictionaries: English, French, and Spanish, two or three rhyming dictionaries, a medical dictionary, and a thin book called *Words, Ancient and Modern.* For relaxation and peace, Porter occasionally escapes to his wife's apartment across the corridor. There, Mrs. Porter, a sleek and finely fashioned woman, lives in an atmosphere untouched by rehearsals, tryouts, or anything less gracious than her own collection of aquamarines.

People who meet Cole Porter for the first time often find his personality baffling. He is by turns pensive, nervous, mercurial, and polite. When he is interested or amused, he talks with a rush of words that betrays him into a slight lisp. At other times his air of boredom verges on the spectacular. While continuing to sit in it, he can withdraw from a room as completely as though he had got up and walked out of the door, and sometimes, during such a silence, he puts in some private work on whatever song he happens to be writing. Once, at a rehearsal of *Red, Hot and Blue* several years ago, Porter passed Russel Crouse, one of the co-authors, some fifteen times in one day without speaking. Crouse wondered what he had done to offend Cole and was about to ask him, when Porter walked up to him at six o'clock in the evening, laid a matey hand on his shoulder, and said firmly, "In my pet pailletted gown." It turned out that he had merely been trying all day to think of the right line to fit into a lyric.

Unlike songwriters who compose over a piano keyboard, Porter stays away from the piano until he has written the words and music of a song in his head and has put them down on paper. Then he plays it and sings it, making changes. He plays cheerfully, with a rhythmic shrug of his right shoulder that suggests at times a hot "I'm Just Wild About Harry" piano player, at other times a simple, ineffable delight in his own work. He has different ways of singing, too. If he is pleased with a lyric, he sings it with a relish that is handsome to see, throwing his head back and closing his eyes. If he is not yet sure about it, he leans forward tensely and listens to each word as it come out of him. His singing voice is high, true, and slightly metallic, and his own comment on it is brief. "I sing unpleasantly," he says. Nearly all of Porter's most successful songs have been written to fit the personality or the voice tricks of the star who is engaged to sing them. He wrote "Night and Day," in *The Gay Divorcée* to fit Fred Astaire's voice, which has a small range and sounds best on a certain few notes. He wrote "I Get a Kick Out of You" for Ethel Merman, in *Anything Goes,* when he discovered that her best notes are A-flat, B-flat, and C-natural, and that she has an engaging manner of throwing herself away in the last few bars of a song. Porter long ago abandoned the song-writer's tradition that a popular number should have a six-teen-bar verse and a thirty-two-bar chorus; some of his songs have had a thirty-two-bar verse and a sixty-four-bar chorus. He likes to add a few extra bars, or "tag," to a Merman chorus, holding some of the notes twice as long as usual, because he knows that Miss Merman can deliberately flat a long note and make it sound brassy and fine, and that she can work up to an exciting finish with a few unexpected bars. He tries, too, to put the words "very" and "terrific" in the lyrics he writes for Miss Merman; no one, he says, can sing these words as she can. The verse of "It Ain't Etiquette," sung by Bert Lahr in the Porter show *Du Barry Was a Lady*, ends with the phrase "Now, for ninstance, Snooks." Porter feels that syllables like those were obviously created so that Lahr could spray them at an audience.

Porter will tell you, with a reminiscent grin, that the source of "for ninstance" is a story about Miss Peggy Hopkins Joyce that entertained certain Americans in France in the happy years before 1939. Miss Joyce, who had arrived in Monte Carlo in one of her statelier moods confided to a friend a few days later that she had simply decided to *leave,* because Monte Carlo was full of such *dreadful* people that season. When the friend protested mildly that a good many attractive people seemed to be around, Peggy drew herself up and loftily inquired, "For ninstance, whom?" Porter treasures things like that, sometimes for years.

Any man who works according to a system as rigorous and as efficient as Cole Porter's may be forgiven a distaste for being referred to in print, by some breathless biographer or other, as "a rich playboy" or, conversely, as "a small-town boy whom the gods have smiled on." Actually he is both. Seven-teen years ago he inherited over one million dollars from his maternal grandfather, J. O. Cole, and during the past ten years his songs have brought him in an annual income of more than a hundred thousand dollars. He likes fashionable people and elaborate parties, partly because they genuinely amuse him, just as poor people and makeshift celebrations honestly depress him, and partly because ideas for songs flow sweetly through him in the midst of a jewelled throng. In contrast to lyric-writers and composers who sweat in lonely toil over a pad and pencil or a piano, Porter relaxes at a party, drinks champagne, and gets home at dawn with a fairly complete outline of a new song, suggested, perhaps, by something someone else has said. "You're the Top," for example, had its origin one night during supper at the Boeuf sur le Toit in Paris, when Porter and the then Mrs. Alastair Mackintosh entertained themselves by making up a list of superlatives that rhymed. Another Porter song, "Miss Otis Regrets," was the result of an evening at Leonard Hanna's New York apartment when one of the guests turned on the radio and picked up a cowboy lament. It sounded so terrible to Porter that he sat down at the piano and began to burlesque it in tortured and nasal strains which gradually formed themselves into a new Cole Porter song. As the music and lyric took shape, Monty Woolley, who was also present, hastily borrowed a morning coat from Hanna's clothes closet and a silver tray from the hall table and, reappearing as a butler, sang the words Porter had just devised: "Miss Otis regrets she's unable to lunch tod-a-ay, Madam." Woolley, that night, had been chiefly prominent as the only guest at the party who had a beard, but "Miss Otis" launched him on the vivacious career as a wit and a mimic that was to lead to the starring role in *The Man Who Came to Dinner.* At all of Elsa Maxwell's parties the rest of that winter, Woolley made a carefully timed entrance in the butler getup and conveyed Miss Otis's regrets in a loud tremolo to the convulsed hostess. The song, a sensation with New Yorkers, never became popular throughout America, but for reasons which nobody connected with it can explain, it sold over one hundred thousand copies in Hungary and Scandinavia, in the days when Hungarians and Scandinavians were still buying songs.

Cole Porter rather cherishes the idea of himself as a small-town boy, and he will sometimes ingenuously show visitors at his apartment the testimonial letter and bronze medal presented to him two years ago by the town of Peru, Indiana, in whose environs he was born. His father, Samuel Porter, had a seven-hundred-and-fifty acre farm near Peru and was a successful fruitgrower. The only rich member of the family, however, was Cole's grandfather, J. O. Cole, who had made some seven million dollars from coal mines and timberland he owned in West Virginia. This gilded relative proposed to leave one-sixth of his fortune to his grandson on condition that he become a lawyer, and he was depressed by Cole's preoccupation with music and by the way his mother and grandmother encouraged him to take violin and piano lessons. At the age of ten, Porter had already composed and dedicated to his mother, *The Song of the Birds,* an ambitious work accompanied by a kind of libretto, written above the notes, explaining throughout what was happening to the birds; "Mother's Cooing," "Echo," "The Young Ones Learn to Sing," and "One Birdling Falls from the Nest (pianissimo, lento)" were among the composer's directions, and they seemed to agitate Mr. Cole. A year or so later, when Porter produced a number called "The Bobolink Waltz" his grandfather stared at him and sent him off to Worcester Academy, in Worcester, Massachusetts, where he prepared for Yale.

At Yale, Porter wrote "Bingo" and "Bulldog," both now a part of New Haven tradition. These achievements and his talent for playing the piano—he had given up the violin—rapidly established him as a social success in one of the most social-minded cliques ever to invade the university. Among the friends Porter made at Yale were, William C. Bullitt, Vanderbilt Webb, Howard Sturges, Leonard Hanna, and Monty Woolley. All were the sons of rich parents, and Porter, whirling through weekends at Southampton, East Hampton, and Newport, learned from them the joys of living colorfully without financial worries, and, by implication, the necessity of becoming his grandfather's heir.

Graduated from Yale in 1913, he entered Harvard Law School, where he played the piano so enthusiastically that Dean Thayer, then head of the School, advised him before the end of his first year to transfer to the Harvard Department of Music. Mr. Cole objected to this plan, but tactful pressure from his wife and daughter finally convinced him that his grandson was not meant to be a lawyer, and he agreed to finance Porter through music school and to keep him in his will in spite of everything. In 1916, while Porter was still at Harvard, he wrote his first show, *See America First,* with book by Lawrason Riggs, a fellow-student, and lyrics by Riggs and Porter. The late Elisabeth Marbury, whom Cole had met in East Hampton, produced the show in New York. One song, "I've a Shooting-Box in Scotland," is still remembered by Porter fans, but *See America First* was a violent failure and closed after two weeks. Lawrason Riggs entered the priesthood soon afterward, and became Catholic chaplain at Yale. Disaster affected Cole Porter in a showier way; he joined the Foreign Legion.

Before Porter sailed for France and the first World War, a friend, Charles Munn of Philadelphia, gave him a portable piano—a kind of combined zither and a harpsichord that could be carried on a man's back like a knapsack. On this instrument, in the next twelve months, Porter played "Over There" and a number of his own, "An Old-Fashioned Garden" (which he wrote within sound of the German guns), to congenial throngs of soldiers in France and Alsace. In 1917, when America entered the war, Porter was transferred to a French artillery school at Fontainebleau as an instructor. In the same year, at the wedding of Ethel Harriman and Henry Russell at the Ritz in Paris, he met Linda Lee Thomas. Mrs. Thomas, at one time a Louisville belle, was beautiful, fashionable, and, through a former marriage to E. R. Thomas, a newspaper owner, extremely well-off. After the armistice, Porter sailed for America with the practical aim of persuading his grandfather to give him an allowance that would be appropriate to the income of Mrs. Thomas, whom he hoped to marry. Another passenger on the boat was Raymond Hitchcock, the comedian, who was planning a new show for New York. One day Hitchcock heard Porter moodily playing "An Old-Fashioned Garden" on a piano in the ship's lounge. Porter was twenty-six years old then, he parted his hair in the middle, and he was in love. Hitchcock asked him to play some of the other things he had written and engaged him to write the score for his new show, *Hitchy-Koo of 1919.*

The show ran two years in New York and on the road, and during the New York engagement alone, about two hundred thousand copies of "An Old-Fashioned Garden" were sold, earning a profit to the composer of some $12,000. Porter saw no harm in going to Indiana anyway and putting the question of an allowance before his grandfather. He explained to Mr. Cole that he needed the money so he could marry Linda, and he described Linda winningly. Mr. Cole refused, pounding the arm of his chair. "I told you," he shouted, "that no good would come of this music business!" Porter returned to New York picked up the royalty checks that were waiting for him, and took the next boat to France. In December, 1919, he married Mrs. Thomas in Paris. The wedding took place in a *mairie,* but it was in a fashionable *arrondissement.*

In the 1920's, the business of writing musical comedy underwent a kind of revolution in America. Until then, songwriters had coasted along with an easy system, spotting a song here and there in a show regardless of plot, and rhyming "moon" with "June" and "love" with "skies above." Then composers like George Gershwin and Richard Rodgers began to write musical comedies with "plot" numbers—songs that came out of situations in the story—and lyric-writers like Lorenz Hart and Ira Gershwin turned out slick, polysyllabic rhymes that had to do with love, all right, but not at the expense of reason. Cole Porter, living in Paris, saw none of this gradual change, but he independently headed in the same direction. He studied harmony and counterpoint with the late Vincent d'Indy at the Schola Cantorum for a while, but he gave that up when he found the influence of the French classical school was interfering with his own sense of rhythm. After that he wrote songs, mainly to entertain himself and to sing at parties. They were perhaps more revolutionary than anything that was being done in America. His melodies were overlaid with European rhythms and his lyrics were, like the party people they were written for and about, smooth, brittle, and full of insinuations. To songwriters in America, "I Love

You" was still a simple declaration; to Cole Porter, musing amid a complicated society of American expatriates, it was beginning to be a smart crack calling for a smart answer. Within a few years after his marriage, Porter had written, and had courteously tossed off at one party or another, such songs as "Two Little Babes in the Wood," "Let's Do It," and "What Is This Thing Called Love?" He turned a bland eye upon his excited friends when they insisted that these songs should be published. He had plenty of money and a vast indifference toward making any more. To one enthusiastic pep-talker, he solemnly explained his fear of commercial success. "Suppose I had to settle down on Broadway for three months just when I was planning to go to Antibes," he said. Some of the things Cole Porter said and did in the twenties have a quaint, Graustarkian ring these days.

The twenties were the years of postwar American gaiety in Europe, and the Cole Porters were happily involved with the shining fleet of vicomtes, contessas, princes incognito, and rich Americans that swept from Paris to London, to the Lido, to the Riviera, with Elsa Maxwell as the tireless tugboat that pulled them forever onward. The Porters' flat in Paris, on the Rue Monsieur, was one of the first to have walls made of mirrors and furniture upholstered in zebra skin. Cole Porter habitually wore in his lapel a kind of blossom which was described by onlookers as the biggest Malmaison carnation in all Paris. He had learned, too, the beauty of a magnificent gesture. One Christmas a friend in New York sent him a pair of gold garter clasps and arranged to have them delivered by Moss Hart, who was sailing for France. Porter met Hart by appointment in the Ritz bar, opened his present, fastened the new garter clasps to his socks then and there, and gave his old clasps to the barman. Hart has never forgotten this incident, because the old garter clasps that Porter tossed across the bar to the barman were gold, too. Mrs. Porter was more conservative in public. People who survived the postwar period in Paris will tell you that her collection of bright jewels and plain dresses was so famous that her name came to be a part of the expatriate language. More than one woman's evening was spoiled when she innocently turned up at a party wearing a classic gown accented by diamonds, rubies, or emeralds and some man said to her, "You're looking very lindaporterish tonight." Generally this comment was preceded by "A-ah!" or "Hm-m"—depending on the speaker's degree of admiration for Mrs. Porter. Either way, Mrs. Porter was the standard of comparison, and the whole thing was very vexing for a number of contemporary belles.

It made the Porters happy to realize that they were almost never known in European society as Mr. and Mrs. Porter. In England, they were the Coleporters; in France, the Colporteurs. This slick union of two Indiana names gave them, early in their invasion of Europe, a kind of cachet that they were careful never to lose. With the Paris flat as their headquarters, they travelled seasonally to all of the right places, and these voyages took on an epic grandeur. They had developed the need of being surrounded by amusing people, and frequently, for a train journey from Paris to Venice, they would engage eight or nine compartments. One compartment was for Mr. Coleporter, one for Mrs. Coleporter, and two more were occupied by a maid and a valet; a fifth compartment was a service room, where the maid and the valet steamed and pressed the Coleporters' clothes. The sixth compartment was turned into a bar, and the remaining rooms were occupied by friends of the Porters who had come along to keep them company. Sometimes these companions bought their own tickets, but more often the Porters paid for everything.

Americans returning from Europe in the early twenties began to bring news of the songs Cole Porter was playing at parties in Paris, on the Riviera, and at the Lido, and Broadway producers, who had not heard from him since *Hitchy-Koo of 1919*, soon began to hanker for him. In 1924, John Murray Anderson persuaded him to come to New York to write the score for *The Greenwich Village Follies.* One of the songs Porter wrote for the show as "I'm in Love Again," which later became a hit, but the *Follies* was only a mild success. When Anderson wanted the composer to do some rewriting on the score before the New York opening, he found that Porter had already started once more on his casual travels. This dispiriting news spread along Broadway, and helped to establish

Porter's reputation for elusiveness—a vivid one, finally dimned only by the war which now limits his wanderings. "This fella Porter," a prominent producer once said, "he's great, great! But where is he?" Another Broadway czar of the time, sitting gloomily in his office a few blocks away, could have told him. "I spend hundreds of dollars in cables trying to get in touch with Cole Porter," he muttered to a henchman. "I beg him to write his own contract. And what is he doing in return?" The producer pointed to a brief cablegram on his desk. "He is faltbooting down the Rhine! First, I am sick and tired," this gentleman declared, "and second, what is faltbooting?"

A good deal of Porter's indifference to producers at this time is traceable to the fact that J. O. Cole had died in 1923, and his grandson had come into his inheritance at almost the same moment Elsa Maxwell undertook (for a fee from the Italian government, it was said) to popularize the Lido. After a respectful pause in honor of Mr. Cole, the Porters embarked on their most fabulous era in Europe. They rented the Palazzo Barbaro in Venice and began giving parties for the colorful folk who had swarmed to the Lido in Miss Maxwell's wake. At one party, tight-rope-walkers swayed in a blaze of colored light above the ancient courtyard to amuse the guests; at another, fifty gondoliers served as footmen. The Porters spent several summers in Venice in one imposing palace after another, and in 1925 they leased for four seasons the Palazzo Rezzonico, where a cardinal had once lived and Robert Browning had died. The parties they gave there have been described as terrible in their grandeur. Guests arriving in the great hall proceeded by way of a mammoth staircase to a room that had twelve windows facing the Grand Canal, then through archways and corridors to a second staircase, more majestic than the first. At the top of these stairs the host could be dimly discerned, small and cheerful, like a cricket in a cathedral. It cost the Porters about $4,000 a month to run the Palazzo Rezzonico, and Porter still thinks of this sum as reasonable. "The lira was cheap then," he explains.

Porter's constant jaunts to Venice, to Morocco, to Bali, Haiti, and other provocative points during this period contributed a good deal to the music he wrote later. He was learning the native rhythms, which in every foreign country penetrate even the roar of American jazz bands. The melodies of the music boats in Venice, the flat wail of an Arab singing from a rooftop in Morocco, and the fast, humorous pace of French popular songs sung in a Paris *boite* were all eventually translated into Porter's own songs. "Night and Day" suggests the monotonous, compelling strains of the Moroccan music; "What Is This Thing Called Love?" was inspired by the rhythm of a native dance Porter once saw at Marrakech; "Begin the Beguine" developed out of an off-beat he detected in another native dance at Kalabahi, a village in the Dutch East Indies; and the business with the brass and drums in "Katie Went to Haiti" originated, of course, in Haiti. "Make It Another Old-Fashioned, Please," from *Panama Hattie,* reverted to a beguine tempo, and the fact that most of the other music from that show was strictly U. S. A. in rhythm holds interesting implications of Porter's rediscovery of America in 1939, after the war began in Europe. Porter's frequent trips down the Rhine in a *Faltboot* also moved him to composition in the old days, and he wrote a good many songs, including most of the score of *Anything Goes,* lying on cushions with his face turned to the sky while Rhine waters flowed musically past him.

Porter's professional return to Broadway, after an absence of nine years (if you disregard his brief skirmish with *The Greenwich Village Follies*), occurred in 1928, and it came about because E. Ray Goetz, the American producer, literally unearthed Porter from the sands of the Lido one morning. Goetz was planning to put on in New York a revue starring Irene Bordoni, and he wanted a score written by an American composer who had a Continental point of view. At the first night of the show, *Paris,* the audience went out happily humming "Two Little Babes in the Wood" and "Let's Do It." In the sixteen years since then, Porter has had fourteen shows on Broadway. *Fifty Million Frenchmen,* in 1929, was followed by *Wake Up and Dream, The New Yorkers, The Gay Divorcée, Anything Goes, Jubilee, Red, Hot and Blue, You Never Know, Leave It to Me, Du Barry Was a Lady, Panama Hattie, Let's Face It, Something for the Boys,* and *Mexican Hayride.*

Until the war obscured such pleasantries, the Cole Porter legend thrived in America as it had done in Europe. Fascinated columnists informed the public that before every opening night, Mr. Porter presented Mrs. Porter with a jewelled token. For *Anything Goes*, it was a diamond-and-aquamarine necklace; for *Red, Hot and Blue*, a platinum cigarette case with rubies, diamonds, and sapphires (red, hot, and blue) on the top and the signs of the zodiac in green gold on the bottom. Audiences still come early to Porter first nights to see the entrance of the Porters and party, who arrive courteously on time and sweep, in a wave of chatter, perfume, and furs, to their seats in the second row. Porter always buys seats for his own first nights and pays for them at the box office, and—unlike many authors and composers who spend such gruelling evenings downstairs in the men's washroom with a bottle of bromide tablets—he enjoys the opening performance enormously, beaming and applauding without restraint. One time, strolling up the aisle at intermission and waving and stopping to chat with friends in the audience, he was heard to say repeatedly, in a tone of honest admiration, "Good, isn't it?"

Seven years ago, Porter's talent for a full life was brought to a grim though temporary halt. He was riding with the rest of a houseparty at Countess Edith di Zoppola's place on Long Island one day when his horse reared, slipped, and fell on him. Both of Porter's legs were broken so badly that doctors at first had little hope of saving either. After eight months in a plaster cast, he had begun to get around a little on his left leg, with the aid of crutches—his right leg was still in a cast—when he fell again, breaking his left leg a second time. With both his legs once more in a cast, his state of mind became almost suicidal, and it still astonishes him to recall that he was saved from melancholia by, of all people, the Shuberts. While he was convalescing physically but was still mentally despondent, the Shuberts asked him to write the score for a show, and his doctor advised him to try it. The piano in his Waldorf-Astoria apartment was raised on wooden blocks so that he could sit at the keyboard in a wheel chair with the plaster casts shoved underneath. Auditions and rehearsals were held in the apartment, and Porter, full of morphia against his constant pain, but cheered by the bounding presence of chorus girls and the stars of the show, Lupe Velez and Clifton Webb, turned out the score of *You Never Know* in less than four weeks. Someone gave him a Persian kitten about this time, and Porter, in gratitude to the Shuberts, named it Jake.

He is still obliged to walk with a stick, but he gets around spryly. At auditions and rehearsals for a show he is a brisk figure hurrying about the dim auditorium, or, with an arm around someone's shoulders for support, climbing the short flight of rehearsal stairs onto the stage. New singers trying out for a job in a Cole Porter show are apt to sing anything, from "Depuis le jour" to "Pistol Packin' Mama," but they never attempt a Cole Porter song; they have heard that he is fussy about the way his songs are sung and that one way to keep out of his shows is to sing them according to any ideas but his own. Porter's trick of tossing a French phrase into a lyric now and then necessitates his carefully drilling the singers until they get the accent right. One of the numbers sung by a girl quartet in *Du Barry Was a Lady* included the line *"C'est pour l'amour de la France."* "Girls, girls!" Porter would cry at rehearsals, clapping his hands for silence in the middle of the number. "You're getting in the habit of saying *'Pour l'amour* dee *la France.'* It's 'deuh, deuh.'" Later he would collect the girls around him in the back of the auditorium while another number was being run through on the stage and rehearse them for twenty minutes on that one line alone. In a *Panama Hattie* number called "God Bless the Women," Rags Ragland and Pat Harrington sang the following couplet:

> You wine them and dine them and buy them bouquets
> And beautiful bonnets from Lilly Daché's.*

During the road tryout of the show, Harrington, who sings the second line, got a series of polite notes from Porter (who likes to write notes), pointing out that he was letting his voice drop on the last word. "Lilly Da-*ché's*. Lift it, lift it," these missives would urge.

---

* Copyright MCMXL by Chappell & Co., Inc., New York.

Toward six o'clock on rehearsal afternoons, Porter generally sighs and murmurs to whatever friends have happened to drop in, "Well, let's all go out and drink ourselves to death." He drinks little, actually—a dry Martini before lunch, an Amer Picon with lime juice at cocktail time, and wine with dinner. He likes to eat and to discuss food gravely with headwaiters and chefs. When he is working alone in his hotel apartment, his lunch, served by the waiter permanently assigned to him, may consist of melon and thin slices of Parma ham, filet of sole *bonne femme,* fresh asparagus, and a green salad. He always eats everything on his plate, and he is indignant at people who leave scraps.

Now that Europe is no longer a playground, Porter's plans for wandering are vague, but whatever they turn out to be, they are likely to include something racy. One summer, he and his wife experimented with a house near the Lido Country Club at Long Beach. The Long Beach Lido bears no resemblance to the Italian Lido, and the house was small, but where the Cole Porters are, there is glitter. Twice a week a dark and shining delivery car with the name "Waldorf-Astoria" in gold letters on its side drew up and waited at the door of the house while the neighbors speculated curiously. What delicacies, they wondered, what strange imported pleasures could the Waldorf be sending the Porters twice a week? They found out, finally. The Waldorf sent the car every Monday to pick up the Porters' laundry, and returned it the same way every Thursday.

8

Big-Time Urchin:

LARRY ADLER

WHATEVER YOUR TRADE or profession is, you seldom get to be better at it than anyone else. Competition is strong, and champions are few. The philosopher who wrote about the better mousetrap and the beaten path made by mousetrap-fanciers would have approved of Larry Adler, a boy who has made the mousetrap gag come true. Adler is the best harmonica player in the world, and the path admirers have made to *his* door is fashioned of beaten gold, plus considerable folding money as well.

Adler is also probably the only soloist appearing in concert with symphony orchestras who, up to two years ago, could not read a note of music and insisted cheerily on the public's knowing it. He learned his pieces from phonograph records and played them by ear until Jean Berger, a French composer, wrote a harmonica concerto for him, and Adler realized darkly that no recording of the work existed. He had to learn how to read the notes, and he has since studied all of his more important new numbers from a score, remarking that he never knew what he was missing. This accomplishment pleases his musical friends, who have long felt that either Larry should be more reticent about his ignorance or, preferably, he should study music. To this Adler replies that he did study music once, at the Peabody School in Baltimore, to which his mother took him when he was eight years old to learn the piano. At the first interview the lady teacher poured a syrupy smile over a shelflike bosom and said, "Play something, my little man." Afire with instant hate, the little man sat down at the piano and tore off "Yes! We Have No

Bananas" by ear, leering at Teacher the while. He lasted at Peabody a couple of terms. At the end of that time the principal informed his mother that he was incorrigible, untalented, and entirely lacking in ear. Larry was removed, with lip curled.

Although Adler is not a diffident man, he takes a certain rather showy pleasure in belittling some aspects of his profession. He likes to emphasize the fact, for instance, that the harmonica is not recognized as a musical instrument by the Musicians' Union, Local 802; the union classifies it as a toy. Last winter, soon after Adler and Paul Draper had given a concert together at Carnegie Hall—the first Carnegie concert to feature either tap-dancing or harmonica-playing—Adler, at a party, ran into James Petrillo, head of the American Federation of Musicians, which includes Local 802. Petrillo intimated that he might be able to fix it so that Larry would be eligible to join the union. "I think I can get you in" was the way he put it. Adler urged him not to go to too much trouble, and added mildly that he was doing all right. This understatement, translated, means that his annual income from playing on the toy of Local 802 is now around forty thousand dollars and has been as high as eighty-five thousand dollars.

Adler enjoys telling vividly modest anecdotes about himself partly because he is a gifted raconteur and partly because he is endlessly diverted by his own objective picture of Adler the musician and the man. The most casual request for information from a newspaper reporter or interviewer will often bring, in reply, a twelve- or fifteen-page typewritten, single-spaced narrative, composed and typed by Larry in person, and containing dialogue and anecdotes. He has such a genuine fondness for seeing his name in the papers that he is constantly writing unsolicited letters to columnists or telephoning them, coast to coast, to tell them about his meeting with Yehudi Menuhin or his experience with Jack Warner or his various reactions to fellow-celebrities. His reports always generously include the names of other famous people, but, as Paul Draper, a devoted and candid friend, once remarked, they are all *about* Adler. This knack of seeming to speak of others while you talk only of yourself indicates a genius for publicity; professional press agents recognize its flowering in Larry and stand back and raise their hats. Nobody objects to his relentless quest after the printed page; it is undeniably part of his trade, and besides Adler is a likeable boy. "I guess you could call him self-centered," a friend remarked recently, "but at least it don't make him a heel, like some.

Adler is twenty-nine years old, slim, excited, and entertaining. He looks fragile and active, something like a very young and slightly sinister kitten, and his forehead and eyes are proportionately larger than the rest of his face, which gives him an interesting air of always appearing to lean forward a little. His fingers are long and compelling, and when he plays, his face, fingers, and slight body all work in dark and violent rhythm to the harmonica. A lot of his flashy work with hands and fingers is necessary, because he uses both to regulate vibration and resonance. To anyone who suggests that the rest of his happy antics may be pure showmanship, he says immediately, "Sure. Didn't I tell you about how I used to play with a shadowgraph showing my profile and hands in silhouette on a screen behind me? What can you lose?" Some of Adler's friends, who worry about his rapid rise to fame, achieved without any of the usual grinding study and without the usual equipment of formal musical knowledge, murmur that he should be called a music-lover rather than a musician. They say that his playing of Bach, Beethoven, and Brahms by ear is a pleasure for Adler rather than a performance by him. None of them deny, however, that his ear is faultless and his memory magic. Not long ago, Paul Draper played a phonograph record of the second movement of a Brahms sonata for Larry, who had never heard it before. Shutting it off, Draper remarked that he thought it might be good on the harmonica. Adler asked him to play it again and, after Draper stopped the record the second time, took up his harmonica and played the music through. Another time, in London a few years ago, an English music critic who had been told of Adler's feats of memory discovered that Larry had never heard the score of *Scheherazade,* and rather belligerently took him to see the ballet and then back to his flat, where he marched Larry to the piano and challenged him to play any theme he could remember from the music he had heard. Adler forthwith played most of the score of *Scheherazade*. He plays the piano in a brooding and spectacular way, so effective that more than one listener, hanging over the keyboard, has asked him why he doesn't take it up seriously and become a concert pianist. "You know what I'd be doing now if I played the piano as well as I play the harmonica?" Larry answers. "Playing in somebody else's band."

Adler knows that being the best harmonica player in the world is a sweet spot to be in, since there is little competition in the field, but he is tender toward his first love, the piano. He was a Baltimore boy, the son of a Bryant Avenue plumber who had never thought much about music. His mother, who had once won a limerick contest sponsored by a local newspaper, was more inclined toward artistic things. Larry's younger brother, Hilliard Adler, also grew up to be a harmonica player and now works, under the name of Jerry Hilliard, in Hollywood, where he lives with the elder Adlers. A year or so ago, Larry was featured in a stage show at Roxy's in New York, which was then showing the film *Pot o' Gold*, and the manager said to him nervously, "You may not like the competition—Jimmy Stewart plays a pretty good harmonica solo in the picture." Adler found later that Stewart's harmonica solo had been played by brother Hilliard and dubbed in. Larry was christened Lawrence Cecil and at the age of eighteen months he had the feeling of being extraordinary. "I had big hair standing out all over the head, and I could carry a tune," he says. When he was two he wandered away from home one day and was found by his father, two hours later, standing on a table in a downtown poolroom and singing a song called "I've Got Those Profiteering Blues" while the enchanted patrons stuffed money into his rompers pockets. Dragged home, he kept on singing so lustily through the years that when he was five his father, goaded, took him to a concert by Rachmaninoff in Baltimore. After that, whenever Rachmaninoff played Baltimore, Larry would turn up at the ticket window, generally alone and always undaunted, though he was usually refused admission because he was a minor and unaccompanied. One time a generous lady just behind him in the queue, seeing his sorrow at being turned away, opened her coat wide and said, "Get in, Sonny." As Adler relates what followed, "Four feet walked in." He always revered Rachmaninoff so deeply that the only time he was introduced to him, several years ago, he was attacked by an unaccustomed shyness and failed to tell the great man his dream. His dream was to have Rachmaninoff write a concerto for the harmonica. This worship mildly worried Adler's modern friends, who considered Rachmaninoff a little old-fashioned, though charming.

At the age of ten, Larry became the youngest boy cantor in Baltimore, and held this position for three years with such excessive piety, chiding his playmates for every lapse from orthodoxy, such as carrying money in their pockets on a Saturday, that soon nobody his age would speak to him. His unpopularity in public school made him unhappy, and he solved that problem by producing enough symptoms of a nervous breakdown to convince the school doctor and his parents, and to get himself transferred to the Peabody School of Music. Ejected from there and mourning the lack of a piano at home, he went downtown alone one day, when he was about eleven, to shop for a Mason & Hamlin, which was the make he had decided on. The startled owner of the music store urged him to settle for a harmonica, and even gave him a new one as a present. Larry accepted the gift, but also persuaded the proprietor to send a Mason & Hamlin home on approval. Delivered the next day, it met with something less than approval from the elder Adlers, but Larry was beginning to show an ability to talk anybody into anything; his parents finally kept the piano, though, he recalls, it took them several years to pay for it. Larry spent his days happily then, playing the piano and the harmonica and peddling magazines on the Baltimore streets to get money for concert tickets and to buy records for the family victrola. His instinct in music was sensitive, and his taste was catholic but good. Next to Rachmaninoff, he loved Al Jolson, and his repertory came to be a triumph of variety, including, "April Showers," "Got a Rainbow 'Round My Shoulder," and other Jolson numbers, as well as the Rachmaninoff preludes and concertos. In 1927, the Baltimore *Sun* ran a harmonica contest with a silver cup as first prize. One after another, the contestants stood before the judges and played either *Turkey in the Straw* or *St. Louis Blues*, two mouth-organ standbys. The judges gratefully awarded the prize to Adler when he rose and obliged with Beethoven's *Minuet in G.* Larry plays it beautifully, in C.

Adler's showmanship in playing the music of Beethoven, Bach, Liszt, and other great composers on a harmonica, and in playing this homely instrument wearing a white tie and tails, probably accounts for a good deal of his success. "It is my boast," he says earnestly, "that I have never imitated a train, or freight cars shunting, or any of those other corny tricks harmonica players are so nuts about. And I have *never* played *Flight of the Bumblebee.*" He looks debonair on the stage, and it was in a somewhat debonair manner, in fact, that he left home at the age of fourteen, fourteen months after the *Sun* contest, and came to New York with his harmonica and seven dollars he had saved. His mother and father did not discover his departure for several hours, but they scarcely had time to worry, because the seven dollars gave out in a couple of days and Larry had to write home for money. A runaway and a rebel, he was nevertheless still a boy who had been brought up in a family of orthodox Jews, and for a long time he was afraid to eat anything in New York. At the St. Regis Cafeteria on Broadway, he shunned the succulent dishes because he couldn't be sure they were kosher, and for several weeks lived mainly on cornflakes and milk. "What can you do to cornflakes?" he shrugs, explaining this. Even now, at dinner parties, he will decline a dish containing too many forbidden items, partly because it pleases his father and mother in California to know that he sticks to kosher food and almost surely because of some inner conviction as well.

When Adler arrived in New York in 1928, he knew all the celebrities on Broadway by name, though he had not met any of them personally. He took a furnished room and spent most of his time away from it, playing his harmonica outside the stage door of the Palace or Roxy's, and hoping that Paul

Whiteman or some other famous orchestra leader would rush out, entranced, and hand him a forty-week contract. One day, when Whiteman was heading the bill at Roxy's, two of his musicians, Frankie Trumbauer and Joe Venuti, did stop to listen to Larry and, influenced by his sales talk as well as his playing, took him inside to see the maestro in his dressing room. "I knocked myself out playing *Rhapsody in Blue*," Adler says, "and Whiteman said it was fine. He didn't give me a job, though. That's the way it always was those days. No jobs. People just kept saying I was a genius." Encouraged, however, by his brief appearance backstage, Larry next crashed the stage door of the Paramount Theatre, where Rudy Vallee was appearing, and played "Button Up Your Overcoat" in the hall outside Vallee's dressing room until the vagabond lover put his head out and inquired what the hell was going on. Vallee, always a kindly fellow, gave Larry a spot in the floor show at his Heigh-Ho Club, but regretfully fired him after two performances because, he explained, Adler was a one-shot novelty and the public soon tired of his kind of entertainment. He helped Larry get a job dubbing in music synchronizations for Mickey Mouse cartoons in an office in the Paramount Building (whenever Mickey rendered a harmonica solo, it was Larry's) and it was no time at all before Adler found his way downstairs and backstage again and was once more playing his harmonica outside the star's dressing room, then occupied by Paul Ash, the orchestra leader.

Ash got Larry a job in a Paramount vaudeville unit which was beginning a thirty-week tour of Paramount theatres, and although this piece of luck set Adler up professionally for thirty weeks, it set him back sartorially about ten years. Sure of a weekly salary, he had begun to think about going to Ben Rocke, a tailor fashionable with theatrical people, and indulging in some correct clothes for both stage and street wear. It was the notion, though, of the orchestra leader who was featured with the unit to introduce Larry to the audience as an urchin he had picked up playing a mouth organ for pennies on a Broadway corner, and Adler therefore appeared in ragged knickers, an old sweater, and a cap with the peak worn backward. Other showmen later recognized this as a good gag and, whenever they engaged Adler, adopted it with a zeal that came to haunt Larry until he was old enough to vote. With Eddie Cantor, Gus Edwards, and in a Ziegfeld show called *Smiles,* he was eternally presented as a gifted urchin whom Cantor, Edwards, or Ziegfeld had discovered playing for pennies in the street. After *Smiles,* Lew Leslie hired Adler for a revue called *Clowns in Clover,* and horridly varied the urchin routine by having Adler come on the stage leading a blind man. The actor who took the part of the blind man would stand motionless and dead-pan while Larry played the harmonica, and then Larry would lead him off. Between performances, Adler (in long pants) was beginning to go about to parties and to meet people. In one large evening he met George Gershwin, Noel Coward, and Howard Dietz, and played for them. Gershwin, that night, advised him never to study music, warning him that formal education might ruin his natural ear and rhythm and set him forever in a cold and classical mold. Coward offered him a spot in a revue he was writing, and Dietz said he wanted him for *Flying Colors,* a show he and Arthur Schwartz had just finished. Adler accepted the last offer because Dietz promised him that he would not have to appear as an urchin. Dietz kept his word and Adler appeared as a bootblack. He had one of the show's hit songs, "Shine on Your Shoes," but Vilma and Buddy Ebsen danced while he played it, and nobody looked at Larry. When *Flying Colors* closed, Larry, suddenly hankering to go to California, sent an enthusiastic wire to Sid Grauman, the Hollywood impresario, announcing himself as a sensational find and cannily signing the name of a theater manager known to Grauman. He got the call to come to Hollywood and was soon appearing in frayed knickers, sweater, and cap at Grauman's Chinese Theatre, where he was introduced to the audience four times a day as an urchin Grauman had discovered playing for pennies at the corner of Hollywood and Vine.

Adler returned to New York in the spring of 1934, and was booked as a single act at the Palace, which had then become a movie theater with incidental stage entertainment. He had developed a certain polish, which included a knack of taking socially desirable young women out to night clubs at no cost to himself. He would unobtrusively tell the manager who he was, reveal that he happened to have his harmonica with him, and respond gracefully to an invitation to play for the customers. After that there was never any check, and besides the girls liked the feeling of being out with a celebrity, no matter how thrifty. At the Palace, Adler took the matter of apparel into his own hands and strolled onto the stage wearing a dinner jacket. One day, during his week's engagement, C. B. Cochran, the English producer, happened to walk past the theater with Elsie April, his musical arranger, and her twelve-year-old son, Peter. Peter saw Ben Blue's act billed outside and begged to be taken in to see the show. After Adler's act, Cochran went backstage and offered him three hundred and fifty dollars a week to go to London and join *Streamline,* a revue of his that was already playing there. What had impressed him almost as much as Adler's playing, Mr. Cochran added, was the novelty of seeing a man wear a dinner jacket to play a mouth organ. Adler sailed the following week, in the wake of advance publicity sent on by Cochran, but considerably altered in one or two cases by British newspaper editors who, informed that the famous producer was importing a young American who played the harmonica, deemed this so unlikely that they prudently changed the word "harmonica," in their columns, to "trombone."

Adler and his harmonica were such an immediate success with London audiences that Larry was soon playing at four supper clubs a night—a fifteen-minute spot in each one—as well as appearing in *Streamline.* In the daytime he made phonograph recordings, the first of which, "Smoke Gets in Your Eyes," sold forty thousand copies the week it was released. He appeared as a guest star on radio shows, occasionally introduced by Cochran, and it was one of these broadcasts that started a legend that has pursued Adler. Cochran, who is nearsighted, mislaid his glasses and, unable to read the announcement of Larry's next number, stalled for time by ad-libbing wildly. "You use a new harmonica every time you play and throw away the old one, don't you, Larry?" he inquired genially. "I-yi!" Larry exclaims now, clapping a hand to his cheek when he tells about it. "What could I do? You don't contradict the boss on a nation-wide hookup." The listening public sent him two thousand letters in the next three days, asking for discarded harmonicas and enclosing stamps, money orders, checks, and cash in payment, all of which Adler had to return with the explanation that he uses his harmonicas time and time again and scarcely ever throws one away. This is even truer now than it was then, since the instruments he plays—chromatic harmonicas with a range of three octaves—were made only by Hohner, a German firm, and are naturally no longer procurable. Adler has about two hundred in reserve and has figured out that it will be about two years before they are beyond repair.

Not long ago Adler remarked to his manager, Fred Schang, that perhaps, now that he was a concert soloist, he ought to call himself by his full name, Lawrence Adler, instead of the less dignified diminutive. "Well, I don't know," said Schang thoughtfully. "We got some pretty good musicians still using diminutives. There's Jascha, and Mischa, and Toscha, and Sascha. . . ." Larry laughed his short laugh, which is scarcely more than a flash of teeth, gave up the idea of calling himself Lawrence, and hurried to tell his other friends what Schang had said. He usually repeats a *mot* better than the man who said it, always tells a story more successfully than the man he heard it from, and never fails to give credit to his source. His own humor depends largely on his flawless dialects (French, British, and Russian, as well as Yiddish), on his fund of dialect stories, which unfortunately lose their charm in print, and on a colorful turn of phrase in simple conversation. "I would like to thank you and thank you and thank you until your teeth fall out," he once said mildly to a friend who had taken him to a particularly boring party. "You must come out sometime for tea and snakes," he suggested graciously to another acquaintance after he had taken a summer house in Katonah one year. His letters to his present agent, Hal Davis, are a fluent combination of Adler the dialectician and Adler the classicist. "Wossamatta wichoo?" he wrote from Miami Beach this February. "You ain't got no conegshins in Flordda? A fortnight awready I been here and wos happening? Bupkis.

A press agent like I got shouldn't happen to a dog-eared edition of *Little Dorrit.*" Sometimes, bored or desperate, Adler uses his dialect to ruin himself in a spectacular way. A year or so ago, for instance, Norman Corwin, the radio writer, asked Larry to appear in one of his radio dramas, *Lip Service.* The story was about a young hillbilly who played the mouth organ, and Corwin planned to have Adler do the harmonica part, with a radio actor taking the hillbilly's speeches. Adler objected, wanting to play the hillbilly as well as play his tunes, and a series of spirited telegrams passed between Corwin, the writer and director, and Adler, the suppliant. Finally Corwin wired Larry, "CALL ME UP AND TALK LIKE HILLBILLY OVER TELEPHONE." An hour or so later his telephone rang, and Adler said softly, "Deed you-all veeshing from me I should do by you-all heel-beely tuk?" Adler played the harmonica in *Lip Service,* and another man played the hillbilly.

After Adler's London success in 1935, Hohner's sale of harmonicas went up two thousand per cent throughout the British Empire, and Adler's salary rose, too, to several hundred pounds a week. He asked, and got, twenty-five hundred dollars in American money one time to go to Monte Carlo and play at a party given by Countess Constantini for King Gustav of Sweden. The King's favorite tune was "The Music Goes 'Round and 'Round," and he would lustily sing the part that went "Oh-ho-HO-ho, ho-ho," tapping his foot and whistling along with the rest of it. Kings, in those dead days, were friendly people, casual and secure, with a taste for light music. Adler remembers that Haakon of Norway liked *Caprice Viennois,* that the late George V of England asked for the *Londonderry Air,* and that the present monarch, George VI, never tired of "Smoke Gets in Your Eyes." Adler, a London idol in the years just before the war, played piano duets with the late Duke of Kent at the Kents' house in Belgrave Square and was once paged throughout most of the town's night clubs on behalf of the Duke, who was telephoning to get Larry to come right over and play a Rodgers and Hart tune called "Lover" for Richard Rodgers, who happened to be a guest of the Kents that evening. "You're the only man in London who plays it right," the Duke said tensely when he located Adler. The British public succumbed to Adler to the extent of organizing fan clubs that soon enrolled three hundred thousand members, and often strangers would appear in Larry's dressing room with their mouth organs and insist on playing faithful renditions of Adler phonograph records—"including mistakes," Larry recalls. After *Streamline* closed, he made a quick trip to Hollywood to play a few numbers in *The Big Broadcast of 1937*, starring Jack Benny; when the film arrived in England it was billed everywhere as "Larry Adler and Jack Benny in *The Big Broadcast of 1937*." Adler, having returned to London, was starring in *Tune Inn*, a revue patterned around him, and had advanced from night-club jobs in his spare time to occasional grave recitals instead. Cyril Scott, the English composer, wrote a serenade for the harmonica, the first serious piece to be composed for that instrument, and accompanied Adler on the piano when he played it at a London concert hall. William Walton, the leader of the modern British composers, stated in an interview that there were only two young musical geniuses in the world today, Yehudi Menuhin and Larry Adler. Adler's fame became so great that nothing about him went unnoticed. It happens, for instance, that a certain vein in his temple distends slightly when he plays fortissimo passages. A London picture paper published a photograph of him in which the prominent vein could be discerned, and printed underneath it the stirring caption, "Defies Death Every Time He Plays!"

Appreciative but always self-possessed in the face of adulation, Adler went on Coronation Day in 1937 to see the procession from the window of a friend's flat. One of the guests was a Miss Eileen Walser, a cool English blonde who worked as a mannequin for a West End couturier. She greeted Adler, the idol, with such calmness that Larry decided there must be some mistake, and rapidly worked the conversation around to a point at which he could, in a flash, reveal his identity, modestly adding that he was, at the moment, appearing in *Tune Inn*. "Oh?" said Miss Walser. "What d'you do in it?" Adler grimly invited her to come and see, and, when she came the next night, wielded his harmonica so grandly that he broke a tooth on it. He married Miss Walser in 1938 at Marylebone, in what he likes to describe as a quiet ceremony. "We *sneaked* away," he says. "With just one teentsy-*weentsy* news photographer," his wife adds, rolling a fond and humorous eye.

The Adlers immediately set off on a tour of South Africa and Australia, where Larry was booked as the starring act at a long list of variety theaters. Mostly fashionable British colonials came to hear him, but in Cape Town he played to an audience of a thousand blacks, whose custom, it turned out, was to leap from their seats and yell "Ow!" when pleased by a performance. In Johannesburg his lips cracked because of the altitude, and he told the customers apologetically that he would have to play out of the left side of his mouth. In the middle of the act he finished a number, stared at the audience, and suddenly said, "Hey! I just discovered that I always play out of this side of my mouth anyway!" The audience cheered, impressed, as people always are, by Adler's unbeatable combination of brassiness and boyish charm. He made his first appearance with a symphony orchestra in Sydney, at a benefit concert, and has since played with the Cleveland, San Francisco, St. Louis, Philadelphia, and other symphonies. One of the things that fascinate him about playing a symphonic program, which usually includes Bach, Liszt, Vivaldi, and also Kern, Gershwin, and his own arrangement of "Blues in the Night," is the contrast among people in the audience; jitterbugs in sweaters sit next to spectacled classic-lovers, and all of them seem to have a fine time. The aspect of an Adler concert that interests Mrs. Adler, in addition to her husband's playing, is a pictorial one. "I never can get used to seeing that great stage with a huge orchestra on it tuning up, the conductor raising his baton, all of them waiting—and then out comes Larry, all alone, and puts that little tiny thing up to his mouth," she says affectionately.

In 1939, Adler returned to the United States with his bride, and found himself almost unknown in his own country. "It was hell," he says simply. "Eileen had known me as a big shot in England and on the British Empire tour, and here I was, a nothing." A few radio guest spots, movie-theater engagements, and an appearance at Lewisohn Stadium with the New York Philharmonic under Alexander Smallens helped to remedy this blindness of the American public and to lead up to the first concert at Carnegie Hall in December 1941, with Paul Draper, whom he had met some twelve years before. Adler's own fondness for being well known has not hindered his American career. A week or so before the Carnegie concert a friendly and admiring writer mentioned him in print as "the world's greatest harmonica virtuoso." Adler called the writer up to thank him, and added seriously, "But look. Why didn't you say 'The world's greatest harmonica virtuoso, who is appearing next week with Paul Draper in a concert at Carnegie Hall'? " Adler is as used to being called the world's greatest harmonica player (or virtuoso) as, say, Hugo Zacchini was used to being called the world's greatest man-shot-out-of-a-cannon, and his eye automatically skips that phrase and gets down to the business angle.

The Adlers live, when they are in New York, in an apartment in the East Sixties containing, besides themselves, their daughter Carole, aged four, an infant son, a nurse, a maid, a grand piano, Larry's two hundred harmonicas, about one thousand phonograph records, and an imperfect portable phonograph borrowed from Paul Draper. Draper himself can often be found in these pleasant surroundings, sitting with his feet higher than his head or engaging Adler in a spurt of boxing or jujitsu. Adler is slight and small-boned, Draper tall and muscular, but Larry is always eager to try anything. "Show me how to do that, will you, Paul?" he will say, watching the exquisite Draper torso writhe and ripple in some feat of strength. Several years ago, when the two were living together in Hollywood and Adler was working in a picture called *Many Happy Returns*, he challenged Draper to a bicycle race from La Brea Avenue to Santa Monica, a distance of about twelve miles, and lost in spite of a couple of spectacular bursts of speed, plunging across the finish line to find Draper leaning against a tree smoking a cigarette while he waited for him. "As for me, I had left a lung on each side of the bicycle," Adler says.

The Adlers like people around them, and their apartment is generally filled with friends: musicians, writers, social celebrities, and an occasional artist—notably Thomas Benton, the painter, who is a harmonica player himself and is fond of playing duets with Larry. Adler's schedule of concerts, theater and night-club performances, and tours of Army camps leaves him little time for such amenities. He has twice been overseas with Jack Benny, in a USO unit, and travelled through Sicily, the South Pacific, and the Near East, entertaining the troops. "Just think," he remarked to his wife in an awed voice once, after he got home, "I actually prayed at the Wailing Wall in Jerusalem!" Mrs. Adler has a feathery wit, arrow-tipped, and she knows her Larry. "What for?" she inquired. "Bigger billing?"

In what leisure Adler has, he likes to sit at home with friends, dreamily playing the piano with one hand, the harmonica with the other, and wearing a bathtowel bound around his head to train the luxuriant curl out of his hair. This towel is practically his sole headgear. He almost never wears a hat, and owns only one, which he keeps for putting on in the synagogue he attends on Yom Kippur.

Students and fans are always wanting to know how Adler manages to make a harmonica sound like a full orchestra, and Adler is always willing to explain. For a trumpet effect, for instance, he stands three feet back of the microphone, opens his hands over the harmonica, and blows a sharp, brassy tone; for a wah-wah muted-trumpet sound he opens and closes his hands slowly, closer to the mike; a violin tone is achieved by fluttering the hands fast and playing into the mike from a distance of ten or twelve inches, a cello tone by blowing softly over the first three holes of the harmonica, about six inches from the mike, and an oboe effect by vibrating the tongue rapidly. Adler agrees that this information sounds pretty confusing, and he prefers the following instructions, recently written on his behalf by Leonard Feather, the English swing critic:

"All you have to do is move the left framiscle on the portisdublе from hardistack with the muscles, using a frammisanic embouchure. Then you bogrulate the ambiscridge in the key of B flat, controlling the reeds by discrovenizing your cyrillis every time you breathe through the meadispule. Just practice this three times daily, but remember the fundamental rule: two stanistrings in the pedigrate of the bordistrich, but *always* with the left hand."

"That's it," says Adler.

❁ 9 ❁

*Words and Music:**

RODGERS AND HART

There's a dame next door
Who's an awful bore,
It really makes you sore
To see her.
a......................
b..................
c......................
d.........
By and by, perhaps she'll die,
Perhaps she'll croak this summer;
Her old man's a plumber,
She's much dumber.

The above incantation is part of what is called, in the song-writing business, a dummy lyric. It is a hasty assortment of words thrown together by the lyric-writer while a song is being composed, generally loony and often bawdy, but always carefully accented to follow the rhythm. Fortunately for the lyric writer, a frenzied toiler, he seldom has to fill in the second stanza, since it repeats the rhythm of the first. The sentimental words that finally grew out of the tale about the dame next door and the plumber were written by Lorenz

* Lorenz Hart died on November 21st, 1943. Because the name of Rodgers and Hart continues to be a part of the American language wherever songs are sung, I have left this piece as I completed it, shortly before Mr. Hart's death.

Hart and accompanying the melody by Richard Rodgers, became a song hit in *On Your Toes*:

There's a small hotel
With a wishing well;
I wish that we were there
Together.

There's a bridal suite;
One room bright and neat,
Complete for us to share
Together.

Looking through the window you
Can see a distant steeple;
Not a sign of people,
Who wants people? *

This seems to be an answer to the ancient question with which the layman badgers songwriters: "Which do you write first, the music or the words?" But Rodgers, who writes the music, and Hart, who writes the words, say that there is no answer to that. Sometimes it happens one way, sometimes another. One day in Paris, in 1926, the collaborators were riding in a taxi with two girls; the cab skittered into a truck and one of the girls, fluttering, cried, "Oh, my heart stood still!" From the floor of the taxi, where the collision had flung him with his hat jammed over his eyes, Larry Hart mumbled, "Hey, Dick, that's a title for a song." The rest was fairly simple (after they got out of the wrecked cab), and "My Heart Stood Still," originally presented in a Cochran revue in London and introduced to New York in 1927 in *A Connecticut Yankee* (which was revived this year), has come to be known reverently in the trade as a "standard"—a song kept on file for continual use and amounting to about the same thing as a "classic." The reverence is due partly to the emotions a good song honestly rouses in the hearts of everybody in the songwriting business, partly to the fact that "My Heart Stood Still" earned around fifty thousand dollars during the seven-

* Copyright MCXXXVI by Chappell & Co., Inc., New York.

teen-year lull between the first performance of *A Connecticut Yankee* and its revival.

Rodgers and Hart have been collaborating for twenty-four years, since Rodgers, then sixteen years old, met Hart, who was twenty-three. Rodgers is poised, immaculate, and humorous. He is under five feet seven inches in height, but he seems tall in comparison with the exact five feet of his partner, a small, tumultuous man, rumpled and amiable behind a large cigar which he takes out of his mouth only in order to make excited gestures with it. Hart's carefree attitude toward his appearance sometimes worries Rodgers, and then, he says, "I take Larry by the hand, lead him into the children's department of any good store, and have him fitted out from head to foot—a short distance." The only other thing about his collaborator that used to furrow the Rodgers brow, until he became used to it, is Hart's gift for getting away from wherever he is. When, for instance, the two are walking along a street, conversing pleasantly, Hart abruptly disappears. "You find yourself talking to yourself" is the way Rodgers describes it. He has learned now to walk along slowly until Hart reappears and chattily resumes the conversation where it was left off. Generally it turns out that Larry has darted into a store for one of his big cigars or to a newsstand for a copy of *Variety*. Several years ago Rodgers came upon Hart in a hotel lobby, fiercely denouncing the manager, who was trying to explain, with outspread hands, why he had not been able to procure the latest issue of *Variety*. His reason, which Hart was finally forced to accept, was that the hotel was in Khartoum.

Nothing about Dick Rodgers worries Hart except his own conviction that Rodgers encourages the orchestra to play too loud at rehearsals and performances. "So you want to drown out my lyrics?" he wails. Rodgers regards him peacefully and inquires, "Do you want the audience to go out whistling the lyrics?" All of this bickering is strictly affectionate, the kind that can go on for twenty-four years between two men who are friends although their lives are curiously different. Rodgers married Dorothy Feiner fourteen years ago and now lives rather formally with his wife, two daughters (aged thirteen and nine), and three servants in a pleasant apartment on East Seventy-fourth Street and in the summers at their farm in Fairfield, Connecticut. A drawing of Central Park which hangs on one wall of the New York apartment was given to Rodgers one Christmas by his wife, who bought it when she saw that it happened to include the towers of the apartment building on Central Park West where Larry Hart lives. Larry is a bachelor and his home life is a happy pandemonium shared by his mother and Black Mary, the general maid, who has been with the Harts some twenty years. One time, when Josephine Baker came to dine with the Harts after her elaborate triumphs in Paris and elegantly requested "*une tasse de café noir,*" it was Mary who stared at her for a long moment and then demanded sombrely, "You talk out of your mouth, you, the way you was born."

Geographically separated (and everyone knows how great is the distance between Central Park West and Fifth Avenue), Larry Hart and Dick Rodgers also differ in their social tastes. Mr. and Mrs. Rodgers, gay, attractive, and sociable, are frequently seen with fashionable friends at first nights, in restaurants, and at parties. Larry likes company, too, but the thought of a white tie dissolves him and he prefers to give parties at home, always loudly and almost tearfully proclaiming any soirée of his a failure if even one guest has departed sober. In spite of this sartorial and social gap between them, the Rodgers family frequently invades the Hart apartment for a visit, and the Rodgers home setting generally includes Larry, waving his cigar from the depths of an armchair and talking rapidly in a high, slightly husky voice. Both men speak softly in conversation, and Rodgers' singing voice, like that of a good many composers, is true but faint.

Except for the agonized periods before the opening of a new show, when Hart flees to Atlantic City to revise the lyrics or to write new ones and Rodgers locks himself into his study in the Fairfield house to score the melodies, they always work together in Larry's apartment or in Dick's. In one or the other of these sharply contrasted surroundings, Rodgers and Hart have turned out over a thousand songs, many of them notable hits, including "Thou Swell," "With a Song in My Heart," "I've Got Five Dollars," "The Blue Room," "Ten Cents a Dance," "Falling in Love with Love," "I Didn't Know What Time It Was," "Lover," and "The Most Beautiful Girl in the World." Another song, "Have You Met Miss Jones?" was in the musical commentary *I'd Rather Be Right,* for which the book was written by George S. Kaufman and Moss Hart, the music and lyrics by Richard Rodgers and Lorenz Hart. Moss Hart and Lorenz Hart are not related, except by mutual consternation in the production of *I'd Rather Be Right.* One scene, in Central Park, included the President of the United States sitting on a bench, members of the cabinet and justices of the Supreme Court gathered around a long table, and a young man in love. The plot required the young man to proclaim his love at this point, and it was mechanically impossible to shift the president, cabinet, and Supreme Court off the stage and whisk them back again for the number with which they immediately followed the love song. So the boy was obliged to fetch his girl, Miss Jones, from the wings and introduce her to the president in song, in the presence of a sizable section of the United States government. "Have You Met Miss Jones?" an engaging number, never achieved popularity outside of New York. Dealers in phonograph records and sheet music throughout the country must, when they buy songs, implacably follow the dictates of the average customer's heart; an embrace, implied or accomplished, is fine for the trade, and so is frustration, as expressed by a slow wrenching apart of persons or by a kind of gay defiance in the face of heartbreak. "Have You Met Miss Jones?" lacking all of these qualities, and suggesting merely a formal acquaintance, left the dealers baffled. "Who is this Miss Jones?" one of them demanded when he was approached with the song. "And why do I want to meet her? Did she do something to somebody?"

Both Richard Rodgers and Lorenz Hart were born into comfortably established middle-class families in New York. Rodgers' father was a doctor, with home and offices on West Eighty-sixth Street, and his mother was a merry, musical woman, who liked to sing and to play the piano. She would sing songs from *The Merry Widow* and *Mlle Modiste*, and when Richard was four he was able to pick out the melodies, by ear, on the piano. Dr. Rodgers didn't play or sing, but he loved music and his house was full of it. During the Doctor's business hours, Richard, temporarily distracted from the piano, ran errands around his father's office, helping with the bandages and iodine, but when the Doctor set out on a round of professional calls, it was Mortimer, Dick's older brother, who was allowed to go along with him and carry his bag while Richard was once more retired to the piano stool in the parlor. His family encouraged him endlessly, as he grew older, to write music, and Richard responded with an enthusiasm that dropped only when they suggested that his music might have some commercial value and that he should leave the home piano long enough to go out and try to get a job composing for money. Mortimer Rodgers, who has never been able to carry a tune, faithfully pursued his father's profession and is now an obstetrician, with offices on Park Avenue. His career is no surprise to his father and mother, but they are occasionally stirred to a slow wonder by Richard, the dreamer.

Dick Rodgers turned out his first song, "My Auto Show Girl," when he was fourteen. In the same year, 1917, Larry Hart was a student at Columbia University and had abandoned his regular course there to study journalism. Rodgers and Hart were not to meet for another two years, and in the meantime Rodgers became precociously active in the amateur-show business. He wrote the music and some of the lyrics for shows put on by the Akron Club, a social organization to which his brother belonged, and for various other benefit performances around town. Between shows he peddled mimeographed copies of his songs to music publishers, one or two of whom listened to a couple of numbers without emotion and then, rising, said, "Thank you very much." This, a courteous phrase, always courteously spoken in the show business and in the song-writing business, is generally a death verdict, and it had a violent and healthy effect upon Rodgers. He entered Columbia University in the fall of 1919 with the determination to write the music for the Varsity Show the next spring. The show was called *Fly with Me,* and Rodgers was the first freshman ever to compose the score of a Columbia Varsity Show. After this achievement he was acclaimed a prodigy by the Columbia faculty and the New York press to such an extent that he never went back to Columbia—partly because he feared an anticlimax, partly because through *Fly with Me*, he had met Lorenz Hart.

Hart, a descendant on his father's side of Heinrich Heine, had grown up on West 119th Street, playing with such boys as Edwin Justus Mayer and Morrie Ryskind, who were both to become playwrights. Larry's father was a promoter, but in spite of the fact that he generally promoted the wrong thing, the Hart household was a lively and a genial one. At Columbia, Larry Hart and Morrie Ryskind entertained themselves by writing verses and passing them around in class, and both became locally famous as versifiers. Although Hart left college in 1918, he was recalled to Columbia to write the lyrics for the Varsity Show for which Dick Rodgers was to compose the music. Another Columbia student who had a hand in its production was Herbert Fields, a son of Lew Fields, the comedian. Herbert Fields knew Larry Hart, and some months before work on the Varsity Show began, he took Rodgers to call at the brownstone house on 119th Street where Hart was at that time gloomily translating German plays and musical comedies into English for the Shuberts. Of that meeting, both Rodgers and Hart say now it was love at first sight. After the considerable triumph of the Varsity Show, they had a small flurry of success on Broadway. Their first professional collaboration was on a song called "Any Old Place with You," which was interpolated in a Lew Fields comedv, *A Lonely Romeo.* The lyric included the lines:

> I'd go to hell for ya
> Or Philadelphia *

and proved that Lorenz Hart was on his way toward stamping out the prevalent June-moon kind of lyric. Next, they

* Used by permission of the Copyright Owners, Remick Music Corp.

wrote the words and music for two more Lew Fields shows and a musical comedy called *Winkle Town,* which was never produced. *Winkle Town* had a song the boys liked, however, and they put it aside for future use; it was called "Manhattan." Their work in those days was signed Herbert Richard Lorenz, in fairness to all three, and for the next eight years Herbert Fields continued to collaborate with them, writing the books for such Rodgers and Hart successes as *Dearest Enemy, The Girl Friend, Peggy-Ann,* and *A Connecticut Yankee.*

In spite of the brief Lew Fields connection, the early 1920's were for Rodgers and Hart mainly a long and futile period of hanging around Broadway. They wrote songs and submitted them to Edward B. Marks, who had published the music written for Lew Fields; when Marks turned them down, they went to see Max Dreyfus, who was then with the T. B. Harms Co. Dreyfus, who had been in the music-publishing business for twenty-five years, told them that they had talent but were too young for the business, and advised them to go somewhere and study. Hart starkly resumed translating plays and musical comedies into English suitable for the Shuberts, and Rodgers went to the Institute of Musical Art to study under Frank Damrosch. Damrosch, George Wedge, and Henry Krehbiel opened up to him a whole new field of music—Wagner, Beethoven, and Debussy—and the young Rodgers travelled passionately, week after week, to concerts at Carnegie Hall. At the end of the year he was chosen, as one of the Institute's most promising pupils, to write the music for its annual show. He speaks of this nowadays with pride, but it is not hard to believe that after a year of listening for the first time to Beethoven and Wagner he was depressed by being asked to write a few catchy melodies for another amateur show.

When Rodgers left the Institute he found once more that, in spite of his success with amateurs, there was nothing for him on Broadway. With Larry Hart, he put on some twenty amateur shows in the next year or two for girls' schools, churches, and synagogues. He lived at home and his father gave him an allowance, but Dick liked to take girls out dancing and, to indulge this mild luxury, borrowed five dollars at a time from a friend, one Earl Katzenstein, until he owed one hundred and five dollars. In something of a panic, he went to his friend's office and said, "I'm through trying to get anywhere in music. I want a job." Mr. Katzenstein led him across the hall to a Mr. Marvin, engaged in the children's-underwear business. Marvin wanted to retire in a few years and was looking for a young man he could train to succeed him; he was impressed with Dick's appearance and by the fact that he had gone to college, and offered him fifty dollars a week on the spot. It was a swift solution of Dick's financial problem, but, confronted with actually giving up music, he hesitated. He told Mr. Marvin he would let him know the next day and went home for dinner. During dinner he was called to the telephone by Benjamin Kaye, whom he had come to know during his amateur career. Mr. Kaye was a lawyer who wrote sketches and plays in his spare time, and he now told Rodgers with some excitement that the Theatre Guild needed some new tapestries and was planning to put on a small amateur show Sunday nights, and matinees, maybe, to pay for them. How would Dick, he asked, like to write the music for it? "Positively no," said Rodgers. "No more amateur shows for me." Kaye explained that it wasn't exactly amateur, that most of the cast would be Theatre Guild understudies, and then he went on to speak familiarly of "Terry" Helburn. The thought that if he did the show he might meet Miss Theresa Helburn, a director of the Theatre Guild, decided Rodgers. "But," he said, "I'll have to have Larry Hart to write the lyrics." Hart, with the money he had earned from translations, had gone into the producing business with two fairly spectacular failures: one a play starring Vera Gordon, and another chiefly notable because Tom Powers and the late Clare Eames were the only people in the cast. The Guild had tentatively hired another lyricist, but after some maneuvering Hart was engaged to collaborate with Rodgers on the Junior Guild show, which was called *The Garrick Gaieties. The Garrick Gaieties* opened on a Sunday night in May, 1925, to the hosannas of public and critics, and soon became a riot at the

Garrick Theatre, with nightly performances and two matinees a week. People went around humming "Sentimental Me" and the song the boys had saved from *Winkle Town*:

> We'll have Manhattan,
> The Bronx, and Staten
> Island too . . .*

Bidding for the publication rights to the score became noisy among music publishers, and the Edward B. Marks Music Co. got the job. *The Garrick Gaieties* played two hundred and fourteen performances on Broadway; its second edition, a year later, played one hundred and seventy-nine.

One night years afterward when Dick Rodgers and Larry Hart attended one of the Theatre Guild's stately first nights, Larry nudged Dick and murmured, "See those tapestries? *We're* responsible for them." "Hell," said Rodgers, "they're responsible for *us*."

A few years later, when the Theatre Guild had all but succumbed to its own stateliness, it was Rodgers who helped to pull it back to prosperity with *Oklahoma!* the Guild production that he wrote in collaboration with Oscar Hammerstein II.

On the afternoon in 1919 when Herbert Fields took Rodgers to the brownstone house where Hart lived on the upper West Side, Fields pushed the doorbell and Rodgers waited, smoothing his tie a little and adjusting the brim of his hat. He was a smooth dresser even then, at the age of sixteen, and he was unprepared for the vision that greeted him when Hart opened the door. Mr. Hart, also a very young man, was wearing an undershirt, a checked jacket, dress trousers, and carpet slippers. However, when he led his guests into the parlor and started talking about lyrics, Rodgers, who had written several songs without any cash profit, forgot his host's unusual appearance and listened devoutly. Hart had not sold

* Copyright Edward B. Marks Music Corporation, RCA Building, Radio City, New York. Used by Permission.

any lyrics at that time, but he spoke freely of such mysteries as exterior and interior rhymes, and male and female rhymes. A male rhyme is generally exterior and accents the ultimate syllable, a female rhyme accents the penultimate syllable and is usually interior, and both are illustrated by the lyric of a song Rodgers and Hart were to write some time later:

> Thou swell! thou witty! thou sweet! thou grand!
> Would'st kiss me pretty? Would'st hold my hand?
> Both thine eyes are cute too; what they do to me.
> Hear me holler I choose a
> Sweet lollapaloosa
> In thee. . . .*

Here, the first two lines are male and exterior, the fourth and fifth female and interior. Hart says nowadays that he has never known much about such things. He has never studied versification, he will tell you, and he has always rejected rhyming dictionaries with the comment that it is more trouble to look up a rhyme than to think up one. Occasionally stirred to some heat by people who try to make a scholar out of him, Larry will wave his cigar dangerously, pull at his explosively patterned necktie, and yell, "Why, I don't even know what onomatopoeia is, or a trope!"

Rodgers and Hart have come to be regarded in their profession as musical dramatists rather than as songwriters. The radio and the phonograph long ago proved equally disastrous to the sale of sheet music and to composers who could turn out single ballads suitable to the sheet-music counters but who were not trained to write an entire score. With a few freakish exceptions such as the "Mairzy Doats" song (a number written by a couple of other fellows that Rodgers, incidentally, liked so much that he went around happily interpreting it to anybody who hadn't yet caught on) most song hits now come from musical comedies or moving pictures, and since *The Garrick Gaieties* Rodgers and Hart have been identified with the theater and with Hollywood. One of their specialties is musical dialogue, which they brought to perfection in *I Mar-*

* Used by permission of the Copyright Owners, Harms, Inc.

ried an Angel, in 1938. In one scene, for example, the Angel said to a visiting sister angel:

> Excuse my lack of hospitality.
> Won't you—sit down? *

The dialogue that followed was spoken in a conversational tone to an engaging and allusive musical accompaniment, and it drifted into song only when a plump angel with overtones of a blonde cutie melodiously referred to her archangelic beau:

> Beauty is truth, truth beauty
> Gabriel, blow your rootie tootie! *

Faithful to their belief that a musical comedy should be as well constructed as a straight drama, Rodgers and Hart also like their songs centered around a situation in the plot. In the fifteen shows for which they wrote the music and lyrics in the five years following *The Garrick Gaieties*—including *Dearest Enemy, The Girl Friend, A Connecticut Yankee, Spring Is Here,* and *Heads Up*—they were seldom able to achieve this ideal; most authors of musical-comedy books and most producers had a theory that any sentence implying the presence of the moon, the month of June, or a feeling of frustration was a sufficient cue for a boy and a girl to walk into a spotlight and sing about love. When Rodgers and Hart wrote the book for *On Your Toes,* with the assistance of George Abbott, they came nearer to a reasonable combination of plot and song, but it was not until the two alone wrote the book, music, and lyrics of *Babes in Arms,* in 1937, that they were able to turn out a show in which, as they like to recall, every number was a "plot" number, including the hit song, "The Lady Is a Tramp." Audiences in general, pleased by the song and by the way Mitzi Green sang it, did not think of it as a "plot" song, but Larry and Dick felt that Mitzi had roamed through the play long enough without any explanation, and they are convinced that audiences would have been confused about her if she hadn't sung the song.

---

* Used by permission of Richard Rodgers.

Rodgers and Hart wrote "The Lady Is a Tramp" in one day, when they decided that *Babes in Arms* needed it. Another time, they wrote "Ten Cents a Dance" in less than two hours, and they completed the score for *I'd Rather Be Right* in three weeks. Perhaps the fastest long distance work they ever did was in connection with a Bing Crosby picture, *Mississippi*, several years ago. They finished the score of *Mississippi* on the Coast, and came East to start work on *Babes in Arms*, arriving in New York slightly in advance of a telegram from Paramount frenziedly announcing that the picture needed another song for Crosby right away. Rodgers and Hart turned out the song the day they got the telegram, but then they hesitated. "If we send the manuscript," Hart said, "somebody out there will play it and sing it the way we don't want it." Rodgers said, "If we send a record, they'll play it in some executive's office with the doors banging and the telephones ringing and nobody paying any attention." For a moment the two were baffled by the hellish intricacies of Hollywood art, but at length they brightened and sauntered over to the Paramount Studios on Broadway. With Rodgers at the piano and a radio singer to give the number the sales quality that the composer's small singing voice could never have instilled into it, they made a sound film and rushed it, special delivery airmail, to Hollywood, where they knew that Crosby and the Paramount producers would have no way of hearing it except in the hushed darkness of a projection room. The song, "It's Easy to Remember," was remembered by a good many people after *Mississippi* was forgotten.

Rodgers, the composer, is more methodical in his work and calmer in his attitude toward it than Hart, the lyric writer. He starts about eleven in the morning. If the collaborators have arranged to work that day in Rodgers' apartment, he puts in a series of telephone calls to Hart, beginning around ten o'clock. Mary, the Negro maid in the Hart household, answers these calls and dutifully rouses her employer, who goes back to sleep again like a little child. Mary is a patient woman up to a certain point, when she becomes picturesque. Once after the third or fourth telephone call, she was heard to slam down the receiver and yell heartily into the bedroom, "Mr. Larry, it's goddam time to get the hell *up*!" Most nights there is an impromptu party at Larry's, with old friends pounding the piano, shouting songs, and screaming amiably at each other. Mrs. Frieda Hart, Larry's mother, mingles happily with the guests on these occasions until she feels sleepy, and then goes quietly to bed. Late one evening Dorothy Rodgers, Richard's wife, went into Mrs. Hart's room to say good night and found her in bed, reading. "Doesn't that noise in the living room ever bother you?" Mrs. Rodgers inquired sympathetically. Mrs. Hart shook her head and smiled. "No," she said, "it has never bothered me." She reflected a moment, and added gently, "Except, maybe, that night Paul Whiteman's band came in."

Whatever revelry enlivens the evening, Larry Hart generally begins work the next morning while he is dressing, sorting out the crumpled fragments of paper which his mother periodically removes from his coat pockets and places on his bureau. These contain lyrics written the day before, or perhaps a week earlier, and the probability is that Larry has composed them in a traffic jam, or in a Turkish bath, or while waiting for an elevator somewhere. Those that he likes on reading them over go back into the pockets of whatever suit he puts on before setting forth for a day's toil at the Rodgers apartment. By the time he arrives, Rodgers may have polished up one of the songs for the show they are working on, or he may have decided whether another should be written in three-four, four-four, or six-eight time to fit a certain situation. If Hart bursts in with a totally different idea about the same situation, there is no friction between them; that, they point out, is where collaboration comes in. When they have roughly completed the score they separate until the show is ready to go into rehearsal, and their collaboration then becomes, for each man, a matter of grim and solitary labor. Hart takes the first version of the book and lyrics and goes to Atlantic City, the Shangri-La of most authors and playwrights. Rodgers puts on a torn, brown sweater buttoned up the front, to which he has become attached, and shuts himself in his study to write the music. Several copies of the original manuscript are made after the show is in its final form; one goes to Robert Russell Bennett or to Hans Spialek (a volatile Czechoslovakian known to the boys as the Bouncing Czech), who orchestrates it for the show; another is sent to the Rodgers and Hart publishers, Chappell & Co., where one "Doc" Szirmai simplifies it for sheet music; and a third goes to the American Society of Composers, Authors and Publishers, for eventual release to the public, and to radio, night-club, and other orchestras. Arrangements for popular orchestras are approved by Rodgers before release, but this is a fairly hollow gesture. With the growth of individualism among orchestra leaders, any successful dance orchestra has come to be known as a "name band," and the melody it offers is increasingly less important than the manner in which the leader swings it, or "schmalzes" it. Benny Goodman, Guy Lombardo, and Wayne King, for instance, play the same tune so differently that it has little relation to what the composer had in mind, and their respective fans worship the maestro rather than the music. Featured singers with name bands also have their individual ways of kicking a song around. Rodgers, a patient man, says that a composer can do nothing about any of this unless he goes into the music publishing business himself and puts out, say, an album of his music played and sung the way it was written. If the public likes the album, he claims, they won't care much for the radio deviations.

A year or so ago Rodgers went into the music publishing business in partnership with Max Dreyfus and Oscar Hammerstein II. The firm, with offices in Rockefeller Center, is called the Williamson Company, Inc. because both Rodgers and Hammerstein are sons of men named William. The Williamson Company's first product was the sheet music of *Oklahoma!* which has also been recorded by Decca with the original company, exactly the way the composer intended. The *Oklahoma!* album of records has sold about 500,000 copies so far, and what pleases Rodgers most about this phenomenon is the knowledge that the half-million people who own the album and play it probably accept it as the best rendition of the songs in the show, and will therefore string along with the composer in sneering at any radio maestro, crooner, or female sobber who tries to make improvements.

Larry Hart had no part in writing *Oklahoma!* but with a team like Rodgers and Hart, one member can disappear for a while without splitting the act. As Hart once said in answer to a frown from Rodgers when he returned from some vague journey or other, "Did Gilbert bawl out Sullivan for giving him the slip and writing 'Onward, Christian Soldiers'?" Larry wrote no hymns and he was often in California or Mexico when Rodgers needed him in New York, but he always turned up in time to write the lyrics that helped to make Rodgers-and-Hart part of the American language.

The long life of Rodgers and Hart songs, and the fact that they continually put out new ones, helped to establish them in the AA class of song writers with the American Society of Composers, Authors and Publishers. AA writers and composers in the Society include Jerome Kern, Cole Porter, Ira Gershwin, and other men who are known in the trade as "smart" song writers, meaning that their work is subtle enough to please the carriage trade and sufficiently engaging to satisfy everybody. The ASCAP grading (from AA to D) is based on the popularity and lifetime of a tune and on the money it has earned, which makes Irving Berlin, though he is not a polysyllabic song writer, an AA member; the late George Gershwin is still listed in the AA class and will remain there as long as his music is played. Proprietors who engage dance orchestras must pay ASCAP from $30 to $2,400 a year—depending on whether the orchestra is a piano, a fiddle, and a saxophone in a beer joint or a name band in a fashionable café—for the privilege of playing numbers written by ASCAP members. At the end of the year, the Society adds up the fees earned by each member and after deducting its own expenses, sends half of the remainder to the composers and authors, half to the publishers. Rodgers and Hart's annual income from ASCAP is about $20,000 apiece. Besides this they get six cents on every copy of their sheet music sold and fifty per cent of the royalties on phonograph records. When they collaborate with one or more authors on a show, their combined royalty is six per cent of the gross box-office receipts—a smaller percentage than they receive for writing an entire show; six per cent is frequently adequate, however, as in the case of *By Jupiter*, which took in $24,000 during Holy Week, when nobody, allegedly, goes to the theater. Moving-picture companies pay Rodgers and Hart from $50,000 to $60,000 to write the music and lyrics for a film, generally over a period of five weeks. All money paid to them jointly is divided on a fifty-fifty basis; there has never been a written contract between them.

One of Rodgers and Hart's biggest song hits was kicked about for a long time through the whims of a Hollywood producer who saw no merit in it. Metro-Goldwyn-Mayer signed Rodgers and Hart in 1934 to write the score for a Jean Harlow picture. One song, "Oh, Lord, Why Won't You Make Me a Star?," was yanked out of the picture at the last minute; Hart thought up a new title, "The Bad in Every Man," and Metro tried it in another film. Once more it was quietly removed when the rushes were shown. Back in New York, Rodgers and Hart could do nothing with the song through Harms, Inc., who at that time published their work, because, good or bad, the song belonged to Metro-Goldwyn-Mayer. Always reluctant to let any number of theirs gather dust, Rodgers and Hart took it to the New York office of Jack Robbins, music publisher for Metro. Mr. Robbins listened and spoke. "Boys," he said, "you've got a beautiful melody there, and I have faith in your song. But boys, boys, give me a title! Something with romance," he pleaded, adding, after a moment's reverie, "like 'The Blue Hour,' maybe, or 'The Hour of Parting.'" Next day the boys came back with the title, "Blue Moon;" Robbins published it as a popular number unrelated to any stage show or movie, and it sold 175,000 copies —their largest sheet-music sale to date.

Auditions for a Rodgers and Hart show generally start while Larry Hart is still at work on the first act. Rodgers attends every audition and he will listen to almost anybody who shows even the first stirrings of talent or personality, but he suffers on these occasions, chiefly because it is his task to say at the end of every number, no matter how deplorable,

"Thank you very much"—that polite and fatal phrase which so frequently shattered him in his own early days of trying to sell songs. Sometimes an aspiring act turns out to be so painful that its conclusion leaves Rodgers in a kind of coma, in which he can only grasp at George Abbott, or whoever happens to be sitting next to him, and mutter, "Say something nice, for God's sake." Mr. Abbott, or whoever, then raises his voice toward the stage and says clearly, "Thank you very much." Boys and girls trying out for the chorus are observed with particular care, since all of the principal roles in Rodgers and Hart shows are understudied by the chorus; Rodgers once saw a performance of *On Your Toes* played entirely by members of the ensemble, and he says it was fine. A chorus daisy who had danced in *Higher and Higher* and understudied a specialty dancer in *By Jupiter* turned up at the auditions for *A Connecticut Yankee* last Spring, and Rodgers gave her a part in the show. "You know who she is?" he says, beaming. "Vera dash Ellen!" To anyone who does not immediately recognize Vera-Ellen's name, Rodgers adds casually, "She just signed a contract with Goldwyn for a thousand bucks a week." Like most good showmen, Rodgers likes to see people, including himself, get ahead in the theater. After a couple of ex-officio passes at the producing business in collaboration with Dwight Wiman and George Abbott, in *By Jupiter* and *Best Foot Forward*, he became a full producer with the revival of *A Connecticut Yankee* this year. When anxious friends inquire why he wanted to add the headaches of a producer to those of a composer, Rodgers replies simply, "Look, when I had a producer we used to have to call conferences to decide every little question. Now that I'm the producer I just call a quick conference with myself and the whole thing's decided. It's simpler."

At rehearsals, Rodgers and Hart are quiet or waggish, according to the pressure or comparative relief from the strain which naturally devours them. One time during rehearsal, a leading man announced his decision that the second act was a disaster to which he declined to lend his presence. "You know why, don't you?" Rodgers said to Hart after the actor had passed by with a fearful frown. "He's only got one number in the second act." Hart was reminded of the story about another actor, who, receiving his part, weighed it in his hand and, finding that his arm sagged beneath its burden, exclaimed, "Ah! An excellent play!" At their own opening nights the false calm which traditionally supports authors, composers, and members of the cast during rehearsals and tryouts temporarily deserts Rodgers and Hart. Rodgers sits with his wife in the last row, on the aisle, so that he can get out into the stage-door alley when the tension threatens to tear him apart. Hart wanders around the lobby in a frenzy; if the show seems to be getting across, he rubs his hands together and passes them wildly over his head, his arms, even his back. Of this habit Rodgers says, "Success starts his blood circulating again, and he begins to itch all over."

Rodgers, an educated and honest musician, goes habitually to the opera and to concerts, and his appearance in the front row at Carnegie Hall is generally a signal for the musicians, who have been tuning up their instruments and glancing idly over the audience, to drop briefly what they are doing and come down to the footlights to shake hands with him. Musicians who are good enough to play in symphony orchestras can play any kind of music, and many have often worked between concert seasons in the orchestra pit at Rodgers and Hart shows. At least once, however, a remark from a long-haired musician has shaken Rodgers to the core. Four years ago he rather tremulously conducted the orchestra of the Metropolitan Opera Company in the first rehearsal of his ballet, *Ghost Town,* which was later presented at the Met, with Rodgers conducting. At the end of the rehearsal the Met's first trumpet stared gloomily at Rodgers and shook his head. "From you I expected hot licks," he said.

Another connection between Rodgers and Hart and the more intellectual realms of entertainment is George Balanchine, former ballet director for the Metropolitan, who has staged all of the Rodgers and Hart ballets since "Slaughter on Tenth Avenue," Ray Bolger's memorable dance in *On Your Toes.* The boys, however, have a knack of mingling their artistic and popular achievements so that the result is pleasing to all customers. The orchestras assembled by Rodgers often include swing harpists and other interesting compromises, and one of the most ambitious Rodgers and Hart numbers, "All Points West," introduced at a Paul Whiteman concert in December, 1936, later became a feature of Rudy Vallee's floor show on the Astor Roof. Mrs. Rodgers suggested the title "All Points West" to her husband, in return for the name he had given her for the profitable business she conducts: Repairs, Inc. Under the direction of Mrs. Rodgers, a slight and graceful blonde, Repairs, Inc., mends everything it is possible for the human hand, the elements, or time itself to break.

No successful song writer can long escape public insinuations that his tunes sound like somebody else's. Some years ago, Gilbert Gabriel, reviewing *Dearest Enemy,* with music and lyrics by Rodgers and Hart, wrote that the song "Here in My Arms" strikingly resembled the Negro spiritual "Nobody Knows de Trouble I Seen." Later another purist remarked that "Where or When," from *Babes in Arms,* was remarkably like certain passages in *La Bohème,* and only a few months ago Walter Winchell nagged Rodgers in his column about the resemblance of some tune to some other tune or other. Both Rodgers and Hart are more interested than distressed by such accusations. They are apt to point out, in the happy discussion that follows, that the army bugle call for assembly is extremely suggestive of the "Ride of the Valkyries" in Wagner's *Ring,* but mostly they are content to explain to skeptics how easy it is for any song writer who wants to write songs the easiest way to think up a melody without treading on sacred ground.

Their favorite method of explanation is the telephone stunt, which consists of asking the heckler's telephone number and then, substituting the note C for 1, D for 2, and so on, rapidly transposing it into a tune. The telephone stunt can be elaborated, for purposes of relaxation, by using the letters of the exchange as well, taking them from the number with which they appear on the dial. The telephone number that has sometimes engaged Rodgers and Hart in their hours of ease is Sp 7-3100 (Police Headquarters), which turns out to be a waltz.

10

The Squarest Little Shooter on Vesey Street:

OSCAR HAMMERSTEIN II

ANY MAN who writes the lyrics of popular songs is generally a forgotten man as far as the public is concerned. People speak of Jerome Kern's "Ol' Man River," "Who?" and "The Last Time I Saw Paris," and they may go on to talk knowledgeably about Rudolf Friml's "Rose Marie" and "Indian Love Call," or Sigmund Romberg's "One Alone" and "When I Grow Too Old to Dream." Hummers of these familiar tunes can usually tell you who wrote the music, but if you ask them who wrote the words, they are apt to look blank. Oscar Hammerstein II wrote the words of all those songs, and has written, or collaborated on, the lyrics of some 1,000 others and on the books and lyrics of forty musical comedies, including *Sunny, Rose Marie, Show Boat, The Desert Song, Music in the Air, Oklahoma!* and *Carmen Jones,* his Negro adaptation of Bizet's opera. Hammerstein is calm about the anonymous lot of librettists. He says that the boys who write the books and lyrics get their rewards sooner or later, although sometimes in a backhanded way. "Take Puccini's librettists," he once said to an interviewer. "Puccini wrote his three most famous operas, *La Bohème, La Tosca,* and *Madama Butterfly* with the same team of librettists. Whenever he changed librettists, his operas didn't do so well." The interviewer, with pencil poised, asked Hammerstein the names of the two librettists who wrote *La Bohème, La Tosca,* and *Madama Butterfly,* and Hammerstein smiled and shrugged. "Who knows?" he said.

It turns out that the two librettists who wrote *La Bohème, La Tosca,* and *Madama Butterfly* were Giuseppe Giacosa and

Luigi Illica, a couple of writers whose names have remained obscure to an interesting degree.

In spite of the number of familiar songs and shows Hammerstein had written before he became famous as the author of the two concurrent sensations, *Oklahoma!* and *Carmen Jones,* the ten years immediately preceding 1943 were, for him, a decade of dismal failure. In one of the slumps that sometimes afflict people in the show business he kept turning out the book and lyrics of one crashing flop after another. He is not a man easily frightened by failure or dizzied by success. Last Christmas, when both *Oklahoma!* and *Carmen Jones* were selling out from five to eight weeks in advance, *Variety* published its annual holiday issue in which actors, producers, and writers traditionally take space to proclaim their most glorious achievements. Flops are not mentioned in this gala number, which combines the flavors of an Academy Award Dinner, the dedication of a battleship, and Prize Day at N.Y.U. Among last year's expansive tributes to Billy Rose, George Jessel, and others, from themselves, Hammerstein's contribution covered a modest quarter-page and read as follows:

Holiday Greetings

Oscar Hammerstein II
author of

Sunny River
(Six weeks at the St. James Theatre, N. Y.)

Very Warm for May
(Seven weeks at the Alvin Theatre, N. Y.)

Three Sisters
(Six weeks at the Drury Lane, London)

Ball at the Savoy
(Five weeks at the Drury Lane, London)

Free for All
(Three weeks at the Manhattan Theatre, N. Y.)

I've Done It Before and I Can Do It Again.

After this desolate record, Hammerstein was not greatly in demand as a collaborator, and he turned to writing *Carmen Jones,* a notion which had occurred to him several years earlier at a performance of Bizet's *Carmen* in the Hollywood Bowl. The opera was sung in French, as usual, and in that vast place nobody could hear a word of the lyrics. Hammerstein, mentally putting himself in the place of a man who had never heard *Carmen,* discovered that the music alone pretty well told the story, and decided that this fact ought to give the opera a universal appeal. He already had, at that time, a passionate concern for lyrics that could be understood by a middling-bright audience—a scruple dating from his first experience of *Tristan und Isolde,* in German, which he had attended at the Metropolitan when he was fifteen. He still describes indignantly the effect this performance had on him. "Here's Tristan propped up against a tree, in pretty bad shape," he says. "He sits up and sings a song and then falls back again, dying. Pretty soon some friend of his comes along, grabs him by the shoulder and shakes hell out of the poor guy. Then in comes a man with a horn and plays it right in his ear, but loud, and all this time the poor fella is just trying to die." Hammerstein pauses here, shakes his head, and continues. "The first time I saw that, I thought it was just silly. Then I discovered that this was really a beautiful musical situation; they're trying to keep him alive long enough to see his love, Isolde, who's on the way back to him. But how are you going to know that if you don't understand the words? Unless you want to cram away at a libretto every time you go out for an evening's entertainment." Hammerstein knows opera as well as the next one, but he is a showman at heart and his convictions are pretty well expressed by a remark he made not long ago. "Four hours of beautiful music alone isn't worth as much as four hours of beautiful music when you can understand the words," he said.

Hammerstein wrote *Carmen Jones* on speculation—an unheard-of thing for a librettist who had always worked on assignment and under contract to a producer. Several producers, including Max Gordon, rejected *Carmen Jones* before Billy Rose, the gold-smeller, agreed to produce it. The box-office receipts during its first week at the Broadway Theatre were forty thousand dollars, and they have steadily improved. According to expert opinion, *Carmen Jones* will probably be another *Porgy and Bess*, revived from time to time, forever.

Searching for the American equivalent of Bizet's Spanish gypsies, Hammerstein decided that the American Negro most completely approximated the gypsy's grace, fire, responsiveness, and humor, and he was happily confirmed by the ease with which songs like the *Habanera* lent themselves to lyrics in Negro dialect. The *Habanera,* in French, contains the lines:

L'amour est un oiseau rebelle
Que nul ne peut apprivoiser,
Et c'est bien en vain qu'on l'appelle
S'il lui convient de refuser. . . .

In *Carmen Jones,* Hammerstein's words to the same tune are:

Love's a baby dat grows up wild
An' he won' do what you want him to,
Love ain' nobody's angel chile
An' he won' pay any mind to you. . . .*

In the course of his research, Hammerstein looked up the standard English translation of *Carmen,* which has been offered on many an opera stage, and it gave him a real jolt. He found, for instance, that the opening scene, in English, goes like this:

What a hustling, what a bustling,
  on the square everywhere,
Oh, what a sight these people are,
Oh, what a sight these people are,
Oh, what a sight,
Oh, what a sight,
Oh, what a sight,
Oh, what a sight,
Oh, what a sight,
Oh, what a sight,
Oh, what a sight these people are!

After a careful reading of this work, Hammerstein changed the scene from Hustle-Bustle Square to the outside of a parachute factory, and, keeping the Bizet music intact, he wrote the following version of "Oh, What a Sight These People Are":

Send along anudder load, an' win dat war, win dat war,
Send along anudder load, an' win dat war, win dat war,
One more to go, and den one more,
One more to go, and den one more,
One more to go, one more to go,
Send 'em along anudder load! *

The only musical change Hammerstein made in adapting *Carmen Jones* from *Carmen* was to cut out the recitatives. Most recitatives, as everybody knows, are makeshifts designed to get a character in an opera upstairs or downstairs, or in and out of a door, when the composer doesn't feel like writing any important music about these moves. Hammerstein, talking about this device, raises his voice unmusically in a perfect recitative. "I-think-I'll-go-upstairs-and-get-a-bicarbonate-of-so-o-da," he will sing, on two notes. Quite often, when he has been talking about his dream of opera translated into intelligible English, he *does* go upstairs in his duplex apartment on East 61st Street and get a bicarbonate of soda. He feels, deeply, that any great music that has words to it ought to have words that can match the music.

While Hammerstein, forlorn and angry, was working on *Carmen Jones,* Richard Rodgers, of Rodgers and Hart, was having his own troubles a few blocks away. The Theatre Guild had got the idea of making a musical comedy out of Lynn Riggs's *Green Grow the Lilacs,* and they had asked Rodgers and Hart to write the words and music for it. Rodgers agreed to write the score and undertook to find Hart, a darting and elusive character, who—it turned out—had gone to Mexico. After Rodgers had tried to get Hart home via letters, telegrams, and telephone, and Hart had declined through the same channels, Rodgers rather sadly asked Hammerstein, whom he knew casually, to collaborate with him on the Guild show. The Guild's production of *Green Grow the Lilacs* was then known as *Away We Go!* Nobody connected with it remembers who first thought of calling it *Oklahoma!*

Richard Rodgers, the victim of a twenty-four-year-old headache from an eccentric partner whom he loved, speaks of Hammerstein as a collaborator the way a man might talk about an angel from heaven. After twenty-four years with Hart, Rodgers thought his eyes had betrayed him when Hammerstein calmly walked in with a lyric on time, and even before it was due. "Oscar wrote nearly all the lyrics for *Oklahoma!* before I wrote the music," Rodgers will tell you. Hammerstein says that a good many of his lyrics were inspired by the Lynn Riggs play. For instance, the stage directions in the opening scene of *Green Grow the Lilacs* read, "It is a radiant summer morning . . . the kind of morning which, enveloping the shapes of earth, men, cattle in a meadow, blades of the young corn, streams—makes them seem to exist now for the first time, their images giving off a visible and golden emanation. . . ." Hammerstein condensed this description into the lyric beginning "There's a bright golden haze on the meadow," and called the song "Oh, What a Beautiful Mornin'." In another passage in the Riggs play Curley, the hero, asked his girl to go for a ride in a "bran' new surrey with fringe on the top." Hammerstein and Rodgers agreed one day that there ought to be a song in *Oklahoma!* about this surrey. Hammerstein then went home to his house in Doylestown, Pennsylvania, and Rodgers, in *his* house in Fairfield, Connecticut, spent the evening working on the song. He had written the beginning and the end, to the rhythm of a carriage-wheel turning over and over and over *and* over, but he was stuck for the middle part when Hammerstein wheeled in next day with the lyrics, including a middle verse which gave Rodgers the meter he needed to complete the tune. The middle part, as everybody knows by now, goes:

> The wheels are yeller, the upholstery's brown,
> The dashboard's genuine leather,
> With isinglass curtains you can roll right down,
> In case there's a change in the weather. . . .*

* Copyright MCMXLIII by Williamson Music Inc., New York.

Rodgers says that words like that are easy to write music to. Hammerstein's lyrics are always so lilting, in fact, that tunes of his own go through his head as he writes them, and he usually hums these tunes to composers to illustrate the meter when he delivers his completed lyrics. Composers unite in saying affectionately that Oscar's tunes are terrible.

The surrey song, "I Cain't Say No," "Kansas City," and "People Will Say" are the only *Oklahoma!* numbers for which Rodgers wrote, or partly wrote, the music before Hammerstein wrote the words. According to Hammerstein and Rodgers a love song always comes out better if the music is written first and the words fitted to it later. The boys don't know exactly why this is true, but they think it may have something to do with music being the language of love.

Hammerstein, the lyricist of love, humor, skepticism, bereavement, rage, dreaminess, contentment, and almost every other human emotion, is a big man with a rugged face, a quick, brilliant smile, a likeable manner, and an angelic reputation in show business. Theater people talk with such feeling about his modesty, sweet disposition, honesty, and thoughtfulness, that even strangers who have never met him sometimes find themselves thinking of him as a lovable character, a little like Skippy's pal in the comic strip, of whom Skippy keeps saying "There goes the squarest little shooter on Vesey Street." Besides Hammerstein's other admirable qualities, he has a trait that amounts to flash news in the show business; he is well-adjusted. His friends and colleagues will tell you that he is a well-adjusted man, and when they make this announcement, they rear back and look amazed. In the show business, where the ganglia quiver and the nerve-ends writhe, a well-adjusted man is a minor miracle.

Hammerstein does not share the general awe about his good self-adjustment. If anybody calls him well-adjusted to his face, he takes it in a well-adjusted way, without bowing. Sometimes, however, he is bothered by his reputation of being a lovely fellow. He once grabbed a press agent who was fashioning garlands for him, and backed him into a chair. "Listen," he said, towering over him, "if you want to know what kind of a guy I am, I once stole a radish from a blind man, see?" Hammerstein *did* once steal a radish from a blind man. At a dinner, he was seated next to a blind composer who had a radish on his butter plate, and apparently didn't know it. Hammerstein sneaked the radish and ate it, and he has felt pretty bad about it ever since.

When Hammerstein deliberately courted obscurity by becoming a lyric-writer and librettist, he already had one strike against him in the theater. He was a grandson of Oscar Hammerstein, the famous impresario of the nineties and early 1900's. A celebrated theatrical name is often an advantage to actors, but to children born into the business end of the theater it can be a handicap. Inherited glamor is of no use to these descendants of business men, and comparisons with their fathers or grandfathers are apt to be harsh when they are robbed of the softening effect of footlights. Oscar Hammerstein I, the patriarch of the Hammerstein family, was a vivid, imperious figure who wore a top hat and a Vandyke beard, and uttered pungent remarks after the fashion of the time. In 1906, he built and opened the Manhattan Opera House, on West 34th Street, as competition for the Metropolitan. Somebody asked him, then, if there was any money in grand opera, and Hammerstein tilted his top hat, stroked his Vandyke, and replied, "Yes, *my* money is in it." Another time, he wanted to engage Melba to sing at the Manhattan, and she was coy about answering his offers. Hammerstein strode to the door of her hotel suite, and, when it was opened, tossed thirty one-hundred-dollar bills on the floor at her feet. It was a gesture full of the kind of grandeur that became fashionable, some twenty years later, among Hollywood producers. Mme Melba, stumbling through the hundred-dollar bills, sang at Hammerstein's Manhattan Opera House. So, at one time or another, did Nordica, Calvé, Tetrazzini, Mary Garden, and John McCormack.

When Oscar Hammerstein I came from Berlin to New York in 1863, at the age of sixteen, the Northern Army, exiled below the Mason and Dixon Line, was sending desperate appeals home for cigars. Cigar manufacturers had more orders than they could fill, and Oscar got a job as a cigar-maker, at three dollars a week. He had studied music, and it was his real love, but it was the cigar business that made his fortune. While he was rolling cigars by hand, he began to think up ways of making them by machinery. Before long, he invented a suction machine to spread and shape tobacco leaves, a cigar-cutter, a rolling machine, and a heading machine. He took out patents on these devices, many of which are still used in cigar-making. With the money his patents earned, he went into the theatrical business, starting as producer and stage manager of a "Living Pictures" act at Tony Pastor's, and progressing to a partnership in Koster & Bial's, the big vaudeville circuit of that day. A growing friction between Hammerstein and his partners came to a head one night when Hammerstein, sitting in a stage box, hissed one Mlle de Dio, a pet of the Messrs. Koster & Bial, and the partnership broke up in a row soon afterward. Hammerstein sold out his share in the company for $370,000, and built the Olympia Theatre on Broadway at 44th Street. That section of New York was then an unsavory part of town, known as the Thieves' Lair, and Hammerstein is generally credited with having given it a start toward becoming Times Square. The Olympia opened in 1895, with a vaudeville bill featuring Yvette Guilbert and other acts. Later, it became the Criterion Theatre, a famous jinx house whose every offering was doomed. The building was finally torn down, in 1935, and the corner site, which is no longer owned by the Hammersteins, is now occupied by a Whelan drug store.

Oscar Hammerstein I had an optimistic sense of real estate values, and he was so convinced that New York's theatrical district would move even farther uptown than Times Square that he built two theaters in Harlem, the Harlem Opera House and the Columbia Theatre. The Columbia has disappeared, and the Harlem Opera House, is now Proctor's 125th Street, an RKO movie theater. At the Lenox Lyceum, Hammerstein staged one of the first performances in America of *Cavalleria Rusticana,* which landed with a dull thud and was thenceforth bitterly referred to by its impresario as *Cavalleria Busticana.* Hammerstein always felt a great impatience with the music he loved when it failed to appeal to the customers. Once, in a fit of pique with opera in general, he bet a musical director named Gustave Kerker one hundred dollars that he, Hammerstein, could write an opera, including music and libretto, in forty-eight hours. Kerker took the bet, and Hammerstein retired to a room in the Gilsey Hotel on 29th Street to write his opus. Kerker, obeying a natural instinct, hired a hurdy-gurdy to play under Hammerstein's window for the whole forty-eight hours, but in spite of this distraction Hammerstein turned out an opera called *Koh-I-Noor* in the required time. Kerker read it and refused to pay the bet, on the ground that *Koh-I-Noor* was terrible. Hammerstein doggedly produced it at the Harlem Opera House, where it ran one week and did a gross business of four hundred dollars. He never spoke to Kerker again.

Hammerstein's best known theater was the Victoria, which he built and opened, in 1899, on Broadway at 42nd Street. The manager of the Victoria was William Hammerstein, a son of Oscar I, and the father of Oscar II. Willie Hammerstein, as he was known, fought a losing battle against his father's custom of dropping in at the Victoria and taking money out of the box-office till to pay his opera singers uptown, and the whole family early developed a deep distrust of opera. "So *this* is what's ruining us" they would mutter, looking around, on their infrequent visits to the Manhattan or the Columbia. Willie belonged to the younger generation of 1899, and he proceeded to make Hammerstein's Victoria famous in a way that soon earned him the title of the "Barnum of Vaudeville." The Victoria was the first vaudeville house to introduce "freak" acts, consisting of well-known murderers, betrayed ladies, and other interesting tools of fate. Evelyn Nesbitt Thaw was booked at Hammerstein's Victoria before Harry Thaw's gun or Stanford White had cooled off. Flossie Crane, a girl with a split voice, was imported from Coney Island and billed as "The Female Baritone." Along with these ghoulish divertissements, there was plenty of gaiety at the Victoria. Lottie Collins sang "Tarara-Boom-De-Ay" there, Maggie Cline sang "Throw Him Down, McCluskey," Rooney and Bent danced their waltz clogs, and Houdini got himself in and out of baskets for the first time on any stage. Hammerstein's Victoria is now the Rialto Theatre, a movie house specializing in horror pictures.

Oscar Hammerstein I married three times and had four sons by his first marriage and two daughters by his second. His third marriage was childless. His sons were William (the father of Oscar II), Arthur, Harry, and Abe. Arthur became a well-known musical comedy producer, and had a daughter named Elaine Hammerstein, who was a star in silent pictures. Harry and Abe had brief careers in the show business, and both died in 1914—the year that Willie Hammerstein also died. Oscar I lived five years longer, and died in 1919. His daughters were Stella and Rose, home-girls who both married non-professionals.

Oscar Hammerstein II was born, in 1895, in a flat on 125th Street, near his grandfather's house on 120th Street, across from Mount Morris Park. He was the older of two sons, and his brother, Reginald, is now stage manager of the Chicago company of *Oklahoma!* Touring companies of successful shows are often stage-managed by the authors' irritated younger brothers. Oscar went to school at Hamilton Institute in New York, and entered Columbia in the class of 1916. His family wanted him to be a lawyer, and he studied law for one year at Columbia. He gave up the idea of being a lawyer when he began appearing in the Columbia Varsity Shows and discovered the pleasures of acting and writing for the theater. In 1915, he played a poet in the Varsity Show, *On Your Way*, and he was a blackface comedian in the next year's show, *Peace Pirates*, a parody of the Ford Peace Ship written by Herman Mankiewicz, a fellow student. In the 1917 show, *Home, James!* Oscar did a dance in a leopard-skin costume, and also wrote most of the lyrics. One song, "Annie McGinnis Pavlowa," rhymed "Pavlowa" with "put one over," and "back alley" with "bacchanale," and it had a success that gave Oscar a feeling of power. He left Columbia in his first year of law school and travelled downtown to look into the show business.

Hammerstein's grandfather, Oscar I, was busy then, in 1917, writing a new opera designed to make a monkey out of the Metropolitan. Oscar I had sold the Manhattan Opera Company to the Metropolitan in 1910, for $1,200,000, with the stipulation that he stay out of the opera business as a competitor for the next ten years. He spent part of that time building the Lexington Opera House (now Loew's Lexington movie theatre), and it was his aim to compose an opera which he could produce there in 1920, and thereby whisk the customers away from the Metropolitan. He died before his opera was finished, and a year before the agreement expired. Oscar II, casting about for a theater job in 1917, appealed to his uncle, Arthur, who put him to work as assistant stage manager of a musical comedy he was producing, called *You're In Love.* For the next couple of years, Oscar worked as stage manager of his uncle's productions, *Sometime,* a musical starring Ed Wynn, in which Mae West did a shimmy number, and *Tumble Inn,* a show that featured Frank Tinney. He kept on writing lyrics and plots and shoving them at his uncle, and eventually he became lyric-writer and part author of the Arthur Hammerstein shows, *Always You* and *Tickle Me.* In 1920, a song Oscar had written with Herbert Stothart, called "If A Wish Could Make It So," was interpolated into *Tickle Me,* and turned out to be his first hit, selling about a million phonograph records—mainly, Hammerstein says now, because "Whispering" was on the other side of the record. In 1923, he wrote the book and lyrics of *Wildflower* in collaboration with Otto Harbach, who was already famous as the librettist of *Madame Sherry, The Firefly,* and other celebrated operettas. *Wildflower,* with music by Herbert Stothart and Vincent Youmans, had two song hits—the title song and "Bambalina"—and it began an association between Hammerstein and Harbach that resulted, two years later, in the musical comedy, *Rose Marie.*

According to the records of the American Society of Composers, Authors, and Publishers, "Rose Marie, I Love You," the song introduced in that show nineteen years ago, has remained steadily so popular that it was played 3,484 times over the air during the first nine months of 1942. "Indian Love Call," another "standard" number from the show, was played 5,244 times during the same period. The longer a song remains popular the more money it naturally earns. Hammerstein, the lyricist of such durable numbers as "Who?", "Why Do I Love You?", "One Alone," "I Told Every Little Star," "Can't Help Lovin' Dat Man," "Why Was I Born?", "Stouthearted Men," "Lover, Come Back to Me," "All the Things You Are," and the *Oklahoma!* favorites, is a top-ranking, or AA, member of ASCAP and receives an average yearly income of about fifteen thousand dollars in royalties from radio and night-club performances alone. In spite of ASCAP's efficiency in collecting royalties for composers, authors, and publishers from owners of radio stations and night clubs who might otherwise feel free to use anybody's music without paying for it, a long-time private moan of composers and lyricwriters has been the fact that the copyright of a song belongs to its publishers and not to its author and composer. Hammerstein and Rodgers recently solved this problem for themselves by establishing the Williamson Music Publishing Company in partnership with Max Dreyfus, a well known music publisher. As publishers, the two collaborators—with Dreyfus—own their own copyrights and get the full amount of the ASCAP royalties, without having to share them with any publisher. Hammerstein, as author, gets three cents on every copy of sheet-music sold and twenty-five per cent of the royalties from phonograph records; as partner in the firm, he also receives twenty-five per cent of all profits from stock-company performances and radio presentations of the shows he has worked on. His earnings from old numbers, apart from the royalties on any new show he may have written, amount to about $35,000 a year. Up to the end of January, 1944, 1,153,000 copies of *Oklahoma!* sheet-music had been sold, and 225,000 Decca albums of *Oklahoma!* records at five dollars an album. The boys expect the sale of albums to pass half a million by fall. With Rodgers and Lynn Riggs, author of the original play, Hammerstein gets eight per cent of the gross box-office receipts of *Oklahoma!*, which amount to about $30,000 a week. Riggs gets one eighth of this share, and Hammerstein and Rodgers each take half of the rest. Three and a half per cent of $30,000 is $1,050. Taxes being what they are, it isn't as magnificent as income as it sounds, but Hammerstein finds no fault with it. "A man can live on it," he says.

In 1924, Hammerstein went to the funeral of Victor Herbert. In the cemetery, Otto Harbach introduced him to Jerome Kern. This graveyard meeting resulted in *Sunny, Show Boat, Sweet Adeline, Music in the Air,* and *Very Warm for May*—all of which Hammerstein wrote with Kern. Kern, like Hammerstein, is a mild-mannered man, and about the only thing he hates is the word "Cupid." Lyric-writers know that Cupid horning into a lyric will make the usually gentle Kern curse and stamp his feet around. One day, while Hammerstein and Kern were working on *Show Boat,* Kern played a tune he had written for the show, gave it to Oscar, and asked him to write the words. The next day, Hammerstein solemnly handed Kern the following lyrics:

Cupid knows the way,
He's the naked boy
Who can make you sway
To love's own joy;
When he shoots his little ar-row,
He can thrill you to the mar-row. . . .

Kern read this repulsive jingle with horror, but soon became his sunny self when Hammerstein whipped the real lyrics out of his pocket. The real lyrics were:

Why do I love you?
Why do you love me?
How can there be two
Happy as we?
Can you see the why or wherefore
I should be the one you care for? . . .*

The difference between a lyric-writer and a librettist is the difference between the man who writes, say, the words of "Pistol-packin' Mama" and the man who writes the lyrics and dialogue of *Oklahoma!* A librettist is a combined lyric-writer and playwright with an extra headache. He has to create, or adapt, the plot of a show, write the dialogue and lyrics, and "spot" the songs so that they are sung at the right time to explain the plot and keep it moving. Modern librettists and composers plan to show as carefully as an architect plans a

* Copyright MCMXXVII by T. B. Harms Co., New York.

house. Usually, they make out a chart, indicating the kind of song they will need at various points in the show, and including notes like "Act One, Finale, love song," or "Act Two, Scene One, comedy song," and so on. When Hammerstein and Rodgers began work on *Oklahoma!*, they decided to have a love song as the first act finale, and Rodgers wrote the music for it. Hammerstein set about writing the words, and discovered that if Curly and Laurey, the boy and girl, sang a song announcing that they were in love at the end of Act One, it would automatically end the play. Everything after that would be an anticlimax. Hammerstein wrestled with this plot problem for a couple of days before he finally thought up a lyric that left things uncertain between Curly and Laurey, and yet made it plain to the audience that the kids were swooning. The song, a masterpiece of tentative romance, is now familiar to practically everybody. It begins:

> Don't throw bouquets at me,
> Don't please my folks too much,
> Don't laugh at my jokes too much,
> People will say we're in love. . . .*

Unlike his grandfather, the impresario, Hammerstein has no fancy ways about him. He wears simple clothes, gets up at eight-thirty every morning, and has never smoked a cigarette. He starts work at half-past nine every day, and likes to work walking around his study or standing up at a waist-high captain's desk, an eighteenth-century piece given to him by Jerome Kern. Tricks with words depress him, and he seldom uses a rhyming dictionary, but he has a favorite rhyme of his own that has, unfortunately, paralyzed every song he has tried to use it in. It involves the word "veranda," and a version of it appears in "The Folks Who Live on the Hill," a number Hammerstein wrote with Kern for the picture, *High, Wide, and Handsome.* Part of this song goes,

> Our veranda
> Will command a
> View of meadows green. . . .†

"The Folks Who Live on the Hill" has a small following of permanent admirers, but it never attained great popularity or a wide sale, and the same hoodoo pursues every Hammerstein song using the veranda rhyme.

Hammerstein has been married twice. By his first marriage, which ended in divorce, he has two children—William, aged twenty-four, who is now in the Navy, and Alice, twenty-two. By his present wife, who was Dorothy Blanchard, an Australian actress, he has a twelve-year-old son, Jimmy, and two older step-children, Susan and Henry. The Hammersteins, an affectionate and busy family, have a house on East 61st Street in New York and a farm near Doylestown, Pennsylvania. Hammerstein spends his time between the two places, with an occasional trip to Hollywood to work on a picture. In addition to *High, Wide, and Handsome,* he has collaborated on the movies, *Swing High, Swing Low,* and *Show Boat,* and, with Richard Rodgers, on a new film adaptation of *State Fair,* the Phil Stong story in which Will Rogers was starred on the screen several years ago. He is a vice-president and a member of the board of directors of ASCAP, and is chairman of the board of the Music War Committee of the American Theatre Wing. The Committee's purpose is to discover new war songs as good as the songs that were written during the last war. It is uphill work, Hammerstein says, partly because the lifetime of a song is so much shorter now than it was twenty-five years ago. "Over There," for instance, was played on pianos and sung by small groups of people, and it grew famous gradually, by word of mouth. Nowadays, a good war song like "Praise the Lord and Pass the Ammunition" is banged out so unceasingly on the radio that the public gets sick of it in a couple of weeks. The Music War Committee meets every Monday night, listens to songs, and picks out a few to endorse and push toward publication and popularity. Two of its selections are "Prayer for a Soldier" and "Has Hitler Made a Monkey Out of You?", a number warning against the dangers of loose talk. Hammerstein feels that the Music War Committee is doing a fairly important job, as popular music is a potent conveyor of home-front morale and international good will. A man who agrees with him is Serge Koussevitsky.

Not long ago, a New York music critic, lunching with Koussevitsky, was deploring the edgy relations between Russia and the United States, and he suggested that even so comparatively small a gesture as an exchange of native music might help. "Americans love Russian popular music, and we hear plenty of it, from 'O Chichornya' to the Russian war songs. But what have we to give Russia in return?" the critic demanded plaintively. Koussevitsky answered him in a word. "*Oklahoma!*" he said.

Hammerstein, a modest and realistic fellow, does not believe that a Moscow production of *Oklahoma!* would magically make everything all right between Russia and the United States, but it pleases him to have people like Koussevitsky say that the show is a true and heart-warming picture of America. Appreciation from experts is one of the rewards that console a librettist for his obscurity. Hammerstein is grateful for such praise, but he still thinks that his most striking accolade was the one bestowed on him, a few years ago, by a rattlesnake in California. He was walking in the hills near Palm Springs, singing some experimental words to a tune of his own, when the snake suddenly reared up and stared at him from a rock a few feet away. Hammerstein went on singing because he was too terrified to stop, and presently the snake began to sway from side to side, not angrily as though it were getting ready to strike, but dreamily and with a happy look on its face, like a snake charmer's pet. Hammerstein backed all the way down the hill, singing fit to burst, and, the last he saw of the rattlesnake, it was still swaying in time to the words and music, hypnotized as anything.

11

The Boys:

JOHN-FREDERICS

LAST SPRING Miss Dorothy Stickney, the actress who played Mother in *Life with Father* so long that most people expect her to turn up in private life with a jabot and a pug dog, appeared at a cocktail party wearing a hat that instantly became the talk of the town. It looked like a wilderness of flowers with a few hearts and other distractions here and there, and it turned out to be made of glass and tinsel paper.

This creation was the work of Lilly Daché, the only rival milliner who can drive John and Fred of John-Frederics, the deans of the custom millinery business, but *mad.* When John and Fred heard about the furor caused by Miss Stickney's Daché hat, they withdrew into a throbbing silence. "What's good about it?" Fred finally emerged to inquire. "*Our* customers wear our *perfume bottles* for hats." Having spoken, Fred tossed his chin toward his right shoulder, and closed his eyes. He was right about the customers wearing the perfume bottles. Miss Hope Hampton, recently presented with some John-Frederics perfume in a pink-and-blue plastic container shaped like a miniature hat, tied ribbons on the container, knotted them under her chin, and wore the little plastic hat to the opening of some war picture or other. John and Fred admire inspirations like that one, and are brought back reluctantly to the cold aspect of millinery as a business.

Women in the United States spent about three hundred million dollars on hats in 1943. Most of the hats they bought were manufactured in New York City, the center of the wholesale millinery trade. Some were machine-made by wholesale milliners along Houston and Bleecker Streets to sell to chain stores and mail-order houses, which retailed them to customers at one dollar or less. Others were made by hand in the wholesale district occupying the West Thirties and were bought, in department stores mostly, at prices ranging from $3.95 to $15. Up to this point the manufacturer of hats is an anonymous toiler, intent only upon modifying the styles set by fashionable Paris and New York milliners to a standard line of charm that will suit the greatest number of women at prices they can afford. The average woman seldom knows who actually made the hat she is wearing, because its label carries the name not of the manufacturer but of the store where she bought it. Contact between milliner and customer becomes direct and dynamic only in the realm of de luxe millinery, where no woman is average, all are sublime. Milliners in this glossy group are located mostly in the side streets in the Fifties and along Madison Avenue, and cater to a small, wholesale clientele in the fancier department stores, and to retail customers who can afford to pay around thirty-five dollars for a hat. These milliners' names on the label of a hat have come to carry authority, and their hats are referred to gravely by name, like Rolls-Royces. Many a hat, for instance, that at first sight has astounded the beholder has been instantly explained and redeemed by the phrase "It's a John-Frederics."

John-Frederics, Inc., at 29 East 48th Street, is owned by two men, John Harburger and Frederic Hirst (now legally John Frederics and Fred Frederics), who are known to their customers as John and Fred, or sometimes as "the boys." Their wholesale business distributes hats to be sold retail, at thirty-five dollars and upward, to eight hundred and fifty stores throughout the United States; to their retail clientele, the women who buy hats in the shop, John and Fred appear more intimately as custom milliners. A custom milliner is one who makes hats on the customer's head, with a good deal of brooding. Often a woman who thinks she looks pretty fascinating in a John-Frederics model, and orders it without any changes, succumbs at the first fitting to pensive decrees from the boys; for her, the flower must be omitted or the brim rolled a little higher. By such nuances a dozen women are suited with the same hat, and each one looks different from the others in it. John and Fred admit to no such levelheaded plotting, however, preferring to have their customers regard them as comical fellows engaged in the millinery business for the hell of it. They have perfected the repertory instinctive to most men who deal professionally with women's clothes—the patter of frivolous news and outrageous comment, the lightning glance of appreciation at a new dress—and they maintain a careful attitude of irreverence toward their own business. John, trying a hat on a customer, will pause with critical hands uplifted and say, "This hat turns out to have been made for a horse," or, discarding it, "What a pretty thing that might be, sculptured in soap." Recently a jewelled matron who had ordered a hat made from her own sables was fussily insistent on having the sable heads and feet returned to her after the skins had been used. Fred listened to her with characteristic calm, his head tilted back over his right shoulder, his eyelids a little weary; then he handed the sables to a passing attendant. "Here," he sighed, "save the giblets for Madam."

John is a lightly built, dark young man of thirty-odd whose alternate moods impel him to breathless small talk or to vast periods of silence in which he thinks about hats. He wears—generally over a canary-yellow sweater—suits of a misty plaid, or a light gray striped with blue; a square gold ring the size of a woman's wristwatch covers a third of his little finger, and his watch is large and chimes the hours. His effect, which might be loud, is softened by his voice, which is pianissimo. John's birthplace is Munich. His parents brought him to this country when he was six years old, and his speech is authentically American. Fred, who is slightly younger than John, knew no English when he came from Frankfort, Germany, in 1925; he speaks it now with a deliberate drawl and a larger indifference to its fussier rules. "Listen, John," he will implore, when his partner has set out to divert a customer with some colorful tale, "let me tell this. I tell it so lovely." Since the beginning of their partnership, in 1929, Fred, who can turn out a notable hat, has concentrated, however, on the financial side of the business. John, something of a dreamer where figures are concerned, designs the hats. Holding the opinion that hats designed in sketches on paper cannot get the feel of the fabric, he works with fabrics on wooden blocks, or on his customers' heads, and he can create a hat out of almost anything. He has been known, when illustrating some point or other about hats, to whisk a giant bandanna handkerchief from his pocket and twist it around his own head, with a puzzling effect of chic. John's hats are less loony these days than they were when his patronage was smaller, but they can still be identified by a kind of measured insanity of design. Most of the hats Marlene Dietrich and Rosalind Russell wear in pictures are made by John-Frederics. They made Ginger Roger's hats for *Lady in the Dark*, and nearly all of the comical feathered confections used by Ed Wynn on the stage. Joan Crawford bought twenty-seven hats at John-Frederics one morning during a recent visit to New York. Helen Hayes, Katharine Cornell, Mary Martin, Greer Garson, Hildegarde, and Bette Davis buy a good many hats there; so did Mme Litvinoff, who likes fur numbers, and Mme Chiang Kai-Shek, who ordered a hat made of one-hundred-dollar bills to raffle off at a China Relief party. Another prominent customer is Lauritz Melchior, who had his *Tannhäuser* and *Siegfried* costumes made, amid hilarious fittings, by John and Fred.

John Harburger was brought up in the millinery business. His mother was prominent in the trade as Mme Laurel, and owned a prosperous wholesale hat company on Fifth Avenue at Thirty-ninth Street from 1915 until she retired, eight years ago. Mme Laurel's specialty was the sensible structure known as the matron's hat, and her idea, an agreeable one to the tastes of her day, was to get everything onto a hat that it would hold. The boy John began to suspect that his mother was overdoing it one time when a customer brought back a hat which, she complained, didn't fit; investigation revealed that the mountain of fat satin roses with which the hat was trimmed had obscured a medium-sized pair of scissors sewn absentmindedly into the crown. Before his thirteenth year John had begun to hurry from the local public school to his mother's workroom to carry out his own experiments in making hats; he followed Mme Laurel's general construction, which he found good, but left off most of the ornaments and depended upon line for his effects. By the time he was sixteen, he had gained an almost embarrassing popularity with the girls in his class by presenting each of them with a hat of his own creation. His father (general manager of Mme Laurel, Inc.) then stated that no son of his should grow up to be a milliner, and got him a job as floorwalker for a department store in Indianapolis. One day a woman came into the store carrying some parcels and a large paper bag, and when she had gone it was discovered that she had taken one of the newest hats along with her in the paper bag—a black felt trimmed with bowknots of orange wool. That night, in a vaudeville theater where he had bought standing room, John recognized the shoplifter as she came into the theater wearing the hat, brave as anything. He approached her and demanded that she give him the hat, then and there. What she did was to raise her right hand and wham John across the face with a handbag heavily framed in silver filigree. She had eluded his blind grasp and left the theater, still wearing the hat, before the marks of the filigree faded from his cheek. John went from Indianapolis to Philadelphia, where, still thwarted in his desire to make hats, he once more became a floorwalker in the millinery department of a large store. Goaded in his first week by the sight of so many hats around him, he marched off the floor into the workroom one morning and more or less defiantly, created his first important hat. It was a delicate arrangement of chiffon pleats in pale shades of green, and when his employers saw it they agreed to let John abandon floorwalking to become a designer. In less than two years after he had been sent away from home for trying to be a milliner, John's preoccupation and skill with hats had become so celebrated in the trade that he was recalled to New York by his mother, who knew a good milliner when she saw one. He spent the next six years designing hats for Mme Laurel, and on his first trip to Europe to buy fabrics, feathers, and ornaments met Frederic Hirst, who was selling women's hats for a wholesale firm in Frankfort. Fred, the son of a Frenchwoman and a German doctor, who had wanted him to study medicine, was, like John, in the millinery business in spite of everything.

In 1925, Fred arrived in New York, selling suède and leather hats for the Frankfort firm. His reunion with John took on a note of sadness when Fred reluctantly showed the leather hats to his friend. "People seem to wear them," he said tentatively. John shuddered. "You and I could do better," he said. From that time both men worked toward the idea of becoming partners. Fred, gifted with a shrewd business sense, stifled it temporarily in a series of jobs as salesman with wholesale milliners in the Thirties, and later as floorman at Russeks, where he was fired because his manner was so debonair that it threw the customers into a panic. By 1929, he and John had saved and borrowed enough money to go into partnership with a capital of ten thousand dollars, of which each contributed half. In the same year, Mme Mercèdes, whose hat shop opposite the Ritz had for some years catered to a fashionable retail trade, unconsciously obliged them by retiring from business. With an eye upon her late customers, John and Fred decided to ignore the West Thirties and set up a combined wholesale and retail business at an address more inviting to women shoppers. In July, three months before the stock-market crash, they opened John-Frederics in one room over Delman's shoe shop on Madison Avenue in the Fifties.

Hard times never noticeably afflicted John and Fred. Fashions in women's hats in 1929 had reached a stage that was favorable to the custom milliner. The passing of the Tariff Act of 1913, which included the Audubon Society's laws for the protection of rare birds, had prohibited the importation of egret and paradise feathers, and other exotic plumage, into the United States. Deprived of these ornaments, hats became increasingly simpler until, around 1922, they had evolved into that triumph of simplicity, the inverted bowl called the cloche. The cloche hat survived, in one form or another, for a good five years, and that period may be remembered as the time when women, dressed in a kind of uniform of cloche hat and chemise dress, all began to look alike. It was not until the autumn of 1932 that the Eugènie hat, derided in its little day, definitely changed the whole shape and angle of women's hats; but in 1927, with the arrival of the off-the-face hat, women took the first step of coming out from under the cloche. Stimulated by a full view of their features, milliners fell into a frenzy of hat-making, and the custom-made hat, designed to suit the individual face, came into its own. Up-to-date stores installed custom millinery departments, making hats for fifteen dollars, cheaper hat shops, in the West Thirties, began to feature hats made on the head for five or six dollars, and it became a fad with a good many New York women to dash downtown and have a piece of felt rammed on the head and slashed becomingly. By 1929, women, pampered by the constant adjustment of fabrics to their features, were in a frame of mind to appreciate John and Fred. Even the depression contributed, in its own way, to the success of John-Frederics. Soon after the crash, department stores found that their biggest volume of millinery business was coming from cheap hats, costing from $2.95 to $6.95, and wholesale manufacturers, to cater to the sudden demand, turned out cheap hats in such quantities that they came to have little variety in style. A woman who wanted a distinctive hat was obliged to go to a custom milliner for it, and John-Frederics became an increasingly popular place to go.

John and Fred sold three thousand dollars worth of hats on their opening day, chiefly to the May Company, a chain of department stores, whose buyer ordered a hundred hats from the first collection. Soon after the opening, Mrs. Frank Case, who had bought hats from Fred in the wholesale district, arrived and brought Mary Pickford with her. After that, nothing much surprised the boys. Within three months they were employing twenty milliners in their workroom and planning one of their earliest gestures—a collection, in 1930, of "rag" hats, made of remnants of cloth. These hats were largely responsible for the subsequent craze for hats that were scraps of soft, crushable fabric, carelessly pulled on. When, later, John-Frederics brought out a felt hat whose only ornament was an ordinary belt buckle, it was copied to such an extent that buckle manufacturers delivered buckles in freight cars to wholesale milliners all over the country. The fact that John and Fred had cannily required the manufacturers from whom they bought their buckles to pay them a royalty on every buckle sold to other milliners helped considerably to swell the tide of prosperity which has attended them right along. John-Frederics sales now average over half a million dollars a year.

Like most milliners with a gift for creating styles, the boys are more or less resigned to seeing their styles copied. The showing three times a year of the newest John-Frederics collections is closely guarded, though, from possible style pirates; and the casual shopper, if she is a stranger to the place, finds her way to the showroom only through a pretty intricate series of doors and reception clerks.

A few years ago a John-Frederics hat swept the country through circumstances which left its creators entertained but a little bemused. One day Lord & Thomas, the advertising agency which handled the Lucky Strike account, asked John-Frederics to send around an assortment of hats in order to select one to be worn by the professional model in a Lucky Strike advertisement. John and Fred sent the hats, adding at the last moment a brimmed felt, with a long quill thrust through the hatband in front, which had proved to be mildly popular with customers. Lord & Thomas chose the hat with the quill because quills, in a picture of an Indian war bonnet, appear on every package of Lucky Strike, and most people concerned with advertising like to tie up everything with something else. The Lucky Strike ad appeared in colors on the back covers of magazines and within a week the American Tobacco Company, maker of Lucky Strikes, was bombarded by hundreds of telephone calls daily from milliners everywhere, wanting to know whether the design of the hat was registered. When they found that it was, a good many of them copied it anyway. Originally a $28.50 hat, it sold, finally, on bargain counters for forty-nine cents. John and Fred had no agreement with the American Tobacco Company, and the advertisement carried no mention of their name, so they gained comparatively little in money or prestige from the hat's success. ("We were fools," they say now, lifting their shoulders.) They couldn't sue anybody for copying the hat, because it turned out that the milliners who copied it from the Lucky Strike ad had been able to duplicate only the front of the hat, which was all that was presented to them in the picture. When they came to the back, they turned it up and let it go at that. The original John-Frederics quilled hat had a tricky arrangement of pleats in the back, and that slight difference protected the milliners who had copied it. John and Fred got a certain artistic satisfaction, though, out of knowing that all of the copies were wrong.

In 1939, John-Frederics moved to its present quarters, where the salon and workroom occupy an entire floor. Part of it is devoted to John-Frederics, Jr., a department for children's hats; the boys are pretty tired of seeing little girls fettered forever to bonnets and plain sailors with rolled-up brims. They have a shop in Miami, and other branches in Palm Beach and Beverly Hills, and they employ seventy milliners in their New York workroom alone. Ten of them are women who worked for John's mother at Mme Laurel's, and their feeling toward her son is one of affection and surprise. Since the war put a stop to their semiannual trips to Europe to buy materials and inspect the Paris trend, John and Fred keep a piercing eye out for possible materials closer to home. Not long ago, Fred, who does precision work in a defense plant two nights a week, noticed a scattering of shiny colored disks lying around the floor of the plant. These disks, used to lessen friction of steel parts in machinery, were waste material, once discarded. Fred gathered them up, took them home and had them cleaned, and they now decorate a new line of John-Frederics hats and handbags. Except for the time they spend cruising around in search of new notions, both boys are continually in the shop from ten in the morning until six or seven at night, drifting among their customers in a controlled flurry of fittings, backchat, blown kisses, and amiable cracks.

The boys lived together harmoniously in an atmosphere of considerable dash until a year or so ago when they withdrew to separate apartments without hard feelings. Fred now has a duplex apartment, crisply done in modern furniture, in East Seventy-fifth Street, and John lives in a pent-house overlooking the East River. At occasional parties for their friends

—writers, painters, and people in the fashion business, mostly —John and Fred entertain with a formal grace definitely removed from their abandon during working hours. In their serious moments, they talk about hats or about possible additions to their accessories department, which features gloves and handbags. Several years ago they added a line of perfumes and skin lotions made from formulas obtained by Fred from his father, the doctor in Frankfort. In August the blended formulas reached a point where the ingredients had to be shaken to the proper consistency, and Fred bought a washing machine for the purpose. The washing machine shook them too hard, and ruined an entire batch; but that mishap found John and Fred, as always, dreamily resourceful. They chartered a fishing boat, anchored it off Long Beach, and loaded the brew aboard in ten-gallon jugs. The perfumes and skin lotions rode gently at anchor for three months over mild autumn seas and, once more ashore, turned out to be quite a sensation.

12

Hollywood Agent:

LELAND HAYWARD

A THEATRICAL AGENT is the businessman who handles matters of contracts and salaries between actors, actresses, or authors who want to work for producers, and producers who want to employ actors, actresses, or authors. His job is not as simple as it sounds. People who write and act are often scatter-brained folk who like to tell an agent everything that is in their hearts, and leave the rest to him; producers are notoriously cryptic fellows who won't tell an agent even how much they are willing to pay, in case he should ask for less. As the medium between the selling and the buying ends of a profession that is pretty capricious anyway, the agent probably works harder for a greater number of people, and gets more abuse for it, than anybody in the entertainment business. Because of the shrewd reticence on the part of producers, he has to find out a great many things for himself. Sometimes he does it by strolling into a producer's office and absorbing all the telegrams lying on his desk by glancing at them upside down; sometimes he leans casually across the desk for a match and shuffles the letters on it with his elbow until the one he wants to see comes out on top. In return for his tireless efforts, the agent has come to be generally regarded in the theatrical profession as one of the low-lifes of all time. Because he collects, as his fee, at least ten per cent of whatever salaries he is able to get for the players and writers who are his clients, he is accused of being a parasite fattening on money earned by people artistically more important than himself. His simple desire for large sums of cash is looked upon, in an obscure kind of way, as knavery. The story about the actor who broke his toe pretty well suggests the accepted idea of an agent; nobody understood how he had done it until a friend, thinking it over, said, "He must have kicked an agent in the heart."

People seeing Leland Hayward for the first time have been heard to say, "Is *he* an agent?" and some have explained their astonishment by pointing out that he looks like a man of gentle birth. He is in his early forties, thin, with graying hair which he wears close-cropped, and a manner at once haggard and debonair. His agency, at 444 Madison Avenue, handles actors, actresses, and writers of all kinds, but the greatest part of its business is concerned with moving pictures. Hayward works according to a conviction that the amount of money an agent can get for whatever it is that he wants to sell is dependent upon the amount of hysteria he can create about it. One morning, in 1935, he read an article in *Fortune* about the play *The Green Pastures* and how much money it had made. Hayward called up Rowland Stebbins, its producer, arranged to handle the play for pictures, and then telephoned the New York offices of Paramount, Warner Brothers, Samuel Goldwyn, and RKO, contriving to leave the executives in each company in that favorable state of frenzy which in the moving picture business passes for approval. Before any of them had time to call back, Hayward went to lunch, and afterward spent a pleasant hour or so shopping. He returned to the office in time to hear the hoarse late-afternoon cries of the bidders and after a few days' negotiations, sold *The Green Pastures* to Warner Brothers for a little over $100,000, cash. Recently he applied the same level-headed system to the motion picture sale of Edna Ferber's novel, *Saratoga Trunk.* Hayward sent a telegram to all the leading Hollywood producers saying that the book was available to the first bidder for $175,000 on a seven year lease. The clause, which meant that the buyer could make the picture only once in seven years, was designed to prevent him from thriftily making it over and over in the hope of persuading himself that he had got the best of the bargain. Twenty minutes after Hayward's telegram went out, Warner Brothers, ever on their toes, wired the first, and winning acceptance of the terms. Since then, Hayward has reposefully achieved such prices as $250,000 for the play *Dark Eyes*, $355,000 plus thirty-five per cent of the profits for *Junior Miss*, and he is holding out for a $500,000 advance against fifty per cent of the profits for *Life with Father*.

Leland does most of his business lying on a sofa in his office with three or four telephones in his hands. He never writes a letter when he can send a wire or a cable, and never wires when he can telephone. He likes to dine at Twenty-One and spend most of the dinner hour calling people up on a table telephone. One night he called up Lily Pons on the *Bremen*, Sam Goldwyn in Hollywood, and Myrna Loy in Chicago, and held long, intense business conversations with all of them. Sometimes, having feverishly put in a cross-country call from his table, he finds he really hasn't much to say when the waiter hands him the phone. He spoke to his client Dashiell Hammett not long ago over three thousand miles of wire, saying, "I wrote you a letter this morning. You'll get it tomorrow. It explains itself." "Is that all?" asked Hammett. "That's all," said Hayward tensely, and went on with his dinner.

Once he took Edna Ferber, another client, to lunch at the Brown Derby, a restaurant in Hollywood which also features table telephones. When the waiter interrupted lunch for the fourth time to bring Hayward a telephone, Miss Ferber, who has foibles of her own, threw it on the floor and cast her own blue-plate luncheon on top of it. They have since maintained the deep and grumbling friendship typical of Hayward's relations with his clients, and Miss Ferber has often spoken of her agent, not without esteem, as the only man she knows except George S. Kaufman whose feet are the only visible part of him when he comes to call. He likes to relax on a couch or in a big chair, with his head resting low on cushions and his feet dreamily arranged over the top.

Hayward's first client was Fred Astaire, whose agent he became, about seventeen years ago, through a negotiation which turned out to be surprising to everybody concerned in it. At that time, Hayward, out of a job, was drifting around New York, spending most of his evenings in night clubs. One night at the Trocadero the proprietor, Mal Hayward (who is not related), sat down at Hayward's table and put his head upon his hand. A new place called the Mirador had opened across the street, and was taking the Trocadero's trade. "If I could get an attraction to bring the people back here," said Mal Hayward, "somebody like the Astaires, for instance, I'd pay them as much as three or four thousand dollars a week." Leland went around to the theater where Fred and Adele Astaire were playing in *Lady, Be Good!* and closed the deal at four thousand dollars. He collected his four-hundred-dollar commission every Saturday night during the twelve weeks of their engagement. He had no bank account, and got the checks cashed by a man he knew named Frank Joyce (a brother of Alice), who ran the Coolidge Hotel on West Forty-seventh Street. As the checks kept coming, Joyce grew wide-eyed. "All that dough every week," he inquired, "just for telling the Astaires that Mal Hayward wanted them to dance at the Trocadero?" Brooding, Joyce eventually went to Hollywood himself, and got into the agency business; until his death in 1935, he was a partner of Myron Selznick in the Joyce-Selznick agency on the West Coast.

Through his own tastes, Hayward was estranged at an early age from everything that interested the rest of his family. His father, Colonel William Hayward, was prominent in New York as a lawyer, a one-time United States attorney, and a commanding officer of the 369th U. S. Infantry, the Negro troops in the first World War. By Colonel Hayward's marriage in 1919 to Mrs. Mae Plant, Leland acquired a fashionable stepmother and a stepbrother, the late Phil Plant, who was frequently mentioned in the newspapers as a millionaire playboy. Leland was neither fashionable, a playboy, nor a millionaire and, although he was a student at Princeton for a while, he managed to rid himself of that distinction too, in 1920, when he flunked out with an almost perfect record of non-passing marks. Returning to New York, he learned that his father had discontinued his allowance and had got him a job as a reporter, at twenty-five dollars a week, on the *Sun*. The next few years, for Hayward, were crowded and unprofitable. In January 1921, he went back to Princeton and talked the faculty into reinstating him as a student. Two months later he married Lola Gibbs and quit college; they were divorced in the second year of their marriage. Seven years later they remarried, and four years after that they were divorced again. Two years after *that,* in 1936, Hayward married his present wife, Margaret Sullavan, the actress, who was and is still a client. The Haywards have three children—Brooke, aged seven, Bridget, four, and Bill, three—who live in a house of their own, converted from a red barn, on the Hayward place in Beverly Hills. The Haywards spend most of their time there, keeping an apartment at the Pierre in New York for business trips East and for the periods of Miss Sullavan's stage engagements. Sometimes Leland, the family man, can scarcely remember the days when he acted like a character out of Scott Fitzgerald.

After his short skirmishes with Princeton and the *Sun,* Hayward went to work for United Artists as a press agent at fifty dollars a week and travelled through the Middle West with photographs of Mary Pickford as Little Lord Fauntleroy, and Douglas Fairbanks in *The Three Musketeers.* Sometimes he whiled away the long days in little, dusty towns by writing purely imaginative articles for fan magazines about all the movie stars he could think of; he picked up a hundred dollars or so every month in that way until he was detected by the late Hiram Abrams of United Artists, who pointed out that a press agent employed by United Artists should write about stars who were working for United Artists, and not about any others. Hayward found himself once more out of a job, but by a series of minor dickerings with various picture companies he managed, a few months later, to get to Hollywood, which had become the city of his dreams. Across the hall from him at the Mayfair Apartments, a lodging on North Wilcox Avenue that is a good deal more modest than its name, lived three men, also struggling for Hollywood careers, whom he came to know; they were Myron and David Selznick, and Lewis Milestone. David Selznick, working for Metro-Goldwyn-Mayer, was the only one of the four who had a job, and they all managed to live suitably on his salary. One day David Selznick came home in a rage. "I told 'em something at the studio today, believe me," he said, darkly, "I *told* 'em." What, the three others inquired, had he told them? "I told 'em I resigned!" Selznick replied. During the next few weeks the four men thought up a plan that enabled them to breakfast regularly without cash. Each room in the Mayfair Apartments had a little recess in the wall outside the door, facing the corridor, where the milkman left the daily milk. Rising every morning when they heard the milkman leave, Hayward, Milestone, and the two Selznicks quietly visited a series of recesses in turn, drank what milk they required, and put each empty bottle back into its little niche. It was quite a mystery to the other tenants, who kept on taking in empty milk bottles without ever finding out where their milk had gone.

In the next three years Hayward obtained, and was fired from, some fifteen or twenty jobs as press agent and contact man in Hollywood and New York, and as talent scout for American pictures in Europe. He had already developed the manner of contagious delirium that marks the great salesman, but he was restless; and his restlessness, too, was so contagious that his employers usually fired him after a little time had passed. In 1927 he was again in Hollywood, and again unemployed. The first talking picture had just been shown, and picture companies became insatiable for plays, and for actors and actresses trained in the theater. Hayward saw opportunities for big deals glittering all around him, but he was hampered by the fact that he had no connection with the theater or, at the moment, with pictures either. In an access of pondering in his room one day, he remembered a manuscript that Ben Hecht, then an obscure writer whom Hayward knew slightly, had given him to read back in New York. Hayward dug the story out of a trunk, sold it to MGM for $1,500, and, with his $150 commission, returned to New York and applied for a job with the American Play Company, in West Forty-second Street. John W. Rumsey was the president of the company, which had been long established as an agency for authors and playwrights, and was concerned with selling plays, books, and short stories to producers and publishers. Mr. Rumsey had little interest in the movies and a considerable distrust of talking pictures. He paid Hayward no salary, but agreed to give him half the commission on anything he sold. From the beginning, Hayward argued with Rumsey that agents could make more money from moving pictures than from any other source, and that the American Play Company ought to have a picture department to sell stories to Hollywood and to get movie contracts for actors. Hollywood was beginning to pay staggering wages to practically anybody who could read and write and speak intelligibly, and he saw no reason some of the commissions involved should not be his. Although there was, and still is, a deep friendship between the two men, Hayward and Rumsey were forever divided upon that point. Rumsey insisted that the American Play Company was doing as well as it had always done by limiting its clients to authors and playwrights of the traditional school; he himself had as much work as he cared to undertake, and anyway, he said, a lot of people were still unconvinced that the talkies had come to stay.

Thwarted, Hayward turned his energy for the time being into another channel, and set about a sweeping rearrangement of the American Play Company's offices. He stacked face downward on the floor all the photographs of old stage favorites that lined the walls, and had the walls painted a new, and tastier, shade. He ordered the ancient green carpets torn up and had new ones, in novelty colors, put down. When Rumsey pointed out that this flurry in interior decoration was costing the firm a good deal of money, Hayward insisted that it would make money for them in the end. "You've got to put up a big front in this business," he said. Hollywood had taught him that. Next he involved the offices in an elaborate system of electrical devices. One contrivance lighted colored lights, green, blue, and orange, signifying various demands, in the office of his secretary, Miss Malley; another controlled a red light in his own office that went on every time there was a telephone call, the idea being to spare himself the harsh jangle of the telephone bell. There were always men from the Telephone Company creeping around the carpet under Hayward's desk, installing one thing or another. When, in 1932, Hayward left the American Play Company to go in business for himself, he wanted to get a good telephone number for his new headquarters. "Who do we know in the Telephone Company?" he asked Miss Malley. "Heavens, Mr. Hayward," said Miss Malley, "we know everybody in the Telephone Company." For his new offices, he got the tidy number of Regent 4-7000.

Possibly to avoid the wear and tear of further ministrations from Hayward, Rumsey at length agreed to let him try to build up a moving-picture department in the agency. Hayward engaged Myron Selznick, who had gone into the agency business in Hollywood, to represent the American Play Company on the Coast; Selznick was to get fifty per cent of the commission on any client he acquired, and the other fifty per cent was to be divided between Hayward and the American Play Company. The first coup brought off by Hayward and Selznick was a contract between Ina Claire and Sam Goldwyn, and the commission on that deal was over $10,000. When, in 1931, Paramount asked Miriam Hopkins to make a picture, she engaged Hayward as her agent. Four years later, he signed her to a two-year contract with Goldwyn calling for over half a million dollars for eighty weeks' work and a percentage of the gross profits, and arranged for her to be loaned to Pioneer Pictures, during the run of her contract, to make *Becky Sharp*. She made about $100,000 in salary from *Becky Sharp*, plus a percentage of the gross. When Ben Hecht, still a staunch Hayward client, started collaborating with Charles MacArthur, Hayward acted as agent for both, and when MacArthur married Helen Hayes, she became a client, too. One time Howard Hughes sent for Hecht to come to Hollywood to write the script for *Scarface*. Hecht didn't want to go to Hollywood. "Tell Hughes I'll come for a thousand dollars a day, cash," he told Hayward. Hughes agreed that Hecht was to receive, each day, a check for $1,000. "No checks," said Hecht, when this was reported to him. "I said cash, and I mean bills, money, tens, twenties, fifties. . . ." Hughes said all right, he would pay Hecht $1,000 in cash every day for the first nineteen days he worked; after that, he would get paid by the week, same as other people. Hecht went to Hollywood, and on the nineteenth day turned in the completed script, gathered up his $19,000, cash, and returned to New York, where he wanted to be.

During his three years with the American Play Company, Hayward had bought thirty-three per cent of the company's stock. In 1932, he gave the stock back to Rumsey, and by an amicable agreement took in return his own clients and Miss Malley, his secretary. His first offices at 654 Madison Avenue, occupied a good part of two floors, and his private office, about seventy-five feet long, had a roof garden, an arrangement of sun lamps, a bathroom with a glass-enclosed shower, and a phonograph that played twenty-four records in succession.

Last year Hayward left these quarters for larger ones at his present address. Owing to the shortage of labor and materials, the move has not resulted in just the grandeur he had planned. The new place is still unpainted in spots, and Hayward's private office has mysteriously turned out to be a small room in the rear. "For God's sake, why did we move?" he demanded of Miss Malley not long ago, looking around him in bewilderment. Miss Malley, who can answer even rhetorical questions, explained that the idea of moving had originated with the bookkeeper, who was not pleased with his own former surroundings.

Two colored maps on the wall of Hayward's office show his former air route between New York and Hollywood (where his offices are all done in leather, even the draperies). Before the war, he flew his own plane back and forth two or three times a month at an average flying time of seventeen hours for the trip, and had a standing bet of $1,000 with Myron Selznick that Selznick would die of the Hollywood pace before Hayward killed himself flying. Hayward, who likes titles as well as he likes flying, soon became a director and member of the executive board of TWA. In 1940, he resigned these posts and with John H. Connelly, a Civil Aeronautics Authority inspector, established Southwest Airways, of which Hayward is now chairman of the board. Southwest Airways, which started with five pilots, six other employees, and seven planes, now operates Thunderbird Field and three other flying schools near Phoenix, Arizona. Since the United States entered the war, the four training fields have turned out thousands of

American, British, and Chinese pilots who have flown the remarkable total of one million hours in training before leaving for combat overseas. Southwest Airways works in co-operation with the Army Air Forces, the A.A.F. contributing men and some of the equipment and Southwest and its stockholders furnishing the other necessities, including money.

Hayward's clients now include Charles Laughton, Myrna Loy, Ginger Rogers, Garbo, Judy Garland, and about one hundred and fifty others. Ernest Hemingway became a client through Donald Ogden Stewart, in a cosy kind of way. Several years ago Hayward got a wire from Stewart, en route from Hollywood, that he and Mrs. Stewart were sailing for Europe that night, at midnight, and needed $1,000 in cash. The wire arrived after the banks had closed, and Hayward hadn't that much cash in the office. He toured nearly all the restaurants and night clubs in town, cashed a small check at each one, and was at the boat with the required sum. Two weeks later a cable arrived from the Stewarts, somewhere in France, asking him to send along the Stewart baby and nurse. Hayward arranged everything, and six months later, when the Stewart family returned, learned that Stewart had, in gratitude, secured him Ernest Hemingway as a client. "I told him all about the thousand dollars and the baby and everything," Stewart said, "and he thinks that you're the greatest agent in the world." Hayward's clients frequently demand these small services unconnected with the agency business. Once Miriam Hopkins telephoned that an actor with whom she had once played was having a nervous breakdown out on Long Island, and had been ordered by his doctor to chop wood. She was too busy to attend to it herself, but she would like to have some trees sent out to him as a present from her. Hayward's secretary telephoned around, and the next day three trees on a truck were delivered to the nervous actor, with Miss Hopkins's compliments.

Hayward's vice-president, in charge of the New York office, is Paul Streger, a humorous and tireless man who is everywhere throughout the organization, like a warm breeze. One day a film producer, talking to Hayward on the telephone, happened to say that he needed a story for one of his stars. Hayward covered the telephone with one hand and whispered rapidly to Streger, "He wants a story for Cagney. For God's sake, think of something." Streger is no author, but with incredible speed he produced the outline of a plot and murmured it to Hayward, who spilled it over the telephone in a fine, enthusiastic frenzy. The producer made a tentative offer for it then and there, and the next week bought the finished script from one of Hayward's clients at a fancy price.

Hayward has the agent's habit of thinking about money in big figures, and encourages his clients to do the same, even when they are broke. Some years ago Jean Muir, now a successful actress and producer, was an obscure client of his; her name was then Jean Fullarton. One day Jacob Wilk of Warner Brothers called up Hayward and said that he had seen Miss Fullarton, and was willing to put her under a contract at sixty dollars a week. Hayward replied to the offer with some irony, and telephoned Jean Fullarton. "Listen," he said to her, "ordinarily Wilk would have started you at a hundred and fifty, at the lowest. What happened, when you saw him, that made him offer you sixty?" Nothing, she told him, that she could remember. "I was about twenty minutes late for the appointment," she said, "but I told Mr. Wilk quite frankly that I was late on account of having to walk all the way from where I lived, because I didn't have carfare." When anything like that happens, Hayward moans a little and runs his hands through his hair. Then he braces up and tries to right the wrong. He can see no excuse for people who have any talent to sell not selling it at the top price.

❁ 13 ❁

Miss Fixit:

FANNY HOLTZMANN

FANNY HOLTZMANN, an American lawyer whose practice embraces New York, Hollywood, and London, has worked up a surefire approach to each place. In London she dines with dukes and duchesses and is invited to meet royalty as an authority on Broadway and Hollywood; in New York she is elusive and fairly highhanded with her clients, because New Yorkers are impressed by the fact that she knows several members of the royal family to speak to; in Hollywood she relaxes and yells at film producers, who respect her because she is a shrewd lawyer and because she knows everybody on Broadway and big people in England besides. Her clients are successful writers, beleaguered actors and actresses, and dreamy British peers—celebrities whose fame has brought them so much money and grief, or grief and lack of money, that they instinctively hire Fanny to worry about everything for them.

Fanny carries their burdens with a strong airiness of manner which she has cultivated, and sometimes speaks of her own wonder that she is able to do it, being, as she is, so little and so comparatively young. She is not much over forty, and five feet two inches tall. Her wavy bob and a trick she has of using her hands in delicate gestures give her an appearance of demureness, but her face is sharp and skeptical and her manner is essentially bold. An interviewer writing about Fanny in the London *Daily Mail* pretty well described her, although less gracefully, perhaps, than he intended. "Seen from behind," he wrote, "she is reminiscent of Janet Gaynor."

Fanny speaks the languages of Broadway, Hollywood, and

Mayfair, and slides from one into another with the ease of a dialect comedian. In 1933, when *As Thousands Cheer* opened on Broadway with a sketch that sensationally kidded the British royal family, Fanny, who happened to be in London, heard that the British government proposed making a formal protest to Washington. Although no one had consulted her legally, she managed to communicate with the Earl of Cromer, the Lord Chamberlain, and to point out to him that a formal protest would be a mistake. "It will simply give the revue tons of publicity," she said, "and one dislikes obliging the producer to that extent." Lord Cromer thanked Fanny, but the protest was made anyway, through the British Ambassador at Washington. Every newspaper printed it, with counter-protests from Sam Harris, producer of the show, and *As Thousands Cheer* got off to a good start under a momentum of nationwide notoriety. Two seasons later, when Harris was rehearsing *Jubilee!* a revue concerned, unmistakably, with King George V and his Queen, Fanny was in London again. In one of her daily telephone calls to New York, she learned that Walter Winchell's Monday column had carried the following item: "England's king and queen will be violently ribbed in *Jubilee!*" A few days later Winchell printed another crack. "*Jubilee!*" he said, "which ribs Britain's king and queen, shows them holidaying incognito, doing the things they've always wanted to do for the last twenty-five years . . . and how they do carry on!" Fanny called up Winchell in New York to verify what he had printed, and then broke the news to Lord Cromer. "Surely, dear Lord Cromer," she said, mildly, "the British government doesn't want to come another frightful cropper like that last one. Why not let me see if I can't wangle something?" Visibly shaken, Cromer authorized her to do what she could, unofficially, and Fanny called up Sam Harris in New York. "Listen, dear," she said, "what are you trying to do, buck the British government? Maybe you don't want to put on a show in London ever again. Listen," she said, while Mr. Harris listened, "suppose you want to sell your lousy show to Hollywood, so what? So the British are laying for you, and they'll see that the picture is banned all over the British Empire." Mr. Harris saw the truth of Fanny's argument, and besides he had no real desire to keep on affronting England. He changed the locale of *Jubilee!* to a mythical kingdom, and trusted his audience to suspect that it meant England just the same. The British were pacified, and after the New York opening, the London *Daily Telegraph* had this comment to make: "Fears that the play would attempt to caricature the British royal family were dissipated, although it is rumored that extensive cuts were made at the last moment at the suggestion of Washington officials." Fanny's name was never mentioned publicly in connection with the incident and she got no fee from the Lord Chamberlain. But the good will was worth thousands.

Fanny Holtzmann began to develop into a picturesque figure among lawyers almost as soon as she was admitted to the bar in 1922, but it was not until the opposing counsel in the Youssoupoff libel suit, thirteen years later, called her a charlatan and a publicity hound that she became famous. Actually, Fanny's buildup of that case included a smooth reticence about her own connection with it, and a determination to allow nobody to be publicly associated with it except people who had royal blood, or at least titles. Princess Irina Youssoupoff, a niece of the late Czar, had been to several New York lawyers with her claim against Metro-Goldwyn-Mayer on the grounds that Princess Natasha in the film *Rasputin* was intended to represent her, and that Natasha's seduction by the mad monk was a libel on her name. The lawyers declined the case as being flimsy, and the Princess at length sorrowfully sailed for England. At a party on the Riviera, Fanny met Princess Youssoupoff, and the Princess then and there told Fanny all about her grievance against the picture company. Fanny took the case on, moved the whole proceedings over to London, and set about going to work on the British public's love of titles and its happy indifference to Metro-Goldwyn-Mayer. The brief that her colleagues finally presented emphasized throughout the blood relationship between the Russian royal family and the British royal family. As character witnesses for the Princess, Fanny rounded up a glittering mass of Russian and British nobility. She was entranced to find that Prince Felix Youssoupoff, Irina's husband, could give a powerful account of how he and the late Grand Duke Dmitri had helped to kill Rasputin. The case, when Fanny had it ready, was a drama of royalty and the murder of a peasant, enlivened and enriched by the sound of noble names from the witness box. Then Fanny brought off her coup. She arranged through friends of the Youssoupoffs to have them live at Frogmore House, in the grounds of Windsor Castle, until the trial was over. Fanny never appeared in court; she knew that the presence of an American lawyer named Holtzmann would strike a wrong note in the fine spectacle she had wrought. She left Sir Patrick Hastings in charge as court counsel for the Princess, and sailed for America a few days before the trial opened. Although she was on the New York-London telephone continually after that, talking about the case, her name might not have been mentioned in open court if Sir William Jowitt, counsel for Metro-Goldwyn-Mayer, had not, on the third day of the trial, shaken his finger angrily in the face of Prince Youssoupoff, who was on the stand, and said, "I suggest that an American lawyer, Miss Fanny Holtzmann, has been exploiting your wife." Storming out of the courtroom at the end of the session, Sir William added bitterly to reporters that he was convinced that Fanny Holtzmann was back of the whole case, and that she was using the Youssoupoffs to gain prestige for herself.

Fanny's picture struck the front pages of the newspapers in New York and in London, and reappeared there regularly as Sir William continued to denounce her. The drama of the countroom proceedings increased, accordingly. On the last day of the trial, the presiding Justice, the late Sir Horace Avory, read aloud a passage from *The Rape of Lucrece* beginning "But she has lost a dearer thing than life . . ." and the jury brought in a verdict for Princess Youssoupoff of twenty-five thousand pounds and costs. With settlements from exhibitors added to this, the Princess collected around $250,000 and costs, and Fanny's fee is said to have been fifty per cent of $250,000. Returning to London after the victory, Fanny gave a party to celebrate it, at her flat in Knightsbridge. The guests included Violet, Duchess of Rutland, and her son, the Duke; Jimmy Walker, Gertrude Lawrence, and crowds of Russian nobles. Princess Youssoupoff wore the Romanoff emeralds, and everybody stayed for scrambled eggs at dawn.

Although she has secretaries working permanently at Claridge's in London and at the Beverly Hills Hotel, near Hollywood, Fanny's only office is in New York—a light-green, dusty suite of rooms in the Bar Building at 36 West Forty-fourth Street, furnished with the same carpets, tables, and chairs that she bought when she opened it in 1923. Pictures of Daniel Webster and John Marshall lend an Old World tone to the entrance hall, but the walls of Fanny's private office are lined with signed photographs of more spirited people, all friends or clients—Ina Claire, Clifton Webb, Noel Coward, Lady Astor, Lord Haldane, Justice Cardozo, Fred Astaire, Mme Wellington Koo, and thirty or forty others. Not long before his restoration to the throne, King George of Greece wrote Fanny a letter in longhand. It arrived while she was out of town, and her secretary had it framed and hung on the wall as a surprise for her when she returned. The letter was simple and chatty, mentioning the wedding of the Duke of Kent and Princess Marina as a pleasant occasion and expressing the hope that George himself might soon be able to go big-game hunting ("which has long been a dream of mine," he wrote). Fanny briskly ordered it taken down as soon as she saw it, but she kept it in a desk drawer, frame and all, and showed it discreetly to somebody almost every day. She is a great one for letting people peek at letters, telegrams, and other messages signed with important names. Not long ago, when George Bernard Shaw cabled her a simple affirmative in answer to her request for his permission to use *Pygmalion* as a radio vehicle for Gertrude Lawrence, Fanny carried the cable around for quite a while, waving it as she entered restaurants or cocktail parties. George of Greece became a good friend of hers in London during the time of his exile, and Fanny understands the dramatic value of keeping their friendship informal. She was indignant, however, when a London newspaper once emphasized its informality by saying that she broiled chops for the exiled King on the frequent occasions when he dropped in at her Knightsbridge flat. "I don't go to London to broil chops for anybody," Fanny would say coldly whenever anyone brought this up. "The King of Greece knew where the saucepans were; when he came to see me, he broiled his own chops."

On New Year's Day, 1936—a month or so after he had been restored to the throne—King George sent Fanny a cable of greeting and a standing invitation to visit his palace at Athens. She has a good many such invitations from royal personages —dethroned, perhaps, but hopeful; and there are generally, in her office in the Bar Building, a few princes and counts wandering around or sitting in the leather chairs, smoking, and talking in unindentifiable accents. "The Romanoffs, you know, can't stand *up* after one drink. They can't drink *anything*," they say, and "Do you remember the time Dmitri served vodka when the Duke of Kent was coming to tea?" Then the details of Grand Duke Dmitri's tea for the late Duke of Kent come back to them in a wave of reminiscence. Vodka, one of them explains, is so strong that it must be accompanied by *chernyi khleb,* a canapé that acts as a sort of blotting paper. On the day of Dmitri's tea, his dog got at the canapés before the guests did, and the Duke of Kent was obliged to down his vodka without a crumb of food to soften the impact. If some newcomer to Fanny's office tensely inquires what happened then, there is a slight movement of lifted shoulders among the others, of eyebrows raised in reverence. "Nothing happened," they sigh. "The House of Windsor—*they* can drink *anything*." Fanny takes little part in these conversations. Usually, she sits with one foot under her in a chair with a high, carved back behind a massive desk and listens, her prominent brown eyes liquid with interest. Sometimes these visitors (to whom Fanny refers proudly as "my royal friends") call her Miss Holtzmann in the office, and that hurts her. "My friends always call me Fanny in London," she reminds them gravely. She is careful not to make many statements to outsiders, however, about her foreign connections. Fanny is grateful to Europe, to England especially, because it has given her an astonishing social life. She knows it would be fatal to her popularity there to say anything so personal about her royal friends, for instance, that they would stop saying "Hello, Fanny" when they meet her.

Fanny's first contact with British nobility came about some twenty years ago. She had attracted a large theatrical following through one of her first clients, Edmund Goulding, an English actor who is now a director in Hollywood. One day Francis X. Bushman, the retired movie star, came into her office in a temper. Lord Auckland, he said, had left his dogs at Bushman's country place in Maryland while he went home to England for a time. In his absence one of the bitches had given birth to a litter, and Bushman had sold the puppies to pay for the other dogs' board and keep. Now Auckland was back in America raging around because he claimed that the litter was his by rights, and that Bushman had had no authority to sell it. He was threatening court action, and Bushman wanted Fanny's advice. Later in the day, when Bushman had gone, Edmund Goulding came into the office on some business or other, and Fanny mentioned the Auckland trouble. "Auckland?" said Goulding. "My dear, we'll fix that up in no time." Sitting on a corner of her desk, he called up Lord Auckland at his hotel, and addressed him briskly by his first name. "Hello, Freddie?" he said, while Fanny gazed at him, wide-eyed. On the telephone Goulding persuaded Lord Auckland to meet Bushman next day in Fanny's office, where Fanny soon talked him into taking his dogs, including the famous bitch, back to England and letting the matter of the litter go. Auckland was one of the first to discover that it is impossible to argue with Fanny, because her gift of talking incessantly in a soft voice is so highly developed that her opponent is conscious not of conflicting sound but only of the fact that he is getting nowhere.

It was at about that time that the other lawyers who had offices in the newly completed Bar Building began to look at Fanny with a certain wonder. There had been some hostility toward admitting her as a tenant; she was female, young—barely twenty-one—and Jewish. She lived in Brooklyn and commuted on the subway, and her clients seemed, to the startled eyes of the other tenants, to be chiefly actors and actresses and wild-haired authors, all pretty spectacular. The

New York Bar had admitted its first woman member only five years before, and was still inclined to look upon women lawyers as unnecessary. Fanny, however, was firm about establishing herself in the Bar Building. Woodrow Wilson and Bainbridge Colby had had offices there; Justice Cardozo, then Associate Justice of the Court of Appeals, had the office directly above the one Fanny wanted for herself. She liked to think of walking the same corridors as these distinguished men, and she felt, too, that a little dignity would add to her own success as a lawyer. The Character Committee of the Building finally admitted her, chiefly through the influence of her older brother, Jacob L. Holtzmann, who was, and is, a prominent lawyer in New York and Brooklyn. Justice Cardozo was the first of the older tenants to speak to her graciously in the elevator. "Well, are you coming or going this time?" he would say when he found that her rapidly growing clientele was taking her frequently to Hollywood and to London; and one day he talked to her for quite a long time in the hall, and said that she was realizing his own youthful ambition, which had been connected not with being a Chief Justice but with rushing around all over the world on behalf of his clients. Fanny never brought a case before him after he was appointed to the Supreme Court, but whenever he saw her in Washington, he always remembered her and made a point of saying, "How do you do?" She treasures that. Some of the older lawyers find themselves occasionally in more solid contact with her. Recently a judge who had been chiefly instrumental in trying to keep her out of the Bar Building twenty years ago was driven by his own domestic troubles into retaining her as counsel in his divorce suit. Fanny has come to be a familiar, hurrying figure to everyone in the Bar Building, and members of the New York City Bar Association next door salute her gravely as she passes, though she is not a member.

Some time ago Fanny persuaded her father and mother to move from the house in Brooklyn where she was born to an apartment in Manhattan, on the upper West Side, and she lived there quietly with them for several years. She has an apartment of her own now, on East 64th Street. She has been careful to maintain an illusion of simplicity about herself, because it is effective in contrast to the gaudy celebrities with whom she is associated. She buys her clothes in the girls' departments of various stores, seldom pays more than six dollars for a hat, and owns no jewelry or automobiles, although she has given her mother a car, with chauffeur. At lunchtime she has sandwiches sent in to the office or goes out to lunch in the restaurant of Stern's department store, in the next block. She seems to like the things they have to eat there, such as fruit salad with whipped cream, and cheerfully tips the waitress fifteen cents. She finds people in New York and Hollywood pretty crass on the whole, and thinks of her life here now as a prelude to getting back to England, where the glitter surrounds her. In London, she used to be invited to tea now and then by the late King George and Queen Mary; concerning those occasions she says, "I behaved to the King as I would to my own grandfather, with dignity and respect. And I let him do the talking."

Shortly after the Youssoupoff trial, Fanny lunched at Frogmore House with Grand Duchess Xenia and some eight or ten other members of the Russian nobility who were living there while the King and Queen were in London. After the first course, Fanny became oppressed by a curious silence which persisted around the table. It might be some form of court etiquette, she thought, and she tried to keep quiet too. But silence, with Fanny, is impossible for any length of time, and soon she began a conversation with a ten-year-old prince who sat next to her, about making toy boats out of wood and a piece of cloth and sailing them on small lakes. To her further confusion, the entire luncheon party leaned forward and listened, and in another minute everybody was talking about making toy boats. Fanny learned later, from Grand Duchess Xenia, that the Russians hadn't quite known what an American woman lawyer would like to talk about, and had been pleased to learn that it was something so simple.

Fanny has become great friends with Grand Duchess Xenia since that time. Driving with an American friend in a London taxi one day, Fanny stopped the cab in front of Buckingham Palace. "I simply must drop in and see the Grand Duchess," she said. "She's staying here." Before her friend's incredulous eyes the gates were opened, the great front doors and successive doors. Liveried footmen bowed and announced "Miss Fanny Holtzmann" in turn, as tranquilly as though they had been doing it every day of their lives. Fanny's American friends are frequently startled that way. Some months before Christmas, several years ago, Lillie Messinger, a talent scout for RKO, who was sailing for England, received a commission from Fanny. "Find out," Fanny told her, "whether the Duchess of Atholl has alternating or direct current in her London house, and get her an electric waffle iron at Harrod's or Selfridge's. I promised her one for Christmas." The Duchess got her waffle iron (D.C.) and is reported to be enjoying American waffles right along.

When it becomes important, commercially or socially, to impress a client with what she likes to think of as her own fundamental simplicity, Fanny Holtzmann dramatizes the fact that she is, after all, a Jewish girl from Brooklyn. Sometimes a particular coup she has brought off may startle her into an air of hard and arrogant pride, but generally the attitude she prefers to adopt is one of humble astonishment at her own success, and she is pleased when other people find this attitude sincere.

In her parents' house, in the Brownsville section of Brooklyn, Fanny was the next to the youngest of eight children. Her father taught in the public schools, and was well known in his district as an active Republican. Now and then, when Fanny was eight or nine, there was a whirlwind day in the Holtzmann household when President Theodore Roosevelt, passing through Brooklyn, paid a chatty visit to his friend and supporter, Fanny's father. Roosevelt took an interest in the eldest Holtzmann son, Jacob, and Jacob, who lunched at the White House when he was twelve and became a Brooklyn lawyer at twenty-five, was tacitly considered the spectacular member of the family. Four of Fanny's sisters were taking courses in teaching; another sister, Stella, and a brother, David, were studying law. Both are now lawyers—Stella, who is Mrs. Honig, has her own practice, less conspicuous than

Fanny's, and David is associated with Fanny, although not as a partner. Fanny has no partners. The Holtzmann house was generally loud with the sound of typewriters battering out theses and briefs, and Fanny, who was doing badly in school, became depressed by the bright activity all around her. She took to arriving at school so late that some mornings there seemed to be no point in going at all, and then she would wander downtown and hang around the court where Jacob was trying cases. She picked up a good many legal phrases that way, and a rudimentary knowledge of law.

When she was fourteen, she privately abandoned the idea of school and, dressed up in her sister Stella's clothes, went to New York to look for a job. After several of these excursions, a lawyer in the Singer Building gave her a week's trial as office assistant at eight dollars a week, but when she had finished her first week's work sent her a special-delivery letter asking her not to come back to work until she was older. Fanny took the subway to New York that Monday morning as usual, because pride kept her from confessing defeat to her family, and spent most of the morning sitting on Robert Fulton's grave in Trinity Churchyard, weeping. Stung to independence by a certain wariness with which her family had come to regard her, Fanny went on working, or looking for work, during the day and started going to night school to finish her high-school course, and to study law. Sometimes she got around to as many as three courses a week in different schools (two nights each), and by 1917 she had finished a preparatory course in law and was established in a good job as office assistant to Keppler & Hochman, attorneys, in the Woolworth Building. The Fordham School of Law, a branch of Fordham University, was on the twenty-eighth floor of the same building, and, with a loan from her grandfather, Fanny entered night school there the following year. After that she worked in the offices of Keppler & Hochman from nine until five, took the elevator upstairs to law school in the evenings, and rode home to Brooklyn about twelve, studying on the way. Soon she was urging her employers to expand into the field of coypright law, pointing out that it was a branch of the profession that was not crowded. "Besides," she added persuasively, "you meet such interesting people—authors and playwrights and moving-picture producers. And a lot of them are rich." Mr. Keppler and Mr. Hochman discouraged her, saying that they had no contacts in the artistic world. "You're the lawyers for the *Morning Telegraph,*" Fanny reminded them.

The *Morning Telegraph* had always had trouble collecting payment due from actors and other people of the theater who inserted in the newspaper notices advertising their talents, or sometimes just their existence. Fanny suggested opening an uptown branch of Keppler & Hochman in a district convenient to actors, with herself in charge, and letting her go to work on the *Morning Telegraph* accounts. When her employers agreed to give the plan a trial, Fanny, with one assistant, moved to an office in the Astor Theatre Building on Broadway. From there she wrote charming dunning letters to all the actors and actresses who were in debt to the *Morning Telegraph,* begging them to come in and see F. Holtzmann. They came in such numbers that her office soon became crowded with people, all pacing up and down and all, apparently, faced with some kind of dramatic disaster. Mostly it was debts that harassed them, but often it was emotional problems, or sometimes simply that they had given all their money to somebody to invest for them and would like to get it back. Fanny decided sensibly that if she was ever to collect the *Morning Telegraph* accounts she would have to help these confused people to get their finances in order. She did, and they liked it. One young actor, whose debts all over town Fanny was trying to straighten out, gratefully brought her a big box of flowers from a fashionable florist's twice a week all winter; in the spring, he turned over to her a new accumulation of papers, including a summons for nonpayment from the florist. Through these indigent people of the theater, Fanny was learning to know others, more solvent. She was invited to lunch with Somerset Maugham, with Richard Barthelmess, with Mae Murray. In the company of celebrities Fanny was impressed but not frightened; shyness has never been one of her characteristic qualities. In the early days, it troubled her, however, when the actors and writers from whom she was collecting money got in the habit of introducing her to their friends, with a flourish, as "my lawyer, Fanny Holtzmann." Fanny was then still attending the night classes at Fordham, and she knew that it would mean ruin if the Bar Association got the idea that she was practicing law before she had passed the bar examination. She had not pretended to any position beyond that of manager of Keppler & Hochman's uptown office, and her services there consisted, besides that, of listening to troubles and giving personal, not legal, advice. She worked on a straight salary. But the people who thought of themselves as her clients were people to whom exaggeration came easily. They liked the idea of having a girl lawyer, and they liked to dramatize her in connection with themselves, even though she insisted she wasn't a lawyer.

Fanny graduated from Fordham Law School in 1922, and the following spring passed her bar examinations, third highest of all the applicants in the state. Ordinarily an applicant for the New York State Bar is obliged to wait two months after he has passed his examinations before he is notified of his official admission to the bar. Fanny couldn't wait. She had left Keppler & Hochman, she had perhaps a hundred potential clients of her own, and she had already bought some furniture from the estate of a lawyer, recently deceased, to decorate the offices she had decided to take in the Bar Building. The clients were clamoring, and the furniture was costing money in storage. Fanny got her brother Jacob to ask a special dispensation from the Court of Appeals in Albany, and to go with her—after it had been granted—to Borough Hall in Brooklyn, where she was sworn in specially by the Appellate Division, second department, less than a month after she had passed the examinations for the bar. Half an hour later Fanny moved the furniture into the Bar Building, where she had taken a three-year lease on an office, and opened up the place for business.

During her first year in practice, she went to night school at Columbia University three times a week to take a course in moving-picture production. Copyright law had come to be her chief interest, and she saw an inescapable connection between that and the movies, which were generally being sued by somebody or other on the ground of plagiarism. On account of her dizzy acquaintance among people of the movies and the theater, Fanny looked forward confidently to a good, stormy career with plenty of pacing up and down and yelling all around her. By a depressing chance, her debut as a lawyer coincided with one of those intervals of peace which come occasionally to people in the artistic world. Nobody seemed to be having much trouble, and Fanny settled down morosely to her first professional case, involving a shipment of onions that the plaintiff claimed were damaged on delivery.

Things looked up, however, when an English actor whom Fanny knew brought Charles B. Cochran into her office one day. Cochran wanted to transport Tex Austin's rodeo to England as an attraction at the Wembley Exhibition, but he was worried about the British law concerning the importation of animals and about the possible reaction of the animal-loving British public to the rigors of a rodeo. The first problem was comparatively easy—principally a routine matter of having the animals examined and pronounced free from disease, but nobody could prophesy anything about the second. In a groping attempt to clear up everything in her own mind, Fanny spent three evenings in the New York Public Library, reading up on subjects like horses, steers, England, sportsmanship, and hoof-and-mouth disease. When Cochran and Austin sailed with their troupe, she went along, too, on a retainer from Mr. Cochran. The animals got into England without any difficulty, but on the second day of the show at Wembley a cowboy threw a steer and broke its leg. The next day another cowboy, throwing a steer, happened to break its neck. The R.S.P.C.A. indignantly filed a complaint against Cochran, Austin, and the two cowboys, and brought them into court on the charge of cruelty to animals. Fanny produced a brief crammed with facts she had absorbed in the Public Library about cowboys, steers, and the Wild West, all pretty staggering to British ears, and to put the whole thing over impressively, she got Cochran to engage Sir Edward Marshall Hall, one of England's leading barristers, to plead the case in court. Cochran and Austin won on the plea of accidental death to the animals, and the rodeo prospered at Wembley, helped not a little by the publicity the case had received in the newspapers.

Through Cochran, meanwhile, Fanny had met Noel Coward, Gertrude Lawrence, and Jack Buchanan, all of whom subsequently became her clients. She looked up Lord Auckland, too, for whom she had settled the dispute with Francis X. Bushman, about some dogs, in New York the year before. London found Fanny a novelty. She was only twenty-two years old, small, and occasionally girlish in manner, but she was Cochran's lawyer, and an able one. Besides, in the presence of noble folk she had a way of becoming slightly brassy that startled them into attention. Long before the Youssoupoff libel suit brought her international publicity in 1934, London newspapers were printing interviews with Fanny referring to her as "the U. S. Portia," and expressing wonder that a lawyer should be so little, so young, and a woman.

When Great Britain was about to go off the gold standard, in 1931, Fanny was in Hollywood, handling Ina Claire's divorce from John Gilbert. She flew back to New York and caught a fast boat to England, arriving in the midst of the national elections and at the height of the "Buy British" campaign. On the night of her arrival Noel Coward's play *Cavalcade* opened in London and moved the British public, already shaken by the economic crisis, to a storm of emotion. The next day Fanny lunched with the Duke and Duchess of Atholl and suggested, in the course of conversation, that a motion picture made from *Cavalcade* would be unbeatable British propaganda throughout the world. The cast, she suggested, should be restricted to British actors and actresses, but the film would have to be made in Hollywood because Hollywood controlled world distribution. Several lady members of Parliament who were present at the luncheon were sentimentally impressed, and when the Duke of Atholl introduced her to Major Walter Elliott of the Empire Marketing Board, things took a sharper turn and Fanny began getting calls from Downing Street. She cabled Noel Coward, who, sated by the success of his opening night, had sailed for South America, and found him apathetic. He cabled back that Hollywood scouts at the opening had reported the play to be nothing but an animated newsreel, unlikely material for pictures. Hollywood producers, approached by Fanny, verified Coward's doubts. But Fanny had worked up considerable excitement about the idea in London, and she could scarcely abandon it so soon. She sailed for New York, where she learned that the Chase National Bank had taken over the Fox Film Corporation and that E. R. Tinker was the new Fox chairman. Fanny called up Florence Strauss, then story editor of Fox, and arranged to be seated next to Mr. Tinker at dinner at Miss Strauss's house a few nights later. "Such a pity," Fanny said to him during the second course, "that Hollywood has lost *Cavalcade*." "What do you you mean, 'has lost?' " Mr. Tinker wanted to know. "Has somebody else bought it?" "Well, naturally, they'll make it in England now," said Fanny. That, Mr. Tinker decided after some thought, was just as well. What possible advantage could *Cavalcade* have for Hollywood anyway? "Money," replied Fanny briefly. "The British sales alone would pay for the cost of making the picture, and the rest of the world would be velvet." She looked at Mr. Tinker and sighed sympathetically, and less than a week later sold *Cavalcade* to Fox for $150,000. The picture made four million dollars for Fox, and—a more important result—the Chase Bank loaned the film corporation, which was nearly bankrupt at the time, fifteen million dollars to go on with the day after *Cavalcade* was released. Noel Coward, who had been sensitive about the play, and had feared that it would lose its effectiveness when magnified to Hollywood proportions, sent Fanny a cable. "I forgive you," he said.

Hollywood, after that, felt a new respect for Fanny, New York got to be a little afraid of her, and London became wildly affectionate toward her. Fanny's flat in Knightsbridge and, later, her house in Belgrave Square so quickly became gathering places for all the celebrities in town that one London newspaper carried a headline, over an account of a party she gave: "When Fanny Holtzmann gives a party, London's night clubs are empty." Fanny never thinks of her social success in England as freakish, and neither, perhaps, do the English. To some of them, highly born but helpless, she represents a quick way out of almost any trouble; to others, who want to go on the stage or into pictures, she is the woman with a million contacts on Broadway and in Hollywood; to a good many she is a mild phenomenon, amusing to know because she knows everybody and it all seems so unlikely.

Fanny gave up her house in Belgrave Square some time before the war. It had four guest rooms, and although her British guests had homes to go to when a party was over, there was always a lot of foreign nobility in town who found Fanny's surroundings more homelike than their small hotel bedrooms. Fanny frequently woke up the morning after a party to find that fifteen or twenty wanderers who had stayed all night, doubling up in the guest rooms and sleeping on couches, were clamoring for breakfast. She stayed at Claridge's when she was in London after that, but she still gave big parties—partly because the people she had come to know in England fascinated her, and partly because a good deal of her business is done through social contacts. Her social maneuvers are far-sighted and sometimes a little frightening. She once gave a party for George of Greece, in New York, and submitted the list of proposed guests to the State Department for approval—not that this was strictly necessary, Fanny's friends say now, but because she felt it would give the gathering prestige. Whether the State Department actually deleted any names is not known, but for some time afterward Fanny would greet anyone who was not high in her favor by saying, "I wanted to ask you to my party, you know, but the State Department crossed you off my list."

A member of the New York State Supreme Court Bar, and of the California Bar, she was once invited to join one of the Inns of Court in London, on condition that she call herself by her formal name, Frances. Fanny declined, though not because of the stipulation about her name. A lawyer who practices and resides in England must pay taxes to England. Also, English lawyers are divided into two classes—solicitors and barristers. A solicitor is the middleman between the barrister and the client; the client engages a solicitor to present his case to a barrister—a pretty distinguished man, generally—who may or may not consent to plead the case in court. Fanny is already something beyond a solicitor, in the opinion of her clients, and although a barrister is a personage in England, his fees are limited by law. As an American lawyer working through British barristers, Fanny gets unlimited fees. In America and in England, she sometimes gets as much as twenty-five thousand dollars for a fairly simple case. Not long ago Fred Astaire paid her ten thousand dollars for spending ten days in Hollywood working on a clause in his contract with RKO. The work she does for her clients among the royalty and nobility of Europe ranges from trying to find the Russian money which Rasputin is said to have acquired and stored away somewhere in the United States to arranging, through the immigration authorities, an indefinite stay in New York for a visiting prince. Recently, looking through a copy of an American fashion magazine, Fanny saw a photograph of a pair of shoes with the caption "These are the shoes that Violet, Duchess of Rutland, has worn for twenty years." What the magazine meant was that the Duchess ordered new shoes made from the same last year after year, but upon inquiry from Fanny, the Duchess stated that she had never seen the shoes in the picture, much less worn them. The case was settled out of court for a reasonable sum, which the Duchess graciously accepted. The Duchess has painted, and has exhibited in her London shows, a portrait of Fanny. It is a highly romantic, rather ethereal likeness, the eyes looking heavenward, the brow topped by a halo of curls.

One of Fanny's celebrated cases was the suit she brought for Francis Hackett against Alexander Korda and United Artists, charging that Korda's film *The Private Life of Henry the Eighth* was plagiarized from Hackett's earlier book, *Henry VIII*. The main question—whether Henry VIII is a subject in the public domain, outlawed by the passage of time from any copyright litigation—was interesting to Fanny, and the case concerned copyright law, which she likes to think of as her specialty. The case was settled out of court, but it led indirectly to a coolness between Hackett and Fanny. Some time afterward, Hackett wrote a fictionized biography of Anne Boleyn and used Fanny's suggestion that Anne be presented as a woman who was willing to be beheaded rather than bastardize her daughter Elizabeth, the future queen. At Fanny's further prompting, Hackett later wrote a play around the same idea, and sent it to Fanny to read. Fanny didn't like the play but she still admires the idea, which she considers her own, and she has been heard, once or twice lately, to talk wishfully of suing Hackett for plagiarism.

14

Sweetheart:

MARY PICKFORD

A FRIEND of Mary Pickford's, going to her once for advice in some personal catastrophe, listened skeptically while Mary besought her to be tranquil and strong and to believe that everything would surely come out happily in the end. At these words, the afflicted one grew bitter. "Pollyanna," she muttered. Instantly a grimness settled over Mary. She was not, she insisted gravely, and never had been a Pollyanna.

But she is, nevertheless, an unremitting optimist. Let disaster and woe rain upon her, on her family, or her friends, Mary never stops reminding herself and everyone else that things might be much worse than they are. To a fellow star whose career lay in ruins and whose private life had been tragically shattered, she once said earnestly, "Think how much more awful it would be if you had lost a leg." Somehow this habit is not as irritating as it sounds, perhaps because she applies the same dogged cheer so relentlessly to herself, and because her optimism has that quality of fierceness which is inseparable from her character. Good will prevail, her charming mouth will tell you, while something in her wide, uncompromising face adds silently that it damn well better.

It was no accident of golden curls that made Mary the richest and most famous moving-picture star in the world. America's sweetheart is a business woman, hardheaded, patient, and positive. The conferences that, in 1919, preceded the forming of United Artists—meetings that included Chaplin, Fairbanks, D. W. Griffith, and their lawyers—were quietly dominated by Mary. She had then, as she has now, the gift of intelligent listening, but at the end of one of these thoughtful silences, her rather high, Canadian voice would announce, "I disagree with you, gentlemen, and I will tell you why." It generally turned out that she was right. The United Artists Corporation was her idea, to start with. Earlier, in 1918, when she was an independent producer, she had released her pictures through First National, but had found this method of distributing her product to be unsatisfactory. Through the system of "block booking" (selling to an exhibitor the picture he wants only if he will buy a certain number of other pictures along with it), First National was making Mary's pictures support a whole train of mediocre productions, and she saw that this was highly uneconomic for her. It occurred to her that she could make much better profits by organizing a de luxe company to release the pictures of only the biggest stars. United Artists was the result.

She has always had a pretty alert idea of what the public wants. Not long after her marriage to Douglas Fairbanks, in 1920, the Victor Talking Machine Company offered them twenty thousand dollars to make a talking record together. Douglas thought it might be a good idea; Mary disagreed. "I know," she said, "what a phonograph record can be like, once you get sick of it. People follow us in the street now, and mob us at theaters, but if they have that phonograph record at home, and children, maybe, who like to play it over and over, they might get sick of the whole thing, and of us, too."

In contrast to this positive attitude toward business, Mary is, in private conversation, astonishingly pliable. Talking to an interviewer who once suggested that, after her separation from Douglas, her situation was pathetic, she worked herself, purely by the power of suggestion, into a state of pathos so acute that she finally believed in it herself until the interview was over. For an interviewer who seems to expect a Spartan gaiety, Mary will be Spartan and gay until he has got his story. She does this unconsciously, almost automatically, because she has tried for so long to be what she thinks the public wants her to be. She is inclined to grow fierce about the magazine and newspaper articles, published still occasionally, which have asked the public to be sorry for her because her starring days are probably over, or because she is fifty years old; she knows that this is damaging publicity. It is true that about half of these stories are written by people whom she has never seen, but the other half, the authentic and equally maudlin interviews, can be traced to Mary herself and to her flexibility in the presence of interviewers.

With her friends, she is equally susceptible. Urged variously by those who are fond of her to be gay, debonair, philosophic, or stately in any crisis, she will promise to try to follow all of this conflicting advice. She is as lacking in conviction about her private life as she is obstinate about the practical side of her career.

In this personal bewilderment which afflicts her, her only positive opinions are concerned with business and religion. Discussing any other aspect of life, her conversation is baffling and consists largely of aphorisms. "Be a guardian, not an usher, at the portal of your thought" is a favorite with her. "Increase of appetite grows by what it feeds on" is, rather strangely, another. She likes to talk in generalities, which, with a disarming air of sincerity, she brings forth as great truths. Other people's thoughts genuinely inspire her, and she conducts her personal life by the application of symbolic phrases to her own problems. Her mind, except where business is involved, is receptive; she is a believer, unhampered by any skepticism. When her mother died, sixteen years ago, Mary turned to Christian Science, and for a time aggressively applied that creed, with all its mottoes, to herself and to everyone around her. Now she says that she has come to have more common sense about it. Certainly in her case, the Christian Science doctrine of ultimate harmony, fondly as she cherishes it, marches hand in hand with an underlying instinct to do something pretty brisk in a crisis herself.

Her life at Pickfair during the first years of her marriage to Douglas was undeniably dull. Both of them worked from six in the morning until night most of the time, and their guests at dinner were a strange company of Douglas's trainers and the professional wits and yes-men who eternally clung to him. Mary sat at the head of the table; Douglas, dark and prankish, sat at her side, sometimes disappearing under the table to frighten people by grabbing at their ankles, occasionally vanishing to be found, later, in the chandelier; always there was, somewhere, a chair wired so that the most important guest would get an electric shock when he sat down. Mary, in the midst of these antics, remained pleasant but curiously grave. She had not then, and still has not, many intimate women friends. Sometimes Frances Marion, the scenario-writer, or Lillian Gish would come to dinner, but Mary was, more often than not, the only woman at the table. Neither she nor Douglas drank anything at all—not from any moral conviction, but because Douglas at that time had never tasted liquor, and Mary had no interest in it; rather bad drinks were served, however, to any guests who wanted them. At ten o'clock, a butler passed a tray with cups of Ovaltine or a dish of fruit. After that, people usually went home.

Outwardly, their life was exciting enough. That they were king and queen of Hollywood was no fan-writer's dream; their position there was unique to an almost fantastic degree. People who had not been asked to visit Pickfair began to refer to it bitterly as Buckingham Palace. No *première* of any picture at Grauman's Chinese Theatre started until Mary and Douglas were in their seats. Once, when Mary arrived a little late at a tea where the screen's most glamorous feminine stars were assembled, every woman in the room stood up as she entered. Hostesses all over town willingly ruined their table arrangements by changing the place cards so that Mary and Douglas might sit next to each other at dinner; it was an accepted rule that they never be separated, at their own or at any other table. At home, Douglas sat at Mary's left, and the guest of honor, whether a man or a woman, at her right; nobody ever sat at Douglas's right except Mary. At parties, they danced only with each other. Mary says now that this strange pact was Douglas's idea, not hers, and that she began to find it less enchanting when he pointed out to her on one occasion, when the late Duke of Kent visited Pickfair, that it also prevented her from dancing with His Royal Highness.

A dinner or a weekend at Pickfair soon became a part of the schedule planned for any visitor of distinction arriving in Hollywood, and with the coming of royalty, things at the Fairbankses' house grew livelier. The Crown Prince (later King) of Siam liked his dinner party there so much that he had his equerry telephone twice during the following week to ask whether he and his Princess might come again, informally. Dinner was always prepared for fifteen, whether fifteen people or three eventually sat down to it; when Mary and Douglas were working, it was served whenever they got home from the studio, sometimes as late as ten or eleven. Mary had fourteen servants, but on one occasion even these were not enough. A certain duke whom Mary and Douglas had, in Europe, casually invited to come and stay with them some time in Hollywood arrived, some months later, and announced that his party numbered seventeen. It was only by persuading Mr. Chaplin to move out of his house nearby that the host and hostess, startled but pleased, were able to provide for the retinue.

This was all pretty good fun, but Mary was not entirely happy. She is half Irish, with the Irish clan feeling strong in her, and she wasn't seeing enough of her own family. She would have preferred having her mother and Jack and Lottie around her to this endless pageantry of noble guests. There is nothing swanky about Mary; her early life was simple to the point of starkness, and she has never lost that simplicity.

The biographical facts about Mary Pickford are already familiar to the public. She was born in Toronto, and her name was Gladys Smith; her father, an impractical Englishman, died when she was four, and in 1899, at the age of six, Mary went to work for the Valentine Stock Company in Toronto. The careers of Lottie and Jack were from the beginning nebulous and uncertain, but Mary had inherited her Irish mother's persistency—that quality which had enabled Charlotte Smith to find work for her children, and an occasional acting job for herself, until Mary was launched as the breadwinner of the family. When she was fourteen, Mary made her first film for Biograph; it was directed by D. W. Griffith and called *Her First Biscuits*. After that, she began to be known as "the Biograph girl," and her pay in one year and a half was raised from $40 a week to $5,000 a year, a lavish motion-picture salary for those days. After a stage appearance under the direction of David Belasco in *A Good Little Devil*, she made, in 1913, a movie of the play for Famous Players. Two years later she became vice-president of the Mary Pickford-Famous Players Company at a salary of $2,000 a week and fifty per cent of the profits, and when, in the following year, her own company was organized under the name of Artcraft Pictures, Mary's salary was more than doubled, and she still received her share of the profits. She became an independent producer in 1918, one year before the organization of United Artists, releasing a series of pictures—notably *Daddy-Long-Legs*—through First National. In the handling of her present fortune, estimated at between two and four million dollars, Mary is practical and shrewd, but money in the form of a twenty-dollar bill or a check for ten times that amount means little to her. When she was ten years old, she played in Chicago in a melodrama called *The Child-Wife;* her salary then was $30 a week, and she did her own laundry in the basement of her boarding house. Thirty years later, in 1934, she made her second stage appearance in that city, for a week, for which she got $15,000. This impressed her when she thought about it, but she lost the check for $15,000 just the same. (A secretary found it later.)

Until her marriage to Charles (Buddy) Rogers in 1937, Mary Pickford's life was less happy than many women's. Through it all—the failure of her marriage to Owen Moore, the loss of her mother and her brother, and her separation and divorce from Douglas—she was sustained less by her optimism than by her passion for work. For months before her stage appearance in a one-act vaudeville sketch several years ago she had four lessons a day in singing and speaking, to develop her voice, which, although improved by talking pictures, still retained a good deal of its natural, slightly breathless tone. It cannot, even now, be called mellow, but its strength and flexibility have increased, and her enunciation is excellent. She took piano lessons at the same time, and would stay for hours in an upper room at Pickfair, practicing breathing exercises, scales, recitations, and songs. The windows of that room, over the servants' entrance, were kept closed because Mary was nervous about having the delivery boys hear her. She did laughing exercises, too, and is apt to do them now when she has a few minutes to spare, beginning with a careful laugh on a low note and ending in a rich peal; it sounds fairly eerie in her suite at the Sherry-Netherland. She likes to try to give as much as possible of a long speech from any play in one breath, and to recite *The Raven,* with expression; her teacher has been scrupulous about the different inflections of "nevermore." Her singing voice, low at first, is getting higher, and she can reach high C now, but it upsets her to have to do it. The first song she learned was "Who's Afraid of the Big, Bad Wolf?" followed by "Gather Lip-Rouge While You May," "My Wild Irish Rose," and the Leland Stanford college song, "Hail, Stanford, Hail!" Her biggest number is "Parlez-moi d'amour," which she sings and plays with considerable dreaminess. At one time she had a French teacher on the set with her every day, and took lessons between camera shots until she had learned to speak the language, as she does today, with a successful lack of accent and a fair fluency. She wants, some day, to act a play in French, possibly Musset's *Il faut qu'une porte soit ouverte ou fermée.*

Estimates of Mary's ability as an actress are varied; she is perhaps, on the whole, a clever actress rather than a thoughtful one. Her gift for mimicry is startling, and one of her stunts, a conversation between two fashionable ladies in the ladies' dressing room of a restaurant, is very funny and a little ribald. Her sense of humor is fitful, but occasionally achieves a degree of lunacy; she used to make up names for Douglas and for herself, and one Christmas her present to him was labelled "From Till de Pewr to Frin de Sprink." She rarely smokes; when she does, she smokes a cork-tipped cigarette, and she is apt to put the wrong end in her mouth. Her imagination is sometimes grimly pictorial, and more than once she has put down a cup of tea half-finished because she has had a sudden mental picture of her insides being slowly and dreadfully toughened, like leather, by the tannic acid in the tea. Since she read *The Jungle,* by Upton Sinclair, years ago, she has been unable to eat red meat, and if it is accidentally served to her at her own table, she will leave the dining room and refuse to eat anything at all. She likes to drink a little port at home, these days, and, when she goes out, occasionally gets very funny on a couple of cocktails or—in another mood—volubly indignant about something or other. Her capacity for indignation is tremendous, but concerned mostly with abstract problems of life and behavior, seldom with individuals. With her friends, she is good-humored and adaptable. She is, fundamentally, a good companion with a gift for making people fond of her.

She is scrupulous about her appearance in public, because she feels that people expect her to look well. The first time she was recognized on a New York street (it was in front of the Strand Theater in 1914), she had on an ugly hat, and it worried her for days—not to such an extent, however, that she forgot to ask for a raise on the strength of the public recognition. At home, she has no personal vanity at all, and will sit talking for hours with a shiny nose and her hair done up in pins or pulled straight back from her face—a style that, quite by accident, is very becoming. Her hair is about three inches long in back and naturally wavy; she has a vegetable rinse with every third or fourth shampoo to keep the lights in it. She weighs, now, one hundred and two pounds, and is exactly five feet tall. Her size, in her own opinion, is one reason public officials like to be photographed with her; it makes them look bigger.

Three months' schooling in Toronto at the age of five was the extent of Mary's formal education, but much of her spare time since has been devoted to learning. Her reading is disciplinary rather than intellectual. When she can, she reads a little, slowly, of a book she has heard about, sometimes taking twenty minutes to a page, because she stops to memorize in order to increase her facility for learning parts. When she lives in a hotel, there are no books and no other evidences of personality to be found about her rooms, except *Science and Health* and one or two current biographies.

She is never idle and never rests during the day. Even when she is playing four shows daily in personal appearances at picture houses, she never lies down until she goes to bed for the night. She is almost never alone; her remaining relatives —Gwynne Pickford, her niece; Verna Chalif, a cousin; and her two adopted children, Ronnie and Roxanne—generally surround her, as well as the usual retinue of a movie personage: two secretaries, two maids, managers, and lawyers. Sometimes, faced with a problem, Mary goes into her bedroom alone and talks out loud to herself. These private monologues are apt to sound very fierce, and Mary emerges from them pale but positive.

United Artists is now controlled by Mary, David Selznick, Sir Alexander Korda, and Chaplin. When Mary bought *Junior Miss* for pictures last winter, she sat in conference over certain technical points of the deal with ten men, some of whom had not met her before. They were Fleischer, the negotiator, Cohen, his assistant, Rafferty and O'Brien of O'Brien, Malevinsky & Driscoll (Mary's lawyers), Grad Sears, distribution head of United Artists, Sol Myers, attorney for the authors, Max Gordon, A. L. Behrman, his attorney, Paul Streger of the Leland Hayward office (agents for the authors), and Howard Reinheimer, Hayward's lawyer. "It took us ten guys about five minutes to catch on to just *who* was going to be the focal point of that meeting, whose business head was going to prevail," Streger said afterward, shaking his head admiringly. "Little Mary was it, all right." Mary bought *Junior Miss* for $355,000 plus thirty-five per cent of the profits.

Buddy Rogers, a tall, likeable man who has successfully lived down his unfortunate nickname and a pretty-boy reputation, is a lieutenant in the Navy Ferry Command, and is on active duty most of the time these days. After the war Mary may act again, possibly with her husband. In the meantime she wants, perhaps more acutely than anything else, to be thought of as a mature and capable person—an achievement difficult enough for any woman between whom and the public the ghost of a little girl with yellow curls keeps on plaintively intruding.

❁ 15 ❁

Dance Team:

THE DE MARCOS

IT COSTS A TEAM of ballroom dancers in the white-tie-and-tails class—such as Veloz and Yolanda, Medrano and Donna, Mario and Floria, or the De Marcos—about $10,000 to produce their act before the public ever sees it and approximately $30,000 a year to keep it going after that, if it is successful. These sums include the rent of a rehearsal studio, accompanists' wages, and money paid out for music, orchestral arrangements, publicity, and clothes. In addition to the financial investment, there is the constant worry about "good will," which means, to the team, that night-club patrons must be pleased, not only by the skill and appearance of the couple, but by their exchange of tender glances, their effect of being soulfully one. This is especially true if the members of the team are married to each other. Something about the spectacle of a man and his wife dancing romantically together moves the customers to a mellowness that can put a pair of married dancers into a terrible state of nerves if things are not going well at home. Of all people in show business—notoriously an emotional calling—they are most rigidly forbidden the frown, the whispered battle cry, the slight kick on the instep that might relieve them. The spotlight is on them, the patrons are at their elbows and all must seem harmonious. The team's profit on the money invested in the act and on the hours of grim rehearsal depends so much on the illusion of mutual enchantment the dancers create that one understands the married hoofer, maddened by domestic cares, who once worked out a routine with his wife to the tune of "Why Do I Love You?" "Two grand a week," he explained to her on opening night, just before they moved graciously onto the floor.

Tony De Marco is a man who knows all about the woes of keeping a team together. Sally, his present partner and wife, is his ninth partner and the third to become Mrs. De Marco. His eighth, and possibly best-known partner was Renée De Marco, who was also his wife for some nine years. Tony and Renée separated twice matrimonially and once professionally during their career together. Shortly before their first separation they appeared nightly at the Persian Room in the Plaza and were generally considered to be the best white-tie-and-tails team in the country, though some dissenters held out in favor of Veloz and Yolanda. The woes that parted the De Marcos had nothing to do with dancing; they were merely the familiar headaches that can threaten any marriage—trouble over money and trouble with in-laws. As a dance team they remained indestructible, even when they weren't dancing, and neither Tony nor Renée De Marco had any thought of taking on a new partner. When they had been apart a year, the Waldorf-Astoria announced the return of the De Marcos ("Together Again!"), and hundreds of people crowded emotionally into the Sert Room to welcome them back. It was a sentimental occasion. Pub-crawlers, always mushy beneath the sable coat and the flowered lapel, like to look at happiness, and the De Marcos had always seemed to be more genuinely pleased about dancing with each other than most fashionable dancers; they were little and likeable and full of affectionate tricks. On opening night in the Sert Room, one ringside matron stood up and kissed Renée De Marco impulsively as she passed the table, and exclaimed, "I'm so happy for you, dear child! Another was seen to weep freely as she grasped Tony by the arm and murmured fiercely, "Now you be *good* to that darling girl!"

Demonstrations like these gratified the De Marcos and startled them, as their reunion was a strictly professional one. They were friendly to the extent that each of them stated this fact emphatically to other people, but they lived apart. Renée had her own apartment at the Delmonico, where she lived in a happy whirl of telephone calls, shopping trips, and friends dropping in. She was—and is still—dark-haired, soft-spoken, beautifully dressed, and feminine to the point of looking fragile. Tony liked to think of his wife as helpless, as enchanted by her new freedom and by a full social life for which he has never had much time or energy. "Renée is only a kid," he would say, "and she's crazy about society. *You* know—A. C. Blumenthal and those people."

Two years later, the De Marcos split up permanently, this time with a divorce, and Renée worked up a successful night-club act of her own with a trio of male dancers as a background. As his new partner, Tony engaged Sally Craven, who had been a ballerina in *Boys and Girls Together,* the show in which Tony and Renée made their last appearance as a team. Sally at once took the name De Marco, as all of Tony's partners do. It became legally hers when she married Tony in May, 1944.

Sally De Marco is a dashing brunette in her late twenties, but Tony, some twelve years older, is far jauntier. He has a flip way of pulling the brim of a soft hat down over his eyes, and he walks like a dancer, quickly and gracefully. Waiting for a green light at a street crossing, he is apt to go into a tap routine at the curb, and when he crosses against the light—as he would rather do—his progress among taxicabs and trucks is a dance number in itself. It is only when he sits down that he looks tired.

He has lived for many years in the apartment once occupied by the late Florenz Ziegfeld, in the Ziegfeld Theatre building on Sixth Avenue. Tony has furnished the apartment with pieces from a house he and Renée once had at Rockville Centre, and the *décor* includes some rather massive furniture, several oil paintings, and a mink coverlet for the bed. The large living room contains almost nothing except a grand piano and a phonograph, and the De Marcos rehearse there before a mirror that covers one wall. The mirror is blue, so Tony and his partner see themselves with a kind of gloomy accuracy, unrelieved by any reflection of light from the windows opposite. At rehearsals, Tony, in a white shirt, gray slacks, and gray suède shoes, shuffles thoughtfully around the floor at first, while Sally, barelegged, in sandals, and wearing print culottes and a backless, halter-neck sweater, sits expectantly on the piano. At the piano is a young man, earnest and spectacled, named Sam or Paul or Charlie. (The De Marcos change their rehearsal accompanists often, so as to surprise themselves into keeping things lively.)

Presently Tony puts a record on the phonograph, and the accompanist listens attentively, his hands off the keys. Tony dances slowly across to the piano. "Do you get it?" he asks the accompanist. "Da da *dee-ee,* dada dum de um hm-m. . . ." For a minute he stands over the boy at the piano, his arms and shoulders and feet moving, his hands conducting the music from the phonograph in the corner. "Pick it up from there," he says suddenly, shutting off the phonograph. "All right, Sally." Sally slides down from the piano and accurately meets him in the middle of the floor. Tony whistles the melody continuously as they dance, except for occasional directions thrown over his shoulder to the piano-player. "Wait. Right there, bring it *up*"—here he curves one hand, lifting it—"now, sh-h-h. . . . Retard. . . . Now! Bring it *up* again." Sometimes Leonard, the colored valet, plods through the room during rehearsal, laden with packages and bound for a storeroom in the rear. "Hello, Leonard," Sally says, her face upside down and whirling. "Hello, Leonard," says Tony, spinning madly, "did you get that suit from the cleaner?" Leonard replies briefly and goes on his way. Sometimes the end of a dance comes out wrong at rehearsal. "Why do you finish over there, dear?" Tony asks mildly. "I'm over here." Sally explains that she thought he had said he wanted to finish nearer the middle of the floor so there would be more room between themselves and the ringside tables in whatever room they are rehearsing for. The De Marcos like to keep the size and shape of their current dance floor in their minds when they practice, and Tony has counted the exact number of steps he can take from various points on the Sert Room floor, for instance, before his coattails begin brushing the customers' champagne glasses. "When in doubt," he tells Sally, "always take the first ending." This is part of the De Marco team language and it means that Tony and Sally dance away from each other for sixteen bars, to finish with

Sally bent backward over Tony's arm; this gives him time to improvise or fill in if anything has gone wrong, or occasionally just for variety.

Sometimes Tony simply happens upon a good finish for a dance. Rehearsing a new number one day during one of his Persian Room engagements with Renée, he took out his handkerchief to mop his brow while he waited for Renée to dance across the floor to him and sink into the low curtsy he had planned. Feeling prankish, Tony bent down as his partner approached and lightly dusted off with his handkerchief the spot on the floor where she was to subside. When he caught this gesture in the mirror it seemed good enough to keep in the act, and it is still a popular finish with De Marco fans—the one in which Tony dances around the floor courteously dusting off one spot after another for his partner to sink onto.

Another number that patrons still call for came about in a haphazard way some years ago. One night Tony learned that Jerome Kern was in the Persian Room; as a compliment, he had Eddy Duchin play one of Kern's current hits, "The Way You Look Tonight." It was a tune the De Marcos had never used, and they set about ad-libbing a dance to it. "You go out on the floor, take out your compact, and fuss with your face and hair," Tony said to Renée, "and I'll come out and dance around you, admiring you." The impromptu dance was a hit, and the De Marcos later worked it up into a waltz, abandoning Mr. Kern's music for Noel Coward's "I'll Follow My Secret Heart."

Generally Tony does not like to dance to the music of popular song hits unless like "Tea for Two"—a standard De Marco number—they have become so popular as to be classics. A dance routine to a current tune becomes quickly dated; also, it is easier for other dancers to copy than, say, a number danced to the music of Chopin or Debussy. De Marco is always as fiercely on the lookout for style pirates as any fashionable couturier.

Two of the team's most popular dances are traceable partly to such shrewd reasoning and partly to a more romantic origin. One spring Tony was living in a Hollywood hotel, spending a good deal of time brooding over his separation from Renée. He had danced only once professionally in nearly two years—a number with Joan Crawford in *The Shining Hour* that sent him to a hospital for two weeks with a sprained shoulder and hip. "It was not Miss Crawford's fault," Tony explains earnestly in his high, husky voice, "she is a perfectly proportioned girl, but you can't get away from the truth. She weighs one hundred and twenty-eight pounds and I weigh one hundred and thirty-seven, with all my clothes on." When he got out of the hospital a friend in San Francisco sent him some phonograph records to cheer him up. Among them were Debussy's *Clair de lune* and Chopin's Waltz in C sharp minor—an odd choice, perhaps, for jollying along a lonely man with sprained muscles, but, as it turned out, a fortunate one. Dancing alone around his hotel room to the music of those two records, Tony began, for the first time in over a year, to think up a couple of new routines.

His association with Sally, unharrassed by domestic cares, has been more prolific, and in various movies in which the team has appeared he has turned out some effective routines including "Make with the Feet," "Intermezzo," "I've Got a Nickel to My Name," and "Poo-Poo-Paducah"—a number which Tony danced with Carmen Miranda in a picture called *The Gang's All Here*. Like most dancers, bandleaders, and other people in the voiceless branches of show business, the De Marcos want to act. One of the engagements that pleased them most was the movie *Greenwich Village,* in which they played a couple of delicatessen proprietors who wanted to be dancers.

For night-club appearances the De Marcos receive $2,250 a week, which is paid to Tony; Sally is under contract to him for five years, at a guaranteed yearly income based on a fixed minimum. "What the minimum is, I would rather not divulge," Tony replies to questions concerning it, "but as far as the *maximum* goes, the sky is the limit." When the De Marcos are working Sally is paid forty rather than fifty per cent of the team's weekly salary, but Tony figures that this is just, since the remaining ten per cent covers about half of the team's publicity and other expenses.

Tony De Marco is Sally's first professional dancing partner; Sally, according to Tony, is his last. He made the same emphatic and hopeful announcement concerning Renée, who was the second of his partners to become Mrs. De Marco. The first Mrs. De Marco was Mabel Scott, from whom Tony was divorced some twenty years ago. The trouble that split the team that time began when the De Marcos—Tony and Mabel—were touring the Keith-Orpheum vaudeville circuit, and Mabel was taken so sick that she had to leave the act. Tony wired the booking office to send another partner to fill in until Mabel got well, and the office sent a girl named Helen Kroner. Helen's dancing suited Tony so admirably that, when Mabel was well enough to stand a bit of news, Tony told her he had decided to engage Miss Kroner as his permanent partner. The battle that followed lasted for more than a year, off and on, until Mabel and Tony were divorced in Chicago, in 1924. Tony was dancing in *George White's Scandals* then, with Helen Kroner as the other half of the act, and he had already persuaded Miss Kroner to abandon any independent ambition she may have had, for the good of the team.

Helen Kroner had danced in a ballet company with Pavlowa, and Tony respected her artistic training, but the De Marcos were beginning to be known to audiences and booking agents, and to change the billing would be bad for business.

Tony rechristened Miss Kroner Nina De Marco, announced that she was his sister, and continued the act with the usual billing. All of his other partners—Peggy Hooper, Maxine Arnold, Albertina Vitak, Patricia Bowman, and Arline Langen—became De Marcos professionally, for the sake of the billing. Some of these girls were trained dancers (Miss Bowman and Miss Vitak were successful later under their own names), but they took instruction willingly from Tony, who has never had a dancing lesson. It takes several days, according to De Marco, just to get the established notions about ballroom dancing out of a new partner's head. For instance, the customary motion of the arm in a waltz is a wide, semicircular sweep in an unbroken line; Tony likes to scatter this gesture into two or maybe three smaller movements, accenting the rhythm of the music. In a fox trot, he likes to time his "breaks" vividly. A "break" in two-four time usually comes at the end of eight or sixteen bars, where the melody changes into another phrase. To take "Tea for Two" as an example:

> Picture you upon my knee
> With tea for two, and two for tea,
> Me for you and you for me
> Alone. . . .*

The break comes after the word "alone." One reason the De Marcos can do a considerable amount of ad-libbing around a dance floor is that they know when the breaks are coming. "I'll take it," Tony murmurs to Sally as a break approaches, and that means that he will improvise a dance around her; sometimes he says, "You take it," meaning that she must ad-lib a few steps around him.

Except for such casual inventions between partners who are sure of each other, exhibition ballroom dancing is an exact business, carefully planned and timed. Tony has found that, training a new partner, he must restrict her to plain fox trots, waltzes, tangos, and rumbas for two or three days before he begins to teach her steps in groups—so many steps for the first sixteen bars, another group for the next sixteen. Generally the girls want to leap high in the air in his arms or to toss themselves onto his shoulders for a spin right away, but he discourages this kind of acrobatics—known in the profession as a "lift"—until his partner has perfected her other steps and has learned to hold her back straight and her hips in when dancing, and to use her hands and arms as entertainingly as she uses her feet. A "lift" in ballroom dancing is accomplished by a method borrowed from the ballet. No dancer could raise his partner high off the floor or let her down again gracefully if his legs were stiffly posed or placed apart, so a lift begins with the *assemblé* (feet together at a slight angle) and ends with the *plié* (knees bent). One of De Marco's early partners was fond of food, and Tony began to find it hard to get her off the floor, even with the *assemblé*

* Used by permission of the Copyright Owners, Harms, Inc.

and the *plié,* though she vowed that she had not altered from her original weight of one hundred and fifteen pounds. That partnership dissolved when, one day, Tony shoved her unexpectedly onto a drugstore scale. "It's a lie!" she cried as the needle trembled at one hundred and thirty. Sally weighs one hundred and six, a nice weight for a De Marco. The tricks of whirling a partner on the shoulders or raising her high on one arm and spinning with her depend less, however, on physical strength than on timing and balance. Nearly all ballroom exhibition dancers wear rubber soles on their dancing shoes, to preserve their balance on waxed floors. The reason they can tap wearing rubber soles, as the De Marcos do, is that they put the full weight of each leg into every tap step, swinging the leg from the hip. Eccentric dancers and solo tap specialists use their feet more than their legs in dancing—Fred Astaire, for example, dances from the knees down, Bill Robinson from the ankles down; ballroom dancers dance from the hips down.

Tony De Marco began to be fairly well known in vaudeville about 1921, when he was presented to trustful audiences as "a native Argentinian dancer." The Valentino fever was approaching its height, and people everywhere were sighing for Argentines. Tony's act with Mabel (who soon became Mabelle) was billed as "The De Marcos from the National Theatre, Buenos Aires, with Their Seven Musical Sheiks." Neither Tony nor Mabelle had ever seen the National Theater or Buenos Aires, and the Seven Musical Sheiks were just seven Filipinos who played on Spanish guitars, but nobody seemed to mind, except possibly the Filipinos, who never got quite used to their long white robes and burnooses. When Nina De Marco (née Helen Kroner) replaced Mabelle in the act, ostensibly as Tony's sister, she added a further exotic tang by giving out arresting interviews about her childhood in South America with her brother, and about riding on muleback across the Andes one time to keep a dancing engagement. In San Francisco a feminine admirer wrote to Tony in Spanish, apologizing for her poor knowledge of the language he had inspired her to study. Tony got a stagehand who knew Spanish to read the letter to him and replied in perfect English, explaining that as the lady had made the flattering gesture of addressing him in his native tongue, he wished to return the compliment by responding in hers. When the National Theatre in Buenos Aires got wind of these goings-on and began writing protests to *La Prensa,* New York's Spanish newspaper, Tony sadly dropped the South American touch from his vaudeville billing. He continued to be known as an Argentine though, and to speak, when called upon to do so in the line of business, with a faint accent which he hoped was South American. It was not until a few years ago that he felt himself sufficiently established as a dancer to drop the accent and reveal the whole truth. "I was born in Buffalo," he told interviewers peacefully then.

Actually, Antonio De Marco was born in Fredonia, New York, fifty miles from Buffalo. His father, an Italian immigrant, operated a small truck farm there and hated all dancers because his own father, Carmelo di Marco, who owned a mill near Palermo, had lost it on account of an uncontrolled desire to leave his business and travel around the countryside dancing at *festas.* (The name di Marco was Gallicized by Tony's father.) It grieved and alarmed the elder De Marco to see his only son, Antonio, with his hair greased and his ears deaf to any sound but dance music, streaking off night after night to compete in one of the amateur dance contests regularly held at the Academy Theatre in Buffalo, and when Tony, at sixteen, demanded long trousers to dignify his social life, his father declined to give them to him. Tony bought them, and other fancy wearing apparel, by delivering meat for Valentine Brothers, a firm of butchers on Main Street, at three dollars a week in winter (for deliveries made after school hours) and eight dollars for full time in summer. One warm payday the butcher's boy took his eight dollars to the race track at Fort Erie and won $160 on a horse named Jim L. With money in his pocket, he then departed without notice to anyone for New York, where he eventually got a job touring with a burlesque troupe called Jean Bedini's Mischief Makers. One night in Wheeling, West Virginia, Tony came off the stage after doing a tango and a maxixe with his partner, a large blonde, and found his father and the principal of the Fredonia High School waiting for him in the wings. Dragged home and slapped into school again, he remained an indifferent scholar and explained to his teachers that he couldn't think sitting down. Nowadays De Marco gets up and moves his feet around in a tentative dance step when he has anything important to say. Most of his thinking is concerned with dancing, and he talks about it better when his legs and feet are in motion.

De Marco *père* at last consented to let his son dance professionally on condition that he change his name, and from 1918 to 1921 Tony and Mabel Scott appeared as The DeMarrs at the Cataract House in Niagara Falls, at the Café Frontenac in Detroit, and on the Pantages vaudeville circuit, where the team got three hundred dollars a week in "The Act Different." The following year Tony resumed his own name and his friendly relations with his father, and, first with Mabel and later with Nina as his partner, whirled through the Keith-Orpheum circuit to the Palace Theatre in New York. The De Marcos began appearing in fashionable night clubs and occasionally in musical comedies. Nina and Tony's partnership, begun in 1922, lasted seven years, though it was split by temperamental differences three times during that period. When they separated finally, in 1929, Nina put on a dancing act by herself. She is still dancing alone, here and there, under the name of Nina De Marco.

After the separation, Tony, temporarily without a partner, went to Hollywood to stage dances for a revue. In answer to a chorus call, a girl named Renée Leblanc applied. She was about eighteen and she was dressed in a sports dress, socks, and sandals. To this casual costume she had added, for the occasion, a brown moiré coat trimmed with ermine tails. Renée, born in Montreal, was the daughter of a French Canadian woman, née Leduc, and an Englishman named Nerny. One of Renée's uncles was George Primrose, the minstrel and soft-shoe dancer. She had had one lesson from Theodore Kosloff, the Russian ballet master, had danced with a Fanchon & Marco unit in vaudeville, and had lately been doing a rather inconspicuous solo number at the Montmartre, a Hollywood night club. She had tried Renée Leduc as a stage name, but because everybody pronounced her last name Leduck, she had changed it to Leblanc—not the happiest selection, since everybody including Mr. De Marco pronounced *that* Leblank. Renée got a job in the revue, and when Tony had taken her out dancing several times after the show, he told her one night that he thought she could learn to dance if she worked at it, and asked her to be his partner. Renée agreed to try and to drop her troublesome French names for the name of De Marco.

The De Marcos rehearsed at odd hours during the run of the show, and when it closed they opened in vaudeville at the Hill Street Theatre in Los Angeles. Tony, who had acquired a sensitive taste in clothes, restrained Renée from a sudden, shouting desire for spangles and ordered for her a simple white chiffon dress with three wide ruffles at the hem. On opening night, Renée, eager to please, danced so hard that she put her foot through the bottom ruffle and tore it to a bandage that clung around her ankles and locked them together throughout the first number a waltz. Although she soon became as accomplished a performer as Tony, things like that continued to happen to her so often that Tony patiently took to carrying two safety pins in his pocket whenever they danced. Besides being a practical precaution against the emergency of a broken shoulder strap, or of an entire dress top's giving away under the strain of dancing, as it once did, the safety pins amused the customers when they were brought to use. Tony still whips them out occasionally, dancing with Sally. They are, in a way, typical of the airy inventiveness that distinguishes the De Marcos from other sultrier ballroom dancers.

In 1934 the Plaza announced the opening of a new room for dinner and supper dancing, with Emil Coleman's orchestra and the De Marcos. Nobody in New York had heard much about the De Marcos. They had appeared briefly at the Central Park Casino and at the Empire Room in the Waldorf-Astoria, and they had been married to each other recently.

The Plaza seemed, to expert night-clubbers, an unlikely place for a supper club anyway. It was a place for tea, for Sunday morning breakfast, for dowagers and potted palms; any excitement it held belonged to the past, when Scott Fitzgerald debutantes danced in the Plaza Grill and the Rose Room was so famous a song was written about it. In 1934 the Grill was occupied mostly by middle-aged people from the suburbs, and the Rose Room had been turned into an automobile salesroom. At the risk of public indifference, the Plaza management moved the cars out of the salesroom, had the place decorated by Joseph Urban, and rather nervously gave out the news that the Persian Room was open for business. For almost three weeks after the opening night, which was principally an invitation affair, almost nobody came. Then business began to improve, partly by way of the Plaza's own elevators, when the calm and opulent residents of the hotel wandered in to see what was going on and later spread the word around town. Night-club explorers, bored by night-club dancers who seemed to be bored with each other, suddenly discovered that the De Marcos were different. The De Marcos were gay, they talked to each other, to Coleman, and to people at the tables while they danced, and they had a way of laughing together when a certain step pleased them, or when another went wrong. When Tony went into an intense tap solo and his partner, Renée, sitting aloof at a small table, said scornfully, "Ha! Six-seven-*eight*, I know *that* one," and got up and did it, the customers were fascinated. The Persian Room took in an average weekly gross of $23,000 during the four years the De Marcos danced there, and it was a popular guess that without that income the Plaza might have had trouble financially. Tony likes to think of himself as the savior of the Plaza, and sometimes refers to his engagements there with a trace of melancholy. "We lived in a two-room apartment in the hotel, free, of course—that was in the contract," he says. "So one day Renée had a fitting, and the place was full of dressmakers and dogs and pins and people, and I had a pain in my back. So I telephoned downstairs and asked for a small room where my masseur could give me a rubdown. They gave me a very small room for an hour and charged me a full day's rate for it. It was unjust." Tony makes these remarks mildly, looking down at his feet and moving them around.

A good many things seem unjust to Tony, who has gone through a lot to achieve success. He cannot understand, for one thing, why his partner, who is supposed to pay for her clothes out of her percentage of the team's salary, is always broke when a bill comes around. His partner's explanation is that she must have a hundred dancing dresses and must keep at least thirty-five in rotation during a six-week engagement. Besides, there is the cost of shoes, stockings, cosmetics, and hairdressers. The rationing of shoes is not as much of a headache for professional dancers as it might appear, as the OPA sympathetically admits that a dancer's livelihood depends largely on his footgear. These days, of course, a dancer has his old shoes repaired as often as any layman, and treasures his rubber soles, which frequently may be attached to new uppers. When a pair of the De Marcos' shoes wear out beyond repair they exhibit the remains to the rationing board, which then issues each of them a special coupon for a new pair. Sally uses about thirty-six pairs of shoes a year, Tony about twenty-four.

Tony's wardrobe consists of twenty-three suits of dress clothes, ten dozen dress shirts, three hundred white ties, and eighty or ninety pairs of shoes in use. Like most dance teams, the De Marcos are sentimental about giving away their old clothes. They give them to friends who, they know, will go out dancing in them. They like to think of their discarded dancing dresses and tail coats still whirling around somewhere, never limp and never still. Tony never gives away any of his old dancing shoes. When a pair is beyond restoring, he pastes a strip of paper bearing the date of retirement inside one shoe and puts the pair away in one of the wooden packing cases he keeps for that purpose. He has some two hundred pairs of retired shoes now, and he was recently overtaken by a gracious idea about them. He would like to have each pair silver-plated by a process he has heard of, and he would like then to send them as gifts to his friends, one pair to each pal. There are drawbacks to this plan. For one thing, the silvering process is not feasible until after the war. "And besides," Tony says, "it's hard to think of two hundred people who would appreciate a present like that."

A NOTE ON THE TYPE

The text of this book is set in Caledonia, a Linotype face designed by W. A. Dwiggins, the man responsible for so much that is good in contemporary book design and typography. Caledonia belongs to the family of printing types called "modern face" by printers—a term used to mark the change in style of type-letters that occurred about 1800. It has all the hard-working feet-on-the-ground qualities of the Scotch Modern face plus the liveliness and grace that is integral in every Dwiggins "product" whether it be a simple catalogue cover or an almost human puppet.

The book was composed, printed, and bound by H. Wolff, New York. The typographic scheme and the binding and jacket designs are by Warren Chappell.